DANCING ON THE CEILING

Valerie Hall is a senior lecturer in human resource management at the National Development Centre for Educational Management and Policy at the University of Bristol. She currently manages the taught doctor of education (EdD) programme at the University of Bristol, the first of its kind in Europe. She has taught in schools, colleges and universities for over thirty years. During the past twenty years she has been involved in a number of research projects, including the POST Project looking at the selection of secondary heads, the CROSH Project (changing role of the secondary head) and the SMT Project (senior management teams in secondary schools). Throughout her career she has had a strong personal and professional interest in gender issues, particularly in the contexts of adult learning and the workplace.

DANCING ON THE CEILING:

A Study of Women Managers in Education

Valerie Hall

National Development Centre for Educational Management and Policy,
University of Bristol

P·C·P
Paul Chapman
Publishing Ltd

Paul Chapman Publishing Ltd
144 Liverpool Road
London
N1 1LA

British Library Cataloguing in Publication Data

Hall, Valerie, 1943–
   Dancing on the Ceiling : a study of women managers in education
   1. Women school principals – Great Britain
   I. Title
   371.2'0082

ISBN 185396 287 2

Typeset by Palimpsest Book Production Limited,
Polmont, Stirlingshire
Printed and bound in Great Britain

A B C D E F G H 9 8 7 6

CONTENTS

To my children

Zöe and Robert

ACKNOWLEDGEMENTS

The research was funded by a grant from the Leverhulme Trust, for whose support I am most grateful.

Neither the book nor the research would have been possible without the willingness of the six women heads involved to undergo the close scrutiny to which they were subjected. They have to remain anonymous, but I am indebted to their willingness, in the midst of already heavy timetables, to find time to explore with me the issues involved in being a head. Their commitment to having their story told so that others might be informed by their experience overcame their concerns at the exposure that might entail. I am also grateful to their colleagues who agreed to being interviewed and observed and the unfailing courtesy and support that I met in all the schools.

My thanks also go to my colleagues at the National Development Centre for Educational Management and Policy for their support when the going was tough. In particular, Mike Wallace's contribution of ideas and feedback in the early stages as well as detailed comments on the final drafts were invaluable. I am also grateful to Myra McCulloch, Geoffrey Elliott, Kate Myers and Anne Donald for commenting on the final draft; and to Zöe Hall, Cliff Hocking, Geraldine Yates and Kay Jackman for keeping my spirits up when they were flagging.

Throughout the project and writing the book, I could not have managed without the help of June Collins, Norma Meechem, Angela Allen and Joan Moore. Their patience and unflappability in the face of tight deadlines were essential in bringing the book together.

Valerie Hall

1.

PROLOGUE: DANCING ON THE CEILING

I love my ceiling more, since it is my dancing floor.
                                                    (Popular song)

INVITATION TO THE WALTZ

This is a book about headship and gender that focuses on women but draws conclusions that are relevant to both women and men in school management. It invites the reader to join a school management dance which is led by women. Reviewing writing and research on women in education management in Britain (Hall, 1993), I noted the danger of perpetuating an image of women as victims, for ever banging their heads against glass ceilings, as they fail to negotiate successfully organizational barriers to their career advancement. In contrast, there are women who, although they still encounter some of the pressures described by other women in senior positions, have broken through the glass ceiling. In the words of the song from which the title is taken, they have made the dance their own, demonstrating the kind of transformations to organizational life that can occur when women lead the dance and (most of the time) love the dance they lead.

The following descriptions and conclusions about women as educational leaders are based on a two-year (1992–1994) qualitative study of six women heads, three in primary schools, three in secondary. They were all white women heads, in order to explore gender separately from ethnic origin as a factor influencing women's approaches to school leadership. A small-scale study by Powney and Weiner (1991) found differences in the management styles of black women and white women in senior positions in education. Their findings were based exclusively on self-reporting but indicated the need for further research to provide a picture of education management from the perspective of black women (and men) managers. The six women in the study were special, in that they were carefully selected as heads who were known to be operating successfully and therefore likely to be able to withstand the sustained scrutiny to which the research project would expose them. They were also special in welcoming the opportunities for critical reflection on their own performance that the research methods provided.

Any book written by a woman that focuses mainly on women courts the danger of being labelled as 'women's studies' or 'feminist' and therefore irrelevant to the mainstream debate about educational management. Acker (1994), for example, has described the professional marginalization that occurs as a result of an expressed interest in gender issues. Delamont (1989, p. 4) asks, in her discussion of 'knowledgeable women', why any man would want to read her book. Her justification is that a study of 'élite women' provides a lens for focusing on society. In the same way, I see a book on women headteachers as a way of making the familiar (education management) strange. Like Acker and Delamont's work, this is a book about women written by a woman. Yet I would claim at least three reasons why it should stand alongside other studies of managers in education, particularly headteachers. First, it is a response to the expressed need from some men writers (e.g. Fullan, 1991; Grace, 1995; Southworth, 1995) as well as women writers (e.g. Schmuck, 1986; Shakeshaft, 1989) for studies which describe and analyse headship as done by women. It sets out, in other words, to be a portrayal of women studied on their own terms. The research itself was a response to increasing exhortations to study school management through the lens of women's performance in the job. Some writers have also associated women with effective school management, drawing on a limited number of research studies, mainly in the United States. Fullan (1991, p. 165), for example, claims: 'As a group women are more likely to evidence behaviour associated with effective leadership.' This, as he points out, refers to women on the average and is not meant to deny that there are many examples of men performing well and women performing poorly. Hargreaves (1994, p. 28) talks of the need for a new mindset in a post-modern age. He comments: 'Many ways of knowing, thinking and being moral, not just rational, logical ones, are coming to be seen as legitimate, not least the knowledge and moral judgement of women.'

Supportive though these are of women's capacity for successful performance as managers and leaders, the research base for the claims is limited and mainly from the United States. Both Fullan and Hargreaves draw extensively on studies such as Rosener's (1990) of women who lead. Her study identifies characteristics usually associated with women in organizations (e.g. encouraging collaboration, consensus-building) with transformational leadership as a panacea for schools' problems. Schein (1989), on the other hand, questions the new priority given to femininity and feminine leadership styles as 'foolhardy and dangerous'. For her, it perpetuates sex-role stereotypical thinking, even when it is expressed through the notion of the androgynous manager, in whom male and female characteristics are blended. In her view, 'the androgynous orientation builds a managerial access bridge for women on a shaky foundation of sand' (*ibid.*, p. 155). Unlike Schein, I prefer to make a distinction between androgyny and feminine leadership styles and argue, on the basis of evidence from the project, for a view of school leadership and management that draws on behaviours that are the exclusive property of neither men nor women.

At the same time this book challenges many ideas and assumptions about leadership in schools, particularly those written by men, mainly about men and implicitly for men. Prescriptions for successful school leadership, such as those outlined in Jenkins (1991), marginalize gender by assigning it to a special category rather than recognizing its pervasive quality. Jenkins claims, for example, that 'the gender issue helps to explain why one of the prescriptions in this book exhorts school leaders to care more for, and to value, their staff' (*ibid.*, p. 25). By implication, the remaining six prescriptions derive from and apply only to men's leadership behaviour.

A second reason for seeing this book as being about more than gender lies in the rationale of the research itself. It was not intended as a 'differences' study (like those by Vinnecombe, 1989; Berman, 1982) which look at how men and women differ in their management behaviours. Like Davies (1992) I adopted a research approach that emphasized gender relations rather than gender differences. Although I looked at how women interact with men, I did not set out to compare women with men, but to construct an account of headship based on how women interpreted and did the job. I assumed that the differences between women are potentially as great as between women and men. I also assumed commonalities in women's experiences of leading schools in Britain which could be attributed to at least two factors: their socialization as girls and women in post-war Britain and the gendered nature of organizations (for example, women's lower pay, unequal promotion opportunities, prevalence of sexual harassment). Both these explanations derive from my view of gender influences on behaviour as socially rather than biologically based.

I found it difficult at first to avoid using men's behaviour as educational leaders as a yardstick for describing women in similar positions. Research studies of headship in Britain (e.g. Hall *et al.*, 1986; Weindling and Earley, 1987; Bolam *et al.*, 1993) have not differentiated men from women. Yet the statistics show men to be disproportionately represented in senior posts in education, thereby contributing to a view of education management as 'masculine'. Putting the picture straight by changing the subject from men to women does not involve saying women are different or better. My purpose is rather to explain how they are in this role (headship), in this context (schools) in this period of time (1990s).

This leads to my third claim for considering this book alongside other discussions of school leadership. It documents and interprets the behaviours of women leading schools. As such, it is equally relevant to women and men in education, since both are concerned with identifying the appropriate skills and qualities for effective school leadership, as we move towards the year 2000. The book explores the values that inform the heads' leadership styles and the extent of their commitment to maintaining or changing the schools they lead. Studies of 'successful' women in employment sectors other than education (e.g. Marshall, 1984; White *et al.*, 1992) pay relatively little attention to the values underpinning the women managers' and leaders' orientation to the purposes of their work. Success is defined almost exclusively in terms of career success rather than contributions to the achievement of organizational goals. It is enough in other work sectors, it seems, to have reached a senior position to earn the label of 'successful woman'. In education, however, discussing leadership without discussing leaders' values is like music without sound, dogma without belief. Professional success in education cannot be, and is not, measured exclusively in terms of career success, but in terms of successful outcomes for children's education. A woman (or man) leading a school which is failing its young people cannot be called successful. Being a successful leader in education means having values about the central purpose of the enterprise. This means that, although the research was funded primarily as a study of women as educational managers, it also had to take account of their contribution to educational leadership.

Some writers have challenged the new entrepreneurial approach which the present Conservative government requires of its school managers and leaders (e.g. Bottery, 1992; Mac An Ghaill, 1994). They see it as antipathetic to educational values and an attempt to replace them with the values of the market place which encourage technicist, rational solutions to human problems. Within this perspective, management, including school management, is potentially the lackey of its government masters and managerialism the unwelcome offspring.

These doubts about the true purposes of management in education are also reflected in questions about whether women have the appropriate orientation to fulfil the 'masculine' role that headship is seen to be. Evetts (1990, pp. 182–3), for example, argues that the changes brought by the Education Reform Act 1988 require managerialist approaches which present cultural dilemmas for women headteachers. In her view, heads have had to become tough, aggressive, competitive, directive and autocratic if they are to deal with the pressures of the new reforms. Implicit in this and others' analyses of the current context of school management is the view that it is not a suitable job for a woman. As a result, women who aspire to, and achieve, headship are in a *Catch 22* position. Within a critical perspective, being successfully entrepreneurial (and thereby demonstrating that women can, after all, do the job) means they have failed as educational leaders, since they have compromised educational values by not challenging entrepreneurialism. Within this model, they may also have compromised their identity as women. Hoyle (1986), for example, suggests that the word management has a symbolic function in encouraging the self-image of teachers as pursuing a 'masculine' task. He asks (*ibid.*, p. 157) whether this self-image appeals not only to men but also to women seeking management roles in schools, who see the term 'management' as symbolic of their capacity to fill masculine roles. In presenting these arguments, both men and women writers are making (unproven) assertions of an association between management and masculinity. These lead them to conclusions about women who become managers and those who do not. It is notable that the same questions are not asked of men who choose not to become managers in schools. Are they, according to this line of argument, less masculine?

However, if women who reach senior management positions in education can be shown to practise what has been described as 'critical leadership' then they might also be seen to have challenged the association of management, masculinity and autocratic control over others. Southworth (1995) draws on Foster's (1989) discussion of critical leadership, to summarize the implications of critical perspectives on educational leadership. Within this perspective critical leadership encompasses school management practice which liberates rather than controls. Its strength is its concern with ethics and morals, not just efficiency and means. It represents 'power to' rather than 'power over'. Leadership and followership are interchangeable. The power of the individual leader is limited. The awareness of non-dominant groups is raised. Finally, critical leadership stimulates organizational change through mutual education. Southworth, though critical of Foster's model, supports an association between emancipatory leadership and gender by referring to women writers like Blackmore and Kenway (1993) and Shakeshaft (1989) who argue that women use power to empower rather than to dominate. He concludes: 'An emancipatory view of leadership is worth pursuing since it addresses both objections to power being understood as power over and the male bias of management theorizing' (1995, p. 192).

Even if, as this study shows, women managers in education behave in ways that contribute to successful educational outcomes, some writers see dangers in assuming that women's day has come. Blackmore and Kenway (1993) suggests that organizations are merely using 'feminine' characteristics to bolster continuing masculine privilege. Their recognition of what women have to offer that is different from men is pragmatically rather than ethically grounded. Poplin and Rusch (1995) criticize the plethora of advice and books for women aspiring to be leaders, which describe how women must look and behave to succeed as a leader in a man's world. The books and seminars become examples of how embedded cultural values of privilege perpetuate ideas of a leader as the embodiment of all that is male, even among women authors. There is little reference to how they might contribute to changing 'a man's world'.

At the same time, there are problems with critical theories that associate entrepreneurialism with masculinity and the appropriation of female characteristics with continued masculine privilege. Potentially they could undermine the contribution of women to school management, which is what this study was intended to address. If entrepreneurialism is viewed negatively, and women school leaders are shown to be effective entrepreneurs, then a reconceptualization of education management becomes as tarnished as the one it is intended to challenge. The waters are muddied even further by evidence that women in positions of power do not necessarily demonstrate the responsiveness to equity issues that it is assumed they will, just because they are women. Any description of women as school leaders has to take account of this additional dimension of the extent of their commitment to emancipatory praxis, even though the same question is not always asked of men leaders, particularly where gender is concerned. Writing on educational leadership as emancipatory praxis, Grundy (1993) distinguishes between the 'technical' leader and the 'practical educational leader'. Drawing on Habermas's (1972) conceptual framework of 'knowledge-constitutive interests', she explores the implications of these theoretical constructs for the work of educational leaders, and shows the links between their 'interests' and their actions. The characteristics she associates with each of these leadership approaches are shown in Table 1.1.

As the following chapters show, the women heads demonstrated some behaviours from both models illustrated in Table 1.1. This highlights the limitations of behavioural descriptions for arriving at conclusions about leadership style, since when their interpretations of their actions are taken into account, their preferred model, and the values on which it is based, relate to those associated by Grundy with the practical educational leader. Their values about control and the distribution of power placed them clearly within a 'practical action' model, yet they sometimes behaved within a 'technical' framework. From Grundy's feminist perspective, practical action is not enough to challenge the inequities of society

Table 1.1   Characteristics of educational leadership

'Technical leadership'	'Practical educational leadership'
• sets unambiguous short-term goals • pre-selects the strategies for the implementation of institutional objectives • structures and sequences implementation strategies clearly • anticipates problems and prepares other strategies • as far as possible supplies answers to staff questions • is well prepared for staff meetings • runs orderly, task-orientated staff meetings • enthuses practitioners through her charisma • defuses conflict and redirects dissatisfaction • identifies areas of staff weakness • arranges staff-training opportunities for the development of skills • rewards staff success	• has an over-riding concern for the welfare of staff and clients • encourages staff to pursue broad professional development options • assists staff to set broad, long-term goals • involves staff in decision-making • facilitates the use of deliberative processes for decision-making • shares leadership roles among staff • encourages staff to adopt an experimental approach to their work • recognizes a variety of evidence of achievement of goals • arranges for shared reflection on and analysis of the outcomes of action

Source: Based on Grundy, 1993, pp. 168–70.

and be truly emancipatory. Moving beyond practical action requires 'emancipatory praxis' in which the leadership engages in practical action within a socially critical framework. She says:

> Emancipatory praxis is not a set of behaviours in which an educational leader can be trained. This form of praxis is grounded in a critical consciousness which will manifest itself in action that will always be becoming emancipatory. The question for the educational leader is not, 'Am I emancipated and how can I emancipate my staff?' but, 'How can I engage in forms of critical, self-reflective and collaborative work which will create conditions so that the people with whom I work can come to control their knowledge and practice?'
>
> (*Ibid.*, p. 174)

While emancipatory praxis is the prerogative of neither men nor women, it is more readily expected of women in power, who are assumed to have experienced the effects of gender inequality. Yet, as Yates (1993) points out, gender is only one form of inequality and emancipatory praxis refers as much to class and race as it does to gender. At present, there is a dearth of research on class, race and education management in Britain. Like Strachan (1994) in New Zealand, Blackmore and Grundy are concerned about the impact of New Right reforms in Australia on feminist women's educational leadership practice. They describe this in terms of the wider emancipatory agenda that emerges from women's experiences and beliefs, which they see as being in conflict with managerialism. From their perspective, there is an incongruity between the type of leadership demanded by New Right policies and the personal philosophy of leadership espoused by women principals who identify themselves as feminists (Strachan, 1994, p. 9). There is an expectation (often disappointed) that when women achieve positions of formal power, they will use it to steer people in the direction of greater gender equity.

This question about school leaders' commitment to equal opportunities is usually asked by other women working within a feminist tradition. It is rarely asked by and of men. There are exceptions – for example, Genovese's (1993) examination of women national leaders. His study uses the criterion of their contribution to emancipatory praxis as a basis for measuring their performance as leaders. Generally, he deems them to have failed in this respect, and provides socio-political (rather than psychological) explanations for their failure. Grace's (1995) study of eighty-eight headteachers provides another example of a man including questions about gender and educational leadership, but it is only in his chapter on women and educational leadership that he asks about their commitment to feminism. A quarter of his sample were women heads and he found relatively few making explicit reference to feminist perspectives, equal opportunities issues or female styles of leadership. He concludes (*ibid.*, p. 189) that these matters were not a central part of their discourse. Implicitly, in only asking women these questions, he appears to assume they are women's concerns. His conclusion, that the women heads' self-distancing from association with feminism implies their accommodation into the largely enduring culture of male leadership, leaves that culture unchallenged. Hearn *et al.* (1989) overcome their problem as researchers and writers of men working within a feminist framework by describing themselves as 'pro-feminist'. In this way, they distinguish the conflicts of 'personal' and 'political' interest between women and men writing about organizations in which 'Women and men continue to approach their areas of concern, and live their personal experience, from their own gendered stances. Men can learn from feminism but cannot be feminists' (*ibid.*, p. 26). In contrast, both Grace and Southworth's studies represent attempts to learn from feminist theory and practice but ultimately fail to integrate it fully into their critical frameworks.

Astin and Leland (1991) write as feminists about feminist educational leaders. They include in their study of 'women of vision, women of influence' only women who had a commitment to feminism. So too do Adler *et al.* (1993) in their study of women managers in education. In both studies, emancipatory praxis was predictably a dominant feature of the leadership approaches described and in line with the Blackmore and Strachan studies referred to earlier. Since this commitment was not a criterion for selection of the women who participated in my study, it was an area to be researched rather than taken for granted. Working as a 'feminist' researcher with women managers who claimed not to be feminist did not, in my view, rule out the possibility that their educational leadership would have many of the features of emancipatory practice associated by other writers with feminist leadership. Based on her own research on gender and organizations, Cockburn (1991) suggests that, unless women have a commitment to feminism prior to achieving formal power, they are unlikely to make addressing gender equity issues a priority, once in post. As the studies by Young (1990) and Webster (1990) show, among the many disappointments about Margaret Thatcher's reign as prime minister was her failure to address equity issues relating to women, even though the likelihood of her doing so was minimal in the light of her other political beliefs. Those who were disappointed in her as a woman leader assumed incorrectly that her identity as a wife, mother and daughter would triumph over her professional identity as a politician (judging what wins votes) and over her political identity as a Conservative (valuing women's place in the home).

The account that follows therefore draws on research evidence to inform the debate about women and education management and the validity of the concept of androgynous management. The heads' performance as educational leaders is viewed through the lens of a critical framework that addresses its ethical as well as its technical aspects. It is argued that, although the women heads in the study had many entrepreneurial characteristics, they operated within a value framework and repertoire of behaviours that were broader and, in some respects, different from that associated in earlier research with men as managers.

EXPANDING THE REPERTOIRE

The concept of repertoire is useful for describing the women heads' performance. An examination of their life histories, career experiences and current performance revealed the evolution and development of the behaviours and values which they drew on as school leaders. A performing artist's repertoire will include all the pieces at which he or she is skilled, to be selected from according to the occasion and audience. In this respect, repertoire is a more appropriate word than the currently popular 'portfolio' which is used as a description of teachers' accumulated learning experiences. Portfolios demonstrate a selection of what has been achieved. Repertoires include the whole range of what can be produced, if required. We can only hypothesize about men's repertoires, since the questions have rarely been asked about, or the links made, between the different aspects of their lives from childhood to performance in managerial jobs. One exception is Mac An Ghaill's (1994) account of the ideologies of men teachers, their roots in early childhood experiences and their impact on professional identities and practices. He says, for example:

> Biographical details, including memories of significant others, were important in shaping male subjectivities. For example, among the Professionals, older male staff frequently recalled and bitterly regretted the passing of uncontested gender identities of the grammar school era, which clearly delineated masculinity and femininity along a commonsense bipolar system of traditional fixed male and female sex roles. Significant elements of their formative experiences included their father's occupation, the sexual division of labour in their parents' home, experience of the army and active involvement in competitive sport.
>
> (*Ibid.*, p. 25)

The additional value of Mac An Ghaill's study to an understanding of men and women in education management is that it explores schooling and masculinities in a way that reaffirms the centrality of sexual identity to our understanding of organizational life.

Southworth's (1995) research-based interpretation of Ron, a primary school headteacher, is another exception, although his promise to address gender as an issue in primary headship is only partially realized. He describes Ron's view of headship as gendered and paternalistic and presents the key to Ron's performance as lying in the beliefs about power and leadership underpinning his leadership style. He does not, however, explore the relationship between individual beliefs and gender identity, or the ways in which Ron's use of power relates to his self-concept as a man. Gender remains an implicit rather than explicit variable for interpreting the case-study material. Ron's 'praxis' is described and explained – there are many resemblances to the women heads' behaviour, as I discuss in Chapter 9 – but it is not interpreted within a gender perspective. Ron also failed the critical leadership test described earlier and Southworth attributes this failure to the relatively unchanging paradigm, in Britain, of school leadership practice. In Southworth's view, the bureaucratic rationale which has characterized the practice of school leadership is not in retreat. The language of accountancy and accountability dominate and efficiency and effectiveness are the bywords (*ibid.*, p. 193). What my study shows is that, even if the women heads appear to do less well on the critical leadership dimension than some feminists would hope, they still constitute a challenge to the bureaucratic model, as a result of the choices they make about preferred strategies to achieve their versions of efficiency and effectiveness. However, I will return to Southworth's study in Chapter 9, since it represents the most recent attempt to make a critique of existing ideas about school leadership in England, using a research base.

ABOUT LEADING AND MANAGING: CHOREOGRAPHER OR DANCING MISTRESS?

So far I have used the words 'leading' and 'managing' interchangeably. In so doing, I have apparently contributed to what Foster (1989, p. 45) has described as the chewing up and swallowing down of the concept of leadership by the needs of modern managerial theory. Grace (1995), on the other hand, attempts to reconstitute educational leadership as a phenomenon distinct from educational management, acknowledging the resurgence of strong school leadership with roots in the culture of the new managerialism in primary and secondary schools in the 1990s. As someone whose own principal work activities have been about developing teachers as managers, I would argue that leadership is potentially pervasive within teaching and managing, not exclusive (Hall *et al.*, 1995). It is important to recognize that, ideally, all managers are leaders and all leaders are managers so that, by implication, all teachers are also managers and leaders. This recognition, which both preceded and was confirmed by my work with the women heads, can then serve to undermine the negative impact of management used as an unquestioning tool for achieving other people's purposes.

As heads they represented not only management but also educational leadership. In the field of education, leadership and management are inseparable, whether in the context of the classroom teacher, the faculty or pastoral head, the deputy or headteacher. Not all teachers welcome management responsibilities. Some fear that being a manager means behaving in unfamiliar or uncomfortable ways, including having undesirable power over others. This fear of management's negative characteristics is often moderated by a welcome for the opportunities it provides for influencing the course of events in ways that might not otherwise have been possible. Teachers are used to having power in the classroom. They have been less used to and have had little preparation for having formal power over other adults, although this is changing with more school-based management development. It is an even bigger step to realizing that being a manager (working to achieve results with and through other people) also means being a leader. Sometimes the words managing and leading are used synonymously. A headteacher may be described as managing a school, a departmental head as leading a subject team. Or the distinction is made pejoratively: leaders do the right thing, managers do things right.

My own position (following Hodgkinson, 1991) is that leadership is philosophy in action, with management an integral part. The women heads in the study were therefore simultaneously leaders and managers. Their approach to modelling leadership included demonstrating the integration of these two functions so that middle managers, for example, were encouraged to be leaders within their own teams. For the heads, their team extended to everyone working in and for the school. Unlike the dancing mistress, whose primary purpose is to coach her charges to 'dance to others" rhythms, the heads saw themselves as having a responsibility for creating the organizational rhythms of their own institution. However, leading and managing are distinguished in the text to reflect the distinctions the heads themselves made between the two processes. For them, educational leadership was a necessary component of entrepreneurial strategies. Managing without leading was unethical; leading without managing was irresponsible.

THE CONTEXT OF HEADSHIP: WHO SETS THE STAGE?

The problem for heads as choreographers is that they have to work with sets mainly designed by others. All heads are working in a broader context of economic, social and political change, as well as the specific context of their school. These contexts both constrain and create possibilities for the successful exercise of school leadership for both women and men headteachers. Constructing a picture of the women heads at work meant taking into account factors deriving from their individual contexts influencing their behaviour. An additional set of constraints lay in the gendered character of schools as organizations. Mac An Ghaill (1994, p. 4) shows them as 'complex, gendered and heterosexual arenas' in which masculinities and femininities are mediated and lived through the school microcultures of management, teachers and students. An association is often made (sometimes without substantiation) of secondary schools with 'masculine' cultures (Cunnison, 1985; Ball, 1987); and primary schools with 'feminine' cultures, for which there is greater empirical evidence (e.g. Acker, 1993). One purpose of the women headteachers' study was to examine the ways in which the gendered character of schools influenced women's behaviour when they reached senior positions; and whether the constraints on their leadership performance were different in primary schools (where most staff are women) from secondary schools (where slightly more staff are men).

CROSSING THE RUBICON

Women who become heads have successfully circumvented the barriers
that traditionally stand in the way of women seeking career advancement
in organizations. They have gone, as Beck and Steele (1989) suggest,
'beyond the great divide'. Unlike the women managers who are the
subjects of other studies, they have not only broken through the glass
ceiling, which is most professional women's 'Rubicon', but have also
taken up leadership positions with the additional possibilities for power
and influence they bring. This makes them different from women
managers in other sectors where, although their number is increasing,
few are obtaining positions of significant corporate power. It also makes
them different from other women teachers who either choose not to, or
fail to, achieve promotion within the school system. The figures relating
to women's under-representation in management posts in schools are well
rehearsed and have barely changed in the past decade, in spite of equal
opportunities legislation and some targeted development programmes.
The position remains that, in 1991, only 20 per cent of secondary schools
had a woman head, although women constituted around 50 per cent
of secondary schoolteachers. In primary schools, where 80 per cent of
teachers are women, just under half have a woman headteacher (DES,
1991). The figures show that, in primary schools, one in three male
teachers become heads but only one in fourteen female teachers; in
secondary schools one in thirty male teachers become heads, but less
than one in a hundred women. The proportion of men and women
with incentive allowances is similarly unevenly distributed, with women
over-represented in posts with no allowances. The women heads in the
study thus constituted a marginal group amongst an already marginal
group of women managers, within the predominantly male enterprise
that educational management has become.

Given what is known about the internal and external barriers to
women's promotion in schools, how did these women cross the Rubicon
and become headteachers? Their careers can only be understood in the
light of the wider social, economic and educational context. As individuals, they cannot be separated from the society and culture in which
they work and in which assumptions about men and women in public
and private, at work or in the family, prevail. Each head's behaviour is
mediated through the national and local context for her headship, as well
as her individual history and predisposition. In particular, these heads
have worked for the past sixteen years within a framework of policy
directives of a Conservative government that has sought to transform
the goals of teaching and education.

The Education Reform Act 1988 (ERA) set in train educational change
on an unprecedented scale, causing selectors to redefine what they were
looking for when they appointed a new head. Concerns were expressed
that the greater involvement of governors in selection decisions might
lead to fewer women being appointed. The POST Project, that looked at

the selection of secondary heads in the early 1980s, found that appointing a woman was seen as making an already risky decision riskier (Morgan *et al.*, 1983). But ERA also brought changes to the management of schools that fitted uncomfortably with the style adopted by many heads appointed in the 1970s and early 1980s. In the wake of the demands of the 1988 Act there was an increase in early retirements and therefore more headteacher vacancies. Seven years on, the discomfort has turned, for many heads, to stress. Heads appointed to schools before the 1988 reforms were barely equipped to take on the massive challenges it represented. Leadership training came after they were in post and concentrated on improving skills off rather than on the job – the common pattern for school management development programmes in the 1980s (Wallace and Hall, 1989).

This, then, was the context in which five of the six heads in the project were appointed. The sixth had become head of her school in 1986, as an internal candidate replacing the male head, who had taken early retirement. Their governing bodies appear to have seen in them the potential for the kind of leadership their school needed to deal with the choppy waters of reform. Each was selected to bring qualities to running the school that were different from her predecessor's, whether a man or woman. As we will see in Chapter 3, the final selection stages were by no means an easy ride, but governors demonstrated their willingness to take the additional risk of appointing a woman. It is often at such moments of transition, as that represented by the late 1980s, that new qualities may be sought amongst hitherto marginalized groups. Even where the women heads replaced women, the main factor contributing to their success in gaining headship was the apparent congruence between what they offered and what the school needed. At the same time, the choice was only possible when they put themselves convincingly forward as ready, willing and able to do the job, as it was being redefined.

Their decision to put themselves forward for headship at this time provides one explanation for the considerable number of commonalities in their behaviour. They were, in effect, responding as women and heads to common national imperatives within the different local constraints of their own schools. In other words, in spite of their different contexts, they shared as women a set of values about leadership, power and influence that framed their behaviour in post. Those responsible for managing schools have responded in diverse ways to the imperatives of ERA and the local management of schools (LMS). For some, National Curriculum, greater powers to school governors, open enrolment, school performance indicators and compulsory staff appraisal represent a strait-jacket, stifling individual initiative. From this perspective, any response (whether to fight or succumb) involves a battle, either publicly or privately. Delegation of budgets brings the threat of not balancing the books when the number on roll falls and fixed costs have still to be met. Tough decisions become the order of the day, as teachers have to be declared redundant and resources reallocated within finite and inadequate budgets. The pursuit of rational management processes takes precedence over enacting a leading professional role, so that headship becomes associated with administration and management and less with teaching and learning.

Others, including the six heads, have a more benign view of ERA, while still lamenting the resource constraints on providing an effective education for young people. This positive perspective sees delegated budgets as giving the school more autonomy in financial decision-making and the choice of making more curriculum-led decisions. Nevertheless, at the time of the study, none of the heads favoured opting out of LEA control and taking on grant-maintained status. Staff appraisal was welcomed as legitimating the contribution of performance review to staff development, though performance-related pay was not considered desirable. They saw the package of reforms as having the potential to strengthen the school's capacity to realize its own goals through the greater integration of financial, curriculum and staffing plans. Of course, responding positively to the challenge of the reforms can also be interpreted as responding uncritically, through failing to challenge the values and assumptions that lay behind the new policies for education. However, the account that follows does not set out to judge the heads' performance, but to trace the links between its different components, and show ways in which it could be said to be idiosyncratic of women.

DIFFERENT TUNE, SAME STEPS?

It is interesting to compare the picture of women headteachers that emerges from this study with that sketched in the only other study exclusively about women heads in Britain. This is the official centenary history of the Association of Headmistresses, which traces the individual careers of the women heads who fought for girls' education, described by Halevy as 'a social revolution of the first magnitude' (in Glenday and Price, 1974 p. 46). The under-representation of women in senior posts in education is often attributed to the absence of role models. This is certainly true where accounts of women leading schools are concerned, whereas the Arnoldian headmaster tradition is familiar to many. Most women of the heads' generation in education have heard of Miss Beale and Miss Buss, but usually as stereotypes of 'old school' leadership, seemingly irrelevant to the modern age. For some girls, including three of the heads in the study, a reflection of this schoolmistress tradition was visible in the girls' schools they attended. Chapter 3 presents some of their testimony to the kind of influence it represented.

There is much in Glenday and Price's account of the women heads' predecessors that reflects the attitudes and qualities of the women heads in this study. The fortitude of the early women heads in the battle for girls' education was acknowledged in the Spens report on secondary education in 1938. There, the success of girls' schools was attributed to the fact that the new mistresses were more responsive to new ideas, more critical and more disposed to adapt themselves to changing circumstances than their male colleagues in the endowed schools for boys (Glenday and Price, 1974, p. 22). This resembles closely the qualities that some governing bodies in the late 1980s also detected in the women heads they appointed, and were confirmed in the research, as subsequent chapters indicate. In the early part of the century, women heads had the luxury of stamping their own personalities on their schools, with almost no external requirements to guide what they should be doing and how. Glenday and Price (*ibid.*, p. 37) describe the pioneers' schools as 'pre-eminently their schools, their own creation, and the history of the school is part of the life history of the founder, reflecting her character'. Now, in an educational management climate that advocates (even if it does not always achieve) collegiality, shared leadership and consultation, this particularly regal type of leadership would be anathema.

The advent of co-educational schools after the Education Act 1902 threatened the autonomy of the women heads as well as the promotion opportunities of women colleagues. Glenday and Price (*ibid.*, p. 70) quote one head at the time: 'It is not enough when a man is the head of a school to place a woman under him as chief assistant, and to say that she is responsible for the girls; for she cannot be responsible unless she is independent of him.' Ninety years later, Litawski's (1993) research on deputy headship shows many women senior teachers still falling into the stereotyped role of the 'nappy and noses brigade'.

By the end of the Second World War, the headmistresses had lost much of their autonomy but 'What they continued to assert was a belief in quality and freedom, a concern for the individual child as a whole person . . . and an intention to serve the community of which the school was a part' (Glenday and Price, 1974, p. 96). So why do the authors call these women headteachers 'reluctant revolutionaries'? At the turn of the century they were forced into the vanguard of social change as advocates of education for girls, at a time when public rhetoric favoured girls and women being seen and not heard. Throughout the century they have, according to the historians, been leaders and catalysts in the radical changes affecting education. The reluctance comes from the tensions created by being pushed into the limelight at a time when woman's place (for the middle classes at least) was still firmly in the home. According to the canons of critical leadership outlined earlier, their behaviour was radical in challenging the status quo but within a framework of values that stressed individualism and achievement through merit. A century later, headship has changed in ways that challenge the talents of both men and women filling the role, but it is still within a framework of individualism and merit. Revolutionary headship is a thing of the past, if indeed it ever existed.

PRESENTING THE MATERIAL

It is not easy to report in-depth research on six people who, by virtue of their position, are in the public eye. Both the heads and the schools have been given pseudonyms to protect their privacy. Personal details of them and their schools can be found mainly in Chapters 3 and 4. The strength of the conclusions rests on the strength of the research methods for collecting appropriate data and the ability to convey enough of the data to allow readers to form their own impressions, as a basis for agreeing or arguing with my interpretation. The findings are presented in a way that demonstrates commonalities between the heads, with differences noted where they occurred. I have tried to achieve a balance of quotations from each. Often a point could be illustrated by reference to any of the six because the commonalities were sufficiently evident. Occasionally, examples are given to show how they were different from each other but such occurrences were less frequent, in spite of the very different context of their schools and lifestyles. The problem with presenting the material in this way, rather than as six separate case studies, is that it appears to suggest they are identical and, by implication, the commonalities are the result of the fact they are women. This was not the intention. Throughout the research, it was apparent that they were six individuals responding to different contexts, but there were strong similarities also. My intention is not to prove that these similarities are the consequence of gender, but to show how gender has an impact on leadership behaviour in the context of education, by focusing on women's experiences.

Chapter 2 considers in more detail questions of the research methods and how they relate to other research traditions concerned with understanding management, leadership and gender. In Chapter 3, 'In search of a lifestyle: choices and dilemmas', the complex and dynamic factors influencing the lifestyles of women heads from childhood to the present are explored. It looks at the choices they made relating to family and career experiences, within the context of the demands and constraints on women's personal and professional lives. Chapter 4 continues the story by examining how they sought to make an impact on the schools of which they had become heads, in ways that met what they saw as the school's needs, without compromising their own values.

Chapters 5 to 8 unwrap the different layers of each head's identity to show how their behaviour as managers and leaders (the outer layer) can be understood in terms of their self-concept, values and beliefs (the inner layers). Picking up the theme from Chapter 3 of the women's 'inner journey to headship' and, from Chapter 4, of 'slaying dragons' during their first headships, the second half of the book looks at how they interacted (Chapter 5), managed people (Chapter 6), interpreted and used 'power' (Chapters 7 and 8). The final chapter, Chapter 9, summarizes the findings and reviews them in the light of discussions of men and women managers and their implications for education management in the twenty-first century.

2.

METHODOLOGY: WATCHING FROM THE WINGS

She [woman] is defined and differentiated with reference to man and not he with reference to her; she is the incidental and the inessential as opposed to the essential. He is the Subject, he is the Absolute. She is the Other.
(Simone de Beauvoir, 1953, p.16)

INTRODUCTION

The test question for any academic discussion which claims to be based on research findings is whether the conclusions are justified by the research design. For that reason, I have considered it important to describe in detail how the research was conducted and the conceptual framework used to inform my analysis of the data collected. This chapter begins by describing the relationship established between myself as researcher and the women heads, and its implications for the kind and validity of information generated. The nature of the sample and sites which provide the accounts is discussed, as well as the players, events and processes characterizing the project's history. Methods of data collection and analysis are reviewed critically to show their appropriateness for the topic, and they are set within the multiple perspectives that constitute the theoretical framework. While acknowledging the study's limitations and strengths, the chapter aims to show the potential of the chosen methodology for research into education management that takes account of a wider range of factors than is usual. These include attention to the life history and gender of managers as a necessary prerequisite to understanding performance in the job, based on observation as well as interview.

CHANGING THE SUBJECT

All research and discussions that put women centre stage of professional activity are, in effect, changing the subject. This includes the subject as person (e.g. women politicians rather than men politicians, women lawyers rather than men lawyers); and the subject as topic (e.g. political behaviour as demonstrated by women, legal activity interpreted by women).

The book from which Simone de Beauvoir's quotation is taken, *The Second Sex*, challenges the taken-for-grantedness of men as men. There are many examples of this taken-for-grantedness in the field of school leadership studies, one of which is Wolcott's (1973) representation of Ed Bell as 'the man in the principal's office'. In this, he takes one individual's experience of school leadership and presents it as universal. In a later article (1982), Wolcott discusses the methodology of his study and regrets having glossed over the broader context in which the principal, as a man, lived, and the links between that context and the type of school he tried to create. Instead, Wolcott's was a man-to-man approach, in which the gender of both researcher and informant, as a basis for understanding headship, was not questioned. In contrast, Southworth (1995) acknowledges himself as male researcher and Ron as male head although, as I show in Chapter 9, he does not explore fully the implications of gender for his findings.

A purpose of this study, therefore, was to change the subject of headship so that women were the players and the script was theirs, albeit in an educational play and an educational stage directed mainly by men. Changing the subject has implications for research methodology too. I chose to work within a qualitative research tradition that aims to capture the subjectivity of individual experience; and within a feminist research tradition that positions the intersubjectivity of researcher and researched centre-stage, as a basis for data collection. This raises questions about the 'objectivity' of the conclusions. Some (e.g. Harding, 1986) see objectivity arising from a feminist standpoint as stronger because it is based on an explicit recognition and examination of the researcher's hidden and unexplicated cultural agendas and assumptions, as well as critical scrutiny of all evidence collected as part of the research process. Although such justifications contribute to validating the research conclusions, they also run the danger of claiming the superiority of an interpretation thus derived over others, including the heads' own. If the researcher is feminist and the subjects are not, whose account counts?

My approach is feminist in so far as I assume the pervasive influence of gender divisions in social life, acknowledging that these are often un-recognized by the players themselves. Choosing to focus solely on women heads represented an attempt to rectify their neglect in the educational management literature, as well as allow for the possibility of constructing an alternative picture of school leadership, based on women's experiences. The relationships between men and women, boys and girls, that are at the heart of leading a school, are viewed through women's not men's eyes. The book is about women's experiences and school management seen from a less familiar perspective. The picture emerging from this study of women heads' leadership and management behaviour reflects my interpretation of their interpretations. A similar study of women heads by a man, that took gender as a central focus, might have looked different. As Wolcott (1982, p. 77) points out, the 'spectre' haunting every case study and serving as a convenient rationale for dismissing it, is how different would the conclusions and recommendations be if another person in another setting were chosen as the subject of the study.

TELLING A GOOD STORY

Although the data collected represent six case studies, I have chosen to present them in a way that integrates them through description, analysis and interpretation. Studies that opt for the descriptive approach and transform their subjects almost into the characters of a novel (such as Blumberg and Greenfield, 1980) rely heavily for their effect on the author's literary skills. As a result, the data can be distorted in order to fit a narrative which is governed by aesthetic as well as academic criteria. Challenging (and more financially rewarding) though it might have been to add to the 'blockbusters' of women at the top, it was both beyond my literary skills and academically inappropriate! It is also difficult in novelistic depictions to disentangle the author's from the subject's interpretation, something I considered important. Southworth (1995), faced with similar issues in writing up his case study of a single male head, usefully distinguishes between three forms of narrative – the everyday, the autobiographical and the biographical:

> The everyday narrative articulates how actors go about their rounds and accomplish their tasks. The autobiographical narrative is the telling of one's own story and how one's past is related to the present. Biography is concerned with the ability to empathize with the life stories of others and with the retelling of the other's life.
>
> (*Ibid.*, p. 51)

The following accounts of six women heads try to integrate all three components of narrative. They do not, however, claim to be fully fledged imaginative biographies, for two reasons. First, the balance of one researcher and six cases prevented the total immersion in each case that a purist life-history approach would require. This limitation arose from the pragmatics of research funding which covered just enough for one experienced researcher. Secondly, the study had gender as an explicit focus, providing a lens (together with power and culture) through which to view the material. Such lenses for a biographer, concerned to tell the whole story of an individual, would create limiting blindspots and produce an incomplete picture. The strength of the gender lens in this study was in highlighting what is usually taken for granted, making sensitive what is often denied and in encouraging people to be self-conscious about something that is often hidden to self. Even though the women heads' striving for self-knowledge as a basis for action emerged as a strong theme, gender constituted a hitherto unexplored area for them.

The book therefore moves between the heads' own words (autobiographical), vignettes of their actions (the everyday) and my interpretation within the conceptual framework of gender, power and culture, which is explained below. Its claims to validity, beyond justifying the sample and methods, resemble those that Wolcott (1990) outlines in his discussion of the challenge of seeking and rejecting validity in qualitative research. He suggests nine ways of satisfying validity's implicit challenge, all of which informed the methodology used in the study described here. They included talking little and listening a lot; recording accurately; writing early; offering informed interpretations; reporting fully; being candid; seeking feedback; rigorous subjectivity; and writing accurately. By following these maxims, I have aimed to provide an account that accurately represents the female world of headship to which it refers. Following Reason and Rowan (1981), I had no reservations about going back to the heads with tentative results, in order to refine them in the light of the heads' reactions.

WOMAN RESEARCHER SEEKS WOMEN HEADS

Finding research subjects is rarely as easy as putting an advertisement in a paper, unless of course it is investigative journalism with aims very different from those informing a serious research study. The relationship among aims, methods, and outcomes is always close in research, but there is a danger that findings may be distorted by how the data are collected. As a woman researching women, I felt particularly vulnerable to accusations that I was merely finding what I wanted to see. Silverman (1993 p. 177), for example, warns of the dangers of gender-based approaches that are 'partisan', seeking to provide theoretical and factual sources for a political struggle.

My reasons for undertaking the research were threefold. Since my doctoral research in the 1970s, in which I looked at women entering the profession of journalism (Hall, 1978), I had continued my personal, professional and academic interest in women and work, in particular their contributions to the professions whose barriers they had overcome. At the same time, I wanted this study to be of interest and use to women and men headteachers, principals and others aspiring to positions of responsibility in schools and colleges. As a lecturer and researcher in a university department, I also wanted to contribute to the theoretical debate about leadership in education, by addressing questions of culture and power through gender perspectives informed by feminism. I saw my experiences as a girl and woman of a similar age to those in the study central to my researcher role. In common with the six women in the study, I was born in the 1940s, educated in schools in the 1950s, and in higher education in the 1960s, and have taught in schools and colleges for all my career. When the research project began, I had been an educational management consultant, researcher and lecturer for twelve years. I was thus a familiar stranger in the heads' worlds, continually juggling familiarity and strangeness, closeness and distance, in order to collect good-quality data.

This recognition of parallels between the heads' personal and professional experiences and my own was an important component of the rapport that developed, as a necessary basis for the joint conversations around which the interviews were structured. Silverman (1993) describes increasing evidence that the gender of fieldworkers is a crucial factor in observational research, although the examples he gives (of nudist beaches, rural communities) rarely represent professional settings. At present we do not know enough about the extent and nature of the impact of the researcher's gender on data collection, other than in discussions of women researching women (e.g. Maynard and Purvis, 1994). The feminist tradition from which these discussions emerge argues for the special quality of researcher–subject relationship. The power hierarchy that commonly exists between researcher and researched is rejected to avoid empowering one (the researcher, through the provision of information) at the expense of the other (the researched, who remain passive). Acknowledging a woman researcher–woman headteacher bond, based not on biology but on a set of common experiences as women, allowed a transforming relationship to develop in the headteacher study. Information was shared and the ideas generated were the outcome of reciprocal influence. The relationship was made easier by the fact that we had in common not only gender but also age, social class, as reflected in present occupation, ethnic origin (we were all white women) and our roles as professional educators. In their eyes, I was already familiar with the phenomenon they represented (successful professional women), the setting (primary and secondary schools) and the task (leading and managing a school). I was accepted as someone who knew and understood what they, as heads and as women, were trying to do.

The challenge of the interviews was that they required my personal involvement as interviewer to obtain good-quality information that would not be judged as biased, as a result of the transforming relationship I have described. I drew on life-history approaches to explore each head's background, in order to develop an understanding of how they arrived at headship and of the source of their interpretations of how they wanted to be as leaders. Woods (1987, p. 124) justifies the value of life-history methods for understanding teacher knowledge by referring to their basis in the subjective reality of the individual 'in a way that both respects the uniqueness of individuals and promotes identification of commonalities among them. It is concerned with whole people in whole contexts'. Such approaches, however, are rarely used in research with those who are powerful, since part of their power resides in their control of information (including information about themselves) and of the public identity they choose to present. Revealing their whole selves and the whole context could be detrimental to their maintenance of power. Getting close to the heads, their biographies and subjectivities, was an important component of the research. They welcomed the opportunities it provided for reflecting on self and coming to an understanding of, among other things, the relationship between themselves as leaders and themselves as women. Unlike other groups of women, who may be empowered by biography and autobiography, the women heads already felt relatively powerful. Their willingness to explore their personal histories was influenced by their desire to help a younger generation of women moving in similar directions, as well as to reach a fuller understanding of themselves.

My awareness of parallels between the heads' and my own personal histories can be justified, as Stanley and Wise (1993) have done, by arguing that the researcher is also the subject of her research, and that her personal history is part of the process through which understanding and conclusions are reached. An important part of recognizing this subjectivity was in being open and honest with the heads, and others, about my purposes and views on gender issues. At the same time, I was continually reminded that they did not necessarily share my prioritization of gender as a feature of organizational life, and often denied its significance. On many occasions they responded to my questions about whether they were aware of being a woman by commenting that they could not know – it might have been an influence but I was in a better position to see that than they were. While their reaction resembled the typical (usually male) politician's disclaimer, they were genuinely interested in the conclusions I reached from the research, for understanding themselves as well as others.

Similarly, they did not share to the same extent my concerns about women in public life. My own research and development work (confirmed by the international research literature) shows that there continue to be both internal and external barriers to women aiming for leadership positions. A few women overcome these barriers, some try to and fail and others do not perceive them in the first place. Where women have been successful in reaching the top, their perceptions of expectations of them as women leaders influence their behaviour. Although it can be argued that men's perceptions of others' expectations of them as leaders include living up to masculine stereotypes, male leadership is rarely discussed or researched in a way that takes gender into account.

HOLDING UP MIRRORS

In searching for a researcher–researched relationship that minimized power hierarchy, it was important for me to share information and thereby empower as well as interpret. As a researcher, I sought to understand and respond to what was in it for the heads to participate in the project. I knew, and they continuously confirmed, that they were extraordinarily busy. 'Time out' to help with research had to be justified to themselves, colleagues and governors. Their reasons for participating were a blend of personal and professional. One typically said that she had a professional responsibility to take part in the project. She had 'a good tale' to tell about being a woman and if there was any way her story would help other women, and perhaps enlighten some of her male colleagues, her participation was justified. My role as researcher required meeting their needs in whatever way I could. Some involved responding directly to the heads' needs, others to colleagues' needs through the access my position in a university school of education provided to resources that could be useful to their own development. I was concerned to demonstrate that, although the study's main focus was on the head, the school would also benefit. Equally the heads were concerned that their participation should bring benefits for others, particularly other women aspiring to management both in their own and other schools. This concern might appear to contradict their denial often of gender as an influential factor but, although consistency was normally a characteristic of their behaviour, attitudes to gender constituted an area where it was not.

Headship is a lonely and powerful position, even when it is construed relationally and democratically. Headteachers' colleagues are often reluctant to give feedback to someone who has control of their working present and future. A strong motive to take part in the project was the possibility of feedback from an outsider on how they were doing in the job. The heads were interested in how I saw their performance as managers (about which they were generally confident) and as women in a senior professional job (about which they had no fixed ideas). On many occasions they referred self-consciously to the impression they might be making on me in either of these roles. These comments usually revealed much about how they saw being a manager and woman in a school. For example, one, referring critically to a male colleague, said: 'Don't I sound terrible, a female chauvinist. I hope you won't dislike me by the end of this interview!'

During and after the project, they described the research process as interesting and useful in helping them reflect on their performance and in seeing how it compared with other women (rather than men) doing a similar job. Reflection and a commitment to self-development were common characteristics. The following comment was typical:

> I think it's been supportive, helping me through quite a difficult time of self-examination, you being here, being around, you've been another voice and another pair of ears during a time when I've been trying to make a big step in my own expertise not as a head but as a manager. I think it's a help to articulate what you are feeling. It's been about the only private professional time that I have had to talk about what I am doing and therefore it's been extremely valuable.

I provided regular written feedback in the form of notes (with my comments) of events in which I had observed them. At the subsequent interview and prior to the next observation, they would confirm, modify or extend my observations and comments, thereby contributing to a full and more accurate picture. The impact was not one way. As a woman manager myself, continual exposure over two years to the six heads' strategies for dealing with demanding situations had a considerable effect on the way I led my own management dance. As Wolcott (1982, p. 133) claims, 'You do not have to be neutral to be objective' and I was prepared to learn from the heads in a way that did not undermine my objectivity, or what Wolcott calls 'rigorous subjectivity'.

PROBING AND RESPECTING PRIVACY

I felt I was negotiating a constant tightrope between probing for detail and respecting privacy. This is a common problem for qualitative researchers. The heads would tell me things which, probed further, would give me greater insight into the relationship between their personal and professional lives. At the same time they might signal, through body language or explicitly, that further probing would not be appropriate. One head chose to tell me of very difficult and emotionally demanding personal circumstances, of which no one else in the school knew. The nub of a critical incident for another was what she saw as her betrayal by two colleagues to outsiders by passing on confidential and inaccurate information. She went through the incident with me many times, but was clearly reluctant to identify the colleagues or the nature of the information. However, as Lipson (1994) reminds us, we are researchers not journalists, and people are important as ends not means. Where it was clear that the heads did not wish to reveal more than they had, I did not push and accepted their willingness to be frank on most other topics. Inevitably this made it difficult to follow through some 'foreshadowed problems', for example, the relationship between personal and public persona, but the advantage of researching six sites was that these issues could often be explored elsewhere.

Together with my acceptability as a researcher and colleague was the heads' trust that their reflections on and my observations of their lives and work would be interpreted accurately. This acceptability and trust was crucial, if the multiplicity of threads making up the tapestry of their lives as headteachers were to be woven into a meaningful picture. On the other hand, it was important to establish enough closeness for them to relax and tell the 'real story' even though it sometimes meant that they forgot my purpose in hearing the account: to build up and publish a portrait of women as headteachers. The dilemma was in whether to remind them of the outcomes, when doing so might stifle the narration.

As we got to know each other better, their self-consciousness diminished, as did their apologies for how they might sound to me. Three of the six heads had recent experience of carrying out educational research and were familiar with my techniques. All increasingly revealed things close to their hearts to the extent that concerns about confidentiality occasionally erupted, particularly when they thought retrospectively about what they had said when talking to me. One discussed with me her perceptions of the unfairness of a selection process she had gone through, and said: 'I know you are taping this but I'd like to talk to you about the confidentiality. Obviously our relationship does take over, there's a certain bonding but there are some things I've thought I must tell you not to put in.' The kinds of comments about which they were concerned usually touched on intimate thoughts and experiences germane to the project, particularly its gender focus. They often revealed how much their formal denial of having experienced discrimination, or being aware of being a woman in the job, was contradicted by their actual experiences. It was not uncommon for them to say 'These are the bits you'll have to censor' or 'Well, perhaps you ought to turn the tape off'; and important contributions to the picture had to be interpreted from what I recalled without being formally recorded at the time.

How, then, should and could this kind of information be used? My approach involved in-depth probing into childhood experiences and influences, and elicited very personal anecdotes, some of which they would not wish publicized. All were frank in talking about their family situations. The dilemma on other occasions, particularly in informal exchanges, was whether to remind them of one of the project's outcomes (i.e. a publication) when they were talking to me outside my research role. One would often ring me to discuss issues or problems in which she thought I might be interested. On one occasion, she rang for advice and 'counselling' as a particular event had upset her. It was a political issue which revealed much about her attitudes to and strategies for dealing with men and power. I was caught between my desire to give helpful advice and, as researcher, to record as much as I could. She said to me later: 'I was like a lamb to the slaughter and that phrase you used when I rang you, about knowing how to play netball and then finding yourself in a rugby game, it was just like that.' So the phone call had been helpful to her and allowed me to try out a metaphor about women and power which seemed to have worked. However, had I provided her with an interpretation or with a means of articulating her own?

INTRODUCING THE DANCERS: SAMPLES AND SITES

The research was conceived as a small-scale, qualitative study over eighteen months. It involved six heads within the state-school sector, providing a spread across infant, primary and secondary schools, inner-city and suburban. Having three secondary and three primary heads also enabled some comparisons to be made within and across phases.

Within the LEA where the research took place, there were far fewer
secondary than primary women heads, thus limiting the range from
which to select the sample. Since the resources were not available
to study all women heads or even a representative national sample,
participants were identified reputationally, mainly through consultation
with the local authority advisers (male) who knew the schools well. On
my request, they produced a shortlist of heads in each phase who met
the criteria I specified: that they were women, had been heads for at
least three years and were seen by those associated with the school to
be performing well. This was interpreted loosely to mean they were
not encountering or generating difficult problems for their schools, as
a result of their leadership styles. I anticipated that three years was time
enough for heads to have gone through the initial stages of either entering
headship or taking over a new school, and to have emerged with a sense
of and confidence in their preferred leadership style in that context. The
six heads therefore had gender, time in post and successful performance
in common. At this stage, I did not know any of the heads personally, so
a relationship had to be forged from the start. Choosing heads who were
coping well with current demands influenced heavily the picture that
emerged, which became one of effective practice, thereby contributing
to an understanding of expert school leadership, as done by women. The
study's focus on gender and on women's performance brought to the
surface an association of these heads' practices with effective leadership
that was not assumed at its inception.

One of the six heads approached was initially reluctant to participate
in the study. Her work commitments were heavy, both within and
beyond the school, and some aspects of her working relations with
senior colleagues were less comfortable than she would have liked.
I persevered in persuading her to participate because I knew of her
reputation as a role model for other women aspiring to headship and she
eventually agreed to become part of the project. At my initial interview
with each head, it was agreed that I should prepare a written statement
for display, describing the project and emphasizing its focus on the head,
not other members of staff or the school in general. The three primary
heads asked me additionally to address the staff as a whole to explain the
project. All the heads knew they would be under close scrutiny, something
they were willing to undergo as long as other staff's time was protected.
It was important to reassure other staff that I was observing the heads,
not them. An important element in the heads' decision to participate was
their interest in the research's gender focus even though, as subsequent
chapters show, they often denied its importance as an influential or
explanatory factor of their behaviour.

We also agreed a code of ethics for the research which included absolute
confidentiality regarding information they or anyone else provided, as
well as the right to view anything written for publication and request
amendments if necessary. In the event, only a few factual errors needed
to be changed in the final draft. There were occasions on which they felt

it inappropriate for me to be present. Although these were relatively few, they were notably more than in my previous research with men secondary heads. These occasions most frequently occurred during interviews with parents about a sensitive staff–student issue. The fact that the women heads excluded me more could have been attributed to their greater sensitivity to the nuances of situations and people's feelings, which I describe in Chapter 5. They always checked first whether others minded my presence. Or, as they suggested themselves, it may have been a sign of the times, when heads were becoming more cautious about the possible outcomes in litigation of difficult situations. The heads were always prepared to discuss with me what had happened or had been said during incidents from which I was excluded.

COLLECTING AND ANALYSING THE ACCOUNTS

The study drew on a range of qualitative methods for understanding the topic, and a number of different sources. These provided a means of focusing on the heads' subjective experiences and meanings. It fell within the tradition of feminist research that pursues a relatively open-ended exploration of women's experiences to see how their world is organized. The purposes of the research were threefold: through observation to document how these women behaved as school leaders; through semi-structured interviews, how they interpreted their behaviour and the values underpinning it; and through life-history approaches, how their behaviour as headteachers related to their experiences of childhood through to their present stage of career.

During site visits, information was collected from and about the heads through a combination of life-history interviews, joint conversations, semi-structured interviews and structured and unstructured observations. Each site was visited up to six times a term over the five school terms of the project. Visits lasted from a couple of hours to a full day. Additionally, semi-structured interviews were conducted with up to six of each head's teacher colleagues, complemented by informal conversations with other people, advisers, teachers, governors, parents, secretaries, during site visits. Prior to each interview I sent the heads a checklist of the topic areas I wanted to cover, so that they could reflect on their responses. This was important since, although they were very generous with their time (some interviews lasted two hours or more), both I and they wanted to use it efficiently. Also, many questions asked them to describe thoughts, feelings and incidents in the past, which could not on the spot easily be retrieved from memory. Finally, I discovered that receiving questions beforehand suited their style since all preferred being prepared for situations rather than improvising. I recognize that time to reflect can also create time to massage responses. Weiler (1988) has observed that female teachers often gloss over the details of their lives, so that they may, for example, 'forget' that they were forced to go out to work to support the family and 'remember' that they had always wanted to teach. There were a number of mechanisms built into the interviews to protect against this doctored recall, including the depth of the probing (questions provided only the initial prompt) and returning to topics at different times.

The first formal interview was the most structured. It lasted up to three hours and explored the heads' careers from early childhood to the present. It concluded with their account of their leadership styles, the context of their school and the structure of their working days. Later interviews returned to issues raised. Subsequent interviews always began with their comments on, and discussion of, the versions I had prepared of a previous observation. These records had three components: description of the observed events, people, setting, talk; comments on my observations (in square brackets), made while I transcribed the observation notes on to tape for typing; and handwritten comments in the margins, after I had read the whole text through. The heads' comments on these were then recorded and formed the beginning of each new transcript. This enabled data analysis to be concurrent with data collection and allowed the interpretation to come from the heads' as well as my own understanding, in the light of the literature on educational management and leadership. Then we would move on to specific themes which included issues relating to leadership and power; deeper probing into early childhood and education experiences; responses to current issues in the school or education generally; experience of taking over the school; combining personal and professional lives; and beliefs about the experiences of women in education. Some questions were put to all the heads, others arose from what they said or I observed them to do.

Early in the project, I observed each head for a full day so that I could begin documenting the relationship between what they said and how they behaved. My earlier experience of observing headteachers at work (Hall et al., 1986) enabled me to construct fairly rapidly the patterns of their working days. The intention of this study was to go beyond description and use the observations to look at the relationship between conception and enactment of school leadership. For example, the heads would express to me an ambivalence about how they used power, but show themselves as politically competent in situations which I observed. Decisions were necessary about selecting events for observation and how far to use structured or unstructured observational techniques.

In his critique of Mintzberg's (1973) reliance on highly structured observations, Gronn (1984) defends a less structured approach for describing the nature of managerial work. He argues (ibid., p. 124) that style is not only behaviour but also a corpus of concepts and analytical constructs which have personal and institutional consequences for both self and others. Observing and recording behaviour is not enough. The actions' meanings for the players are crucial. My observations of each head were written up and passed back to the head concerned for comment at our next meeting. Although other actors' definitions of the situation were thereby excluded, the method enabled the subjective meaning attached to the event by the head to play a key part in its interpretation. A few simple rules guided the selection of events to be observed. All the heads were seen in some common tasks and settings such as governor meetings, meetings with senior colleagues, other heads, parents, selecting staff. Other observations were specific to each head, either individually or within her school context. They sometimes proposed events to be observed or, within events, specific phenomena as foci, thereby contributing to the research framework rather than having it imposed. For example, it was important for one head that I observed her involvement in education–business partnerships since they were a central part of her interpretation of the job. Another was moving to a new school and identified initial events during her 'takeover' as potentially significant in understanding her leadership style.

TALKING TO OTHERS

In order to obtain a broader picture of each head in her context, I also talked with other staff. Data collected in this way are always fraught with difficulties. While it may be true that our understanding of leadership starts by looking at and listening to followers, each follower's account tells us more about the speaker than the leader. What they say reflects their values and how they evaluate the head, so that the head's behaviour might be interpreted very differently according to the respondent's gender, status, personality and history of personal relations with her. The purpose of the formal interviews with other teachers was therefore limited to exploring different people's responses to common issues arising from my analysis of their headteacher's style. Rather than providing hard data, it allowed me to check my picture against their daily experience of working with the head. Interestingly, the degree of consensus in their positive views of their head was high. This was surprising in view of the differences in gender, status and personality of those interviewed. It suggested consistencies in each head's behaviour as she interacted with different individuals and groups.

I interviewed between four and six men and women teachers on each head's staff, exploring their responses to different facets of the head's behaviour. The interviews were sensitive, since those involved were concerned about what might be fed back to the head and, simultaneously, about being loyal. At the same time, I had to be careful not to reveal to them anything the head had told me in confidence. Each interview lasted about an hour and was taped. They included questions about differences in the head's style from her predecessor's, her impact on coming first to the school, her vision and how it was communicated, her style, examples of critical incidents, and their and others' responses to her as a woman.

INTERPRETING THE DATA: FRAMEWORKS AND PERSPECTIVES

The framework for analysis in this study was complex and problematic. A major focus of the research was on women's interpretations of their experiences of managing schools. Their interpretations were then reinterpreted in the light of theoretical frameworks that address issues of power and culture in education management. This combined recognizing the validity of their accounts and setting them within a broader theoretical position that uses theory to make sense of experience. After all, encouraging women to talk about their experiences as a way of legitimizing women's voices does not necessarily guarantee greater authenticity, since people's accounts of their lives are culturally embedded. Given their professional task and status, both men and women educators learn how to construct and represent their lives for public consumption, and the rhetoric may bear little resemblance to the reality.

My decision to provide one account of six individuals could be seen to fail to do justice to any single account, since what they had in common appears to take precedence over how they differed. In the final stages of analysis, commonalities were identified within each of the coding categories that I developed, but differences were also noted whenever they occurred, for example, in how they carried out tasks or responded to people. In fact, commonalities were marked to the extent that, when each head read the final draft, they commented on how much what others were quoted as saying and doing reflected their own sentiments and behaviour; they also said how relieved they were to find this was the case. The point of studying six women heads was not to provide a basis for generalizing to all other women heads, but to contribute new information and ideas to theories of education management. The research aimed to construct an accurate picture of headship as done by these six women. It is a question for further research whether a similar picture would emerge if the study was replicated with six other women or six men headteachers. Additionally, a quantitative study across a large number of men and women senior managers in schools is needed to explore further questions raised in this research.

In a study of teamwork in secondary school management (Wallace and Hall, 1994), we developed a dual perspective or 'power-culture' metaphor as a lens through which to view and interpret the phenomenon. Gender was included as a factor for consideration, but not a specific focus for our observations of the teams' operations. We concluded that teamwork had the potential to undercut gender-based behaviour by proposing different norms and rules that make some behaviours legitimate, and a priority, particularly those stressing collaboration, equity and consensus decision-making. Within a very small sample, we found women and men equally committed (or not) to collaborative values, either as team leaders or team members. Individual responsibilities and status were defined in terms of the management hierarchy and team membership, rather than gender (*ibid.*, p. 39).

Table 2.1   Key concepts employed within different perspectives

Cultural (Nias, 1989)	Political (Ball, 1987)	Cultural and political
Culture of collaboration	Power	Culture of teamwork
Beliefs	Control	Beliefs
Values	Goal diversity	Values
Understanding	Ideology	Norms
Attitudes	Conflict	Role
Meanings	Interests	Status
Norms		Rituals
Symbols		Consensus
Rituals		Power
Ceremonies		Resources
Negotiation		Hierarchy
Consensus		Interests
		Dialectic of control
		Authority
		Influence
		Conflict
		Contradiction
		Coalitions

Source: Based on Wallace and Hall, 1994, p. 24)

The project on women headteachers provided a further opportunity for using the power-culture metaphor, but this time gender was added as a significant factor. The now triple metaphor provided an orientating frame for negotiating the territory of headship and gender, and identifying the questions which data collection needed to address. The justification for a dual metaphor in the school management team (SMT) study was the inadequacy of either 'political' or 'cultural' perspectives (as used, for example, in the writings of Ball, 1987, and Nias, 1989) for explaining the phenomenon of teamwork. Both approaches offer valuable insights but, in focusing the research, each may be constrained by its emphasis on one set of concepts to the detriment of the other. Similarly, a study of women managers would be incomplete unless it drew on key concepts represented in both these perspectives. These are shown in Table 2.1, together with those that comprised our own dual perspective in the SMT study.

Concepts from all three columns in Table 2.1 provided relevant lenses for focusing on the different ways in which the women heads interpreted and used power, and their impact on the workplace culture as, through their leadership role, they worked towards changing schools in order to improve children's educational experience. Shakeshaft (1989, p. 167) argues that successful women have, in addition to their ability to negotiate the world of white males, a socialization as women that they bring to the job. While agreeing that this constitutes a distinctive feature of their leadership repertoire and reflects a female culture and female world, I would argue that patterns of power in organizations constrain the creation of a 'feminized' workplace. Acker (1993), for example, describes the workplace culture of the elementary school which is the focus of her study as a 'feminized' culture, in so far as it incorporated values of caring, participation, commitment. The presence of a female leader was relevant but, in her view, no guarantee of a collegial, caring environment (*ibid.*, p. 18). By using a cultural perspective in the study of women heads, I aimed to explore whether and how far women leaders' beliefs and actions contributed to feminized workplace cultures. In her research in The Netherlands on leadership and gender in different schools' cultures, Krüger (1994) concludes that differences in leadership between men and women are determined by gender in combination with school culture. She describes cultures as 'gender-own' and 'gender-opposite' and sees differences in whether a leader runs an organization in which the rules of conduct, norms and values are established by the leader's own gender or by the opposite gender (*ibid.*, p. 132). On this basis, given the mainly token presence of men in the primary schools, a difference between primary and secondary school cultures might have been anticipated, if 'feminized' cultures depend on a majority of women. School leaders may want to see themselves as primary determiners of school cultures but that does not mean that those cultures necessarily reflect their values. As Sarason (1982, p. 177) points out, 'a person's orientation toward himself or herself and the world is important, but equally important are the ideas and values to which the orientation is related'. For him, the important point is not what the school leader is like (personality, style, experience, etc.) but whether he or she is constantly confronting and encouraging others to confront their own and others' values about the nature of life in a school.

Sarason's is essentially a cultural perspective, although it is political in its advocacy of the need to challenge the organizational status quo. A more political perspective reminds us of the pervasiveness of power relations, whatever the setting. The resulting school culture is the outcome of the complex dynamic between power and culture in organizational life. In the SMT study (Wallace and Hall, 1994, p. 27), we suggested 'that interaction may be an expression of both the shared values of a culture and the differential use of power to realize particular interests'. The headteachers' position of authority gives them greater power than their colleagues to shape aspects of the school's corporate culture, even though their influence on the many subcultures that make up any organization is more limited. When a further lens is added, of gender, the picture shifts again so that both power and culture separately and the interaction between them take a different form and meaning. This analysis uses Giddens's (1984) definition of power as 'transformative capacity': the use of resources to secure desired outcomes. In any interaction, individuals make different use of resources to achieve desired goals, according to their beliefs and values, which they share to a greater or lesser extent with others and of which they have only a partial awareness (Wallace and Hall, 1994, p. 27). The additional use of a gender perspective raises questions about the resources women school leaders use to achieve desired goals; the form these goals take; their beliefs and values; the extent to which the fact that they are women influences others' use of resources to achieve their desired goals, and creates acceptance of or resistance to women as leaders.

Women heads are faced with the duality of expectations of their behaviour as leaders who are also women. Schools are no less involved in the reproduction of gender relations than other organizations. The apparent value neutrality of 'management' obscures not only its political character as a process of power relations but also its gendered associations, for example, the claim that 'management is masculine', discussed in Chapter 1. The advantage of the triple 'power-culture-gender' metaphor is in ensuring that the gender-centred perspective does not ignore the situational variables in organizations that affect women managers' experiences, actions and impact.

Other research suggests that the beliefs, values and norms underpinning women's interpretation of leadership and power are rooted in their earlier experiences as girls and women, in response to the cultural expectations (including those relating to the use of power) of their families, schools, colleges and other work settings (e.g. Astin and Leland, 1991; Cantor and Bernay, 1992). These expectations (discussed in Chapter 3) include their attitudes towards 'status', 'consensus', 'hierarchy', 'authority' and 'conflict', which are embodied in their symbolic leadership behaviour (discussed in Chapters 5 and 6) and their use of power to empower (discussed in Chapter 7). For example, Chapter 6 describes each head's symbolic leadership behaviour, as demonstrated in their approaches to selecting, motivating and developing staff. These human-resource management strategies provide the head with vehicles for strengthening some parts of the school's culture and undermining others, depending on what she and senior colleagues consider desirable. Within the context of each strategy, they use authority, power and influence to contribute to desired cultural outcomes, and combat conflict and dissent as they arise.

CONCLUSIONS

In conclusion, only an in-depth qualitative study could have explored the issues of power, culture and gender in education management as they are described here. The conclusions arising from the research findings set the agenda for future research using the triple metaphor to examine both men and women managing schools. Whether the methods used, drawing as they do on the relationship between the gender of the researcher and subject, are appropriate and necessary for future research in this area is best judged by the quality of the story that follows. Changing the subject from woman as 'other and inessential' to woman as 'subject and essential' does not necessarily mean redefining woman rather than man as 'absolute'. I hope the change will contribute to the possibility of viewing, in training and development programmes at least, women and men's management behaviour in the light of women as well as men.

3.

IN SEARCH OF A LIFESTYLE: CHOICES AND DILEMMAS

INTRODUCTION

A book looking at women as headteachers would be incomplete without a discussion of how they reached their current position and the implications of their chosen career path for their personal lives. How people behave at work needs to be understood together with their life outside work, although the concentration of most school leadership studies on the workplace environment suggests otherwise. This chapter describes the complex and dynamic factors influencing the lifestyles of women headteachers and the relationship between the personal and professional sides of their lives. Research evidence from studies of women managers outside education (e.g. Marshall, 1984; Fagenson, 1993) shows that, in their search for a well rounded life, women managers make choices relating to family and career experiences which influence their success in both spheres. The question is whether women in teaching who seek career advancement resemble women managers outside education in the dilemmas they face and the choices they make. Or, does education as a work arena have a different impact on women's career development? Further, are women who achieve headship different from their women teacher colleagues, in the strength of their commitment to being a leader and their confidence in their ability to take overall control? If so, where did that commitment come from and how was it nurtured and sustained?

An NUT/EOC study in 1980 of women teachers' career aspirations showed they were as career ambitious as male colleagues but estimated their chances of success as lower. More recent studies (Grant, 1989; Evetts, 1990; Acker, 1994) highlight the need to reconceptualize 'career' in the light of women's experiences. They challenge as 'masculine' Lyons's (1981) description of the career-orientated teacher as one who is single-mindedly purposeful in the pursuit of career goals, following a linear progression through carefully planned steps. This model ignores the competing pressures of home and family circumstances on career, which act simultaneously as constraints, demands and choices. How individual women teachers respond to them will depend on their personal identity and the influence of family and educational experiences on their career decisions. Like those in the study, women who become headteachers have responded to conflicting pressures in ways that have allowed them to realize their ambitions. They did not feel their chances of success were less because they were women, nor were they necessarily more career ambitious than other teachers. This chapter will argue that their path to headship evolved alongside the development of an 'inner locus of control' that enabled them to deal with obstacles they encountered to self-realization.

TRACING THE PATHS

In order to understand how these women arrived at their headship positions, I traced their experiences from family of origin, through school, college and early work experiences to family, educational and career experiences as adults. These experiences are set within the context of values about power, culture and gender that played a part in the choices made, and provided a basis for future leadership action. The relationships are traced between the formation of personal identity (who you are), career decisions (what you want) and subsequent leadership behaviour (how you act). I assumed that, at different stages of their lives starting in childhood, women who had become headteachers had made choices about the relative importance they would attach to the following behaviours:

- Being academically successful at school.
- Being a leader at school.
- Gaining higher-education qualifications.
- Having a career.
- Whether and/or when to marry.
- Whether and/or when to have children.
- Seeking promotion.
- Becoming a school leader.

I argue that the choices they made were influenced and at times constrained by factors that in turn created dilemmas at different points in their careers. The influences and constraints included

- social class and parents' educational background;
- division of labour in the household and expectations regarding men and women's public and private roles;
- sibling relations;
- the availability of role models at school, college and work;
- other non-family members' influences;
- type of career chosen;
- type of support available from husband or partner where applicable;

- other types of support;
- number and ages of own children; and
- demands of the job.

Each woman's experience is unique, and common dilemmas can call forth diverse responses. This chapter aims to show the life experiences of these six women which led to their entry into headship. It describes how they responded to the dilemmas they faced in choosing a lifestyle that was acceptable to them and enabled them to be effective in the job.

OTHER ACCOUNTS OF WOMEN'S CAREER HISTORIES

I was interested in the extent to which the women heads' career development and lifestyles resembled those described in other studies of women managers. The strong similarities that emerged, in spite of their different personal and professional contexts, would suggest gender as a significant factor in shaping their career paths. Some studies include discussions of the impact of childhood experiences, others do not. For example, Marshall (1984) concentrated her examination of women managers' employment histories and personal identity on their experiences as adults. Their responses to her core questions 'what do you want?' and 'who are you?' were framed within the context of what the women had already become when taking their first career steps. She acknowledges the role of sex-role stereotypes in early and later socialization, but questions their relevance to understanding women's decisions to become managers. She challenges simplistic accounts of women entering 'a male world', which see them as breaking the stereotypes of 'masculinity' and 'femininity' that conventionally shape career choices. For her, this kind of explanation is based on judgements about what constitute 'masculine' and 'feminine' that derive from other societal values about what is more important: public or private life; career or family; reason or emotions. It is more important to look at how successful women have interpreted the social constraints on forming their self-identities and how they use power differently from men to shape their own and others' lives.

Another study of women 'high flyers' in management (White *et al.*, 1992, p. 226) concludes that successful women are most realistically seen as a self-selected population of highly career-orientated survivors. Their study includes childhood and education experiences as relevant to women's career development, emphasizing the reciprocities among the individual, her environment and the active contribution the individual makes to her own development over time. While many of its conclusions reflect my own findings, my incorporation of the power-culture perspective (described in Chapter 2) suggests some variations in the agendas for understanding women in educational management and women managers in the private sector. These and other writers are concerned with women as managers outside education. Their focus is on women as managers not leaders, i.e. as people who are in senior positions but not necessarily at the top of their organization. As an educationalist studying management and leadership in education, I also wanted to understand the ways in which the dynamic of each woman's career was influenced first by its location in education and, secondly, by the desire eventually to be a leader.

Two other studies were helpful in providing a context for arriving at conclusions about the contribution of key influences and experiences to becoming a leader in education. Evetts' (1990) framework derives from interviews with twenty-five married women primary and infant headteachers. Her emphasis is on how they constructed their careers and what strategies they devised in pursuing them. Central to her reconceptualization of 'career', in the light of women's as well as men's experiences, is the need to include factors relating to teaching as a profession, representing both an occupational culture and a labour market. She concludes that women's paths to infant and primary headships are hardly less fraught than those of women in male-dominated occupations. Their career strategies have had to take account of managing the same competing claims of family and paid work in a labour market for primary teachers, which has been variably supportive of women's attempts to work outside the home.

Evetts develops her concept of 'subjective career' mainly in the context of individuals' working lives. Astin and Leland (1991) look additionally to the families of origin of the 'women of vision, women of influence' who are the focus of their study. In reviewing their relationships with parents, grandparents and siblings, as well as mentors and role models, the authors seek to explain what gave these women the strength to overcome discrimination, harassment and rejection, and become advocates for educational reform. Like White and her colleagues, Astin and Leland identify in successful women an assurance and belief in self that enables them to lead as well as manage. The difference between the groups of women represented in these two surveys, i.e. 'women high flyers' and 'women of vision', is that questions about the values for which the high flyers are flying high do not inform the analysis of the sources of their ambition and motivation. In White et al.'s study, the women come from different commercial and industrial settings, but little reference is made to the relationship between the values that motivate them towards 'extraordinary levels of career success' (ibid., p. 5) and those that drive the enterprise with which they are associated. Childhood experiences are linked to whether they choose to be successful or not, but not to the goals towards which the successful behaviour is directed.

In contrast, Astin and Leland show how the values and leadership potential of the women in their study stemmed from their family and educational roots. Similarly, my understanding of women's career paths towards, and behaviour as, educational leaders takes into account their subjective careers which led them first into teaching and then into educational management and leadership. The women heads' accounts of how and why they took the paths they did in their personal and public lives show that, far from being the victims of stereotypes encountering obstacles based on gender, they made choices at each stage about what they wanted for themselves and for their chosen profession: to educate young people. Their accounts are presented in terms of the phases and stages of each headteacher's life, to show the dilemmas they encountered and the choices, compromises and sometimes sacrifices they made.

FAMILY RELATIONSHIPS AND INFLUENCES

The following profiles of each head comprise reconstructions of their early years from much longer conversations, to highlight what I saw as recurring themes. They summarize the nature of the heads' relations with their parents and siblings, who had power in the family and the origins of their career ambitions. I begin with the three primary heads, Barbara, Heather and Susan. They shared a commitment to becoming a teacher from early childhood, drawn to it as a pleasurable activity as well as a career.

Barbara was in her early forties, married to another teacher and had two school-age children. She lived in a large modern house in a village a few miles from the infants school where she became head in 1989. Her mother, who was nearly ninety, died during the study. Her father had died much earlier. She was born in 1950 in Kent, the youngest of nine children (four sisters and four brothers), with the next sibling up some eight years older. She attributed her desire from an early age to teach young children to being surrounded by her sisters' babies, for whom she was like a big sister. Being the youngest was like being an only child, mainly on her own with her parents and particularly her elderly grandfather, with whom she spent a lot of time. 'When you're number nine you're just one on the end and I think I was probably just left to get on with it.' It was a 'very working-class, very tough sort of existence' in which she 'was always out playing and in her own world'. She combined a certainty that she would teach with a strong streak of independence, looking from about thirteen 'for some route to freedom' through education. Neither of her parents knew anything about education and just said 'do your best'. Her mother took for granted that, if she wanted to be a teacher, that's what she would be. Her father, who worked in the dockyards, could not understand the ambition and wondered why she wanted to work with children, when she could be a hairdresser and 'buy a nice salon'. He was strict, 'very Victorian with a thing about people having a place in society'. Although her mother appeared like 'the power behind the throne', when her father died she 'crumbled'. She hardly knew her brothers who were all much older. The effects of her position in such a large family were to confirm her sense from an early age of wanting to be different. She was uneasy with the domestic lives of her sisters: 'I was aware that life was something more than living in a terrace Victorian house, getting married at eighteen, having children and buying a three-piece suite. I thought my sisters have got married, had babies and the shutters have come down.' Her mother had a string of odd jobs including shopwork. Barbara's early intention to be different was combined with the model presented by all the men in her family (father, brothers and brothers-in-law) of hard work, which she did too, 'slave labour in the paper factory and waitressing on the seafront'. Along with the desire to be different and get an education came the need to justify her deviant choices by being perfect. She assumed that others thought 'you can't have a job and family so you can't be seen to have any cracks'.

Heather was in her mid-forties, married for a second time with a grown-up daughter and grandchildren. She first became a head in 1989 and lived with her husband and father in a modern semi-detached house a few miles from the junior school where she worked. Her mother had died some years earlier. She too wanted to be a teacher from an early age, influenced by her father who would have loved to have been one. He would spend hours patiently helping her and her younger brother with school work: 'I'd come home from school in a state about my work, and he'd put it right'. They lived in London, where her father was a tailor, 'a very working-class background', and her mother worked part time, mostly in catering work. Both parents were very supportive of their children's education, but it was her father whose influence was strongest. From him she learned her 'love of teaching and sitting on the fence'. He was not a dominant man and she felt she learned a lot of skills from her mother about quietly getting her own way. She was not aware of competition with her brother (who became a solicitor), although he told her later that he had been jealous sometimes because she was her father's favourite. It was a harmonious household in which neither parent dominated, providing a secure environment from which to go forward. Heather commented:

> The supportive nature of my management style comes from the supportive nature of my parents. Until late in life I had learned to take everyone on trust and I believed everyone had my best interests at heart. I had to learn that not everyone's life revolved around me. I suppose why I found it so difficult to become a leader was because neither of my parents had these leadership qualities. Neither would dominate others and my style is always to lead from behind and be supportive from underneath and so it was against my nature to lead from the front.

Susan was in her late forties, had not married and lived close to her sister and father. She became a head in 1989 and lived on her own in a modern house a few miles from the primary school where she worked. She had lived her whole life in the same city where she was now a head. From an early age she wanted to be a teacher and would play teachers at home with anyone she could find. She would provide the books and make the registers. Her father, a printer, was proud of her intention to contribute to educating the young but tended to favour her twin sister, who became a homemaker rather than career woman. He was not an easy man to please and Susan looked for his approval well into adulthood. 'His word was the last word and you didn't question it.' Both parents valued a strong work ethic, so that she and her sister felt that whatever job they did, it must be done well. 'We both of us always felt we had to hear people say "you're a good worker".' Although her mother did not work outside the home 'she was a good housekeeper and ran a good ship'. Within this tight structure of discipline, high standards and hard work, the household was a happy and supportive one. Her father was self-educated, very intelligent, and she felt her own capacity for self-motivation came from his example. She was driven to succeed by her own ambitions rather than being pushed and by the high standards she set herself as well as those set by others.

Vanessa was in her early fifties, divorced with two grown-up sons. She lived on her own in a modern detached house a few miles from the inner-city comprehensive school where she had been head for seven years. Her mother lived about forty miles away and Vanessa visited her regularly. Her father died a few years previously. As a child, she and her younger brother had accompanied their parents when they played sports. She was good at physical education and, encouraged by the school, drifted into it later as a career choice. Her parents were supportive but neither had had higher education and their main concern was that she should be happy doing whatever she chose. Her mother was more assertive than her father and tended to favour her brother who was often poorly: 'She would never tell me how well I'd done, only him.' She did not work outside the home, other than churchwork to which she was very committed. Vanessa had a close relationship with her father, a leather chemist, who was gentle and understanding, 'very respected as a manager by all the people who worked for him'. In spite of her considerable lack of confidence as a teenager, she was determined to go her own way, carve her own niche and show she could succeed. She was always a perfectionist, and later she sought the same respect from others that she saw given to her father, as a person and manager.

Pauline was in her late forties, married, with no children. Her mother lived nearby but her father died when she was fifteen. She lived with her husband in a modern house some thirty miles from the mixed comprehensive school where she worked. Although she had wanted to teach since primary school, it was not her immediate goal as a career. She described her origins as lying in her grandfather's advocacy of women's education 'because, he'd say, you never know what's going to happen to you'. As a result her mother received a good education and trained as a shorthand typist. Her father, an accounting clerk, was self-educated, forced to leave school at fourteen and diabetic. She was an only child and, though disappointed that she was a girl, he was very anxious she should be well educated. Lacking the son through which he could relive his sport, he would play cricket with her for hours and take her to the Oval cricket ground. She attributed her own competitiveness to not liking to fail and always wanting to please her father: 'He set so much store by my success but wasn't good at showing approval. That came from my mum who was always "whatever makes you happy".' Although his word was law, it was not oppressively so and she would negotiate with her mother to get what she wanted or to persuade her father. After he died when she was fifteen, it was her mother's sacrifices that enabled her later to go on to higher education. She saw her mother working from five in the morning until seven at night, helping her grandmother run her newsagent's business next door. Unashamed of her working-class origins, she also wanted to use education to better herself as well as have the safety net advocated by her grandfather.

Diana was in her late forties and lived with her husband and two school-age children some distance away from the mixed comprehensive school where she worked. She commuted weekly between home and school, not wanting to disrupt her children's schooling, as well as having difficulties in selling the house. Her mother lived in another part of the country and she would visit her in the school holidays. Like Pauline, Diana was an only child (of elderly parents) and spent most of her teenage years at a mixed Quaker boarding school. It was her father's influence and encouragement that made her go on to higher education and a career.

He had a great respect for education and came from a family which, through the generations, had had a great love of learning. As a result, Diana had always felt 'education is the greatest gift we can give young people'. Her mother, on the other hand, would have preferred her not to work and she felt, in many respects, she did not meet her mother's expectations. Both parents were disappointed when she decided to do voluntary service overseas when she was twenty-one but she valued the fact that they did not stand in her way. At one stage when she wanted to do law, an uncle who was also the family lawyer intervened and said that she should not because 'it was a male profession and not the right thing for a girl to do'. Looking back she felt that perhaps she had been very weak at the time to let herself be influenced so easily. Her decision to go overseas at twenty-one was an early demonstration of the single-mindedness that characterized her approach to life later. Within the family, domestic and behavioural expectations were set by her mother but the major decisions and priorities were determined by her father. His influence on her was definitely the greater. 'He was a very reasonable, very gentle person, always looking at things in a balanced way, always seeing the good in people.'

While recognizing the dangers of generalizing, the profiles demonstrate common themes about significant influences on the women's personal and career development, although the actual experiences may have differed. The nature of the influences can only be hypothesized, since it would require a more extensive study to establish precise relationships between early experiences and later behaviour. There is a considerable literature on parental influences on career choices and adult lifestyles which White *et al.*

(1992) draw on to analyse the parent–child relationships of the successful women in their survey. For example:

- Parental behaviour promoting achievement, striving and independence in female children includes warmth, moderate permissiveness, encouragement for and reinforcement of achievement-related efforts.
- Problematic relationships with mothers lead to a lack of bonding in the parent–child relationship that encourages a separate sense of identity among successful women.
- It is more common for fathers to train their daughters in traditional femininity; that is, they show greater concern with the affective and interpersonal development of their daughter than with achievement-related behaviour.
- Senior women managers recall happy childhoods, closeness and warmth in relations with parents and a special relationship between fathers and daughters.
- Although the mothers of successful women shared the father's aspirations for their daughters, their relationship was not so prominent.

A general conclusion emerging from these findings is that, as a result of the different influences of each parent, women are exposed to a diverse set of role options. All women, as girls, will absorb some of the feminine strengths and abilities which their mothers provide as role models. Mothers who have a full-time career outside the home may also provide the additional stimulus to continue in their footsteps. Only one of the heads had a mother who worked full time and she, together with grandparents, constituted a strong influence on Pauline's attitudes to having a career. Overall the heads' accounts gave the impression of families in which tasks and roles were clearly differentiated along gender lines. In this respect they differed from Astin and Leland's women educational leaders, many of whose mothers represented self-actualized women outside the home. The women heads' role models for self-actualization through work outside the home, as well as through personal relationships, did not come from their mothers. Generation is also likely to have played a part, since they grew up at a time when fewer women had careers outside the home. A younger generation of women heads might demonstrate a different pattern.

Marshall suggests that women who positively value their mother's role within the private world of home (which these heads did) develop an appreciation of their own feminine strengths and abilities that does not depend on male approval. None of the women heads felt a need either, when a child, to be more like a boy or, in adulthood, to be more like a man, in order to progress or win approval. Deciding to follow a different career path and lifestyle from their mothers was the result largely of their fathers' special influence. It is clear from the literature and from this study that women, unlike men, take both their mothers and their fathers as role models. This provides them with a broader range of behaviours or repertoire on which to base their own actions later in life. Harris's (1995, p. 42) analysis of 'becoming a man' claims that, at the age of six, boys make clear distinctions between the concepts of male and female and begin to no longer model their mother, who in most cases has been their most nurturing parent. At that point they have to figure out how to act like men and start modelling the behaviour of men they admire.

In his study of 'messages men hear', he draws on a sample of over five hundred men to construct a theory of masculinity by exploring how men form their gender identities and how these identities influence their behaviour. He confirms that men are driven by social messages that encourage them to be 'duteous workers, to obey the law, to become technically competent and to work in order to earn a living' (*ibid.*, p. 89). As a result, they have fewer opportunities to achieve identities independent of their job titles. When it comes to being 'successful', he shows how reaching positions of power (becoming the boss) enables them to achieve and feel good about their masculine identities (*ibid.*, p. 135).

He concludes that what men learn about relating to others from male messages 'presents a picture of emotional tragedy' (*ibid.*, p. 106). It would seem that, as a result of the loss of women as role models, men's repertoires are more limited than those of women who are drawing on both parents. Men headteachers of the same generation as these women heads are unlikely to have had mothers who worked outside the home, since that was far less common in the late forties and fifties. Their model for future work patterns will have come from other men, including the assumption that boys when adult will go out to work (assuming employment opportunities exist). Harris describes how work defines men, playing a key role in constructing their identities. He quotes as typical one craftsman: 'The messages I received from my environment were that men were only important as providers, that work came first and work was where one's true identity as a man came out and was judged' (*ibid.*, p. 73).

The women heads' biographies suggest that, for some girls at least, choices are available. They include choices about whether to work and about which aspects of each parent's behaviour to accept or reject as part of their own identity. Whilst not denying the myriad constraints on both women and men's personal and public lives, the theme of choosing how one wants to be and act emerged strongly in the six heads' careers. None of the women heads had parents in teaching or any other profession and all but Diana were the first in their generation in the family to have a career as opposed to a job. Even Diana was the first woman in four generations to enter a profession. It was important for them not to be seen to fail in their chosen path, and this concern explained some of their reluctance to display any weaknesses in the job. Parental influences (particularly fathers) were therefore significant influences on the women heads' early independence, self-sufficiency and desire to succeed.

LEARNING ABOUT POWER

Listening to their accounts of family life for clues about the origins of
their conceptions of power suggests that they interpreted and used
power in specific ways, because that is how they had learned to use it,
not because of innate 'female' characteristics. Although family of origin
is by no means an exclusive influence on future values and behaviour, it
shapes perceptions of which resources achieve which results. In their case,
fathers provided the dominant role model (both positive and negative)
for how formal authority might be used, and mothers were a source of
other strategies for exercising influence. As adults, the women combined
formal authority as heads with informal influence deriving from their
other public and private roles. There emerges from their accounts a picture
of formal authority lying with the father and informal influence lying
mainly with the mother. Generally, their fathers' enactment of authority
was benign rather than Draconian. The ways in which family attitudes
to power and influence were manifested varied between individuals,
but as daughters they were exposed to a wider range of strategies for
using power and influence (including those used by women) than sons
might be.

Relationships with parents and siblings extend, of course, beyond
childhood, and the women heads continued to be conscious of how
their successful careers appeared to other family members. All were
involved in close, continuing care for a remaining parent. Over the years
their relationships with their fathers had changed, but the patterns set in
early childhood continued. Fathers were still looked to for support and
approval. The four heads whose mothers were still alive suspected that
their mothers had little understanding of what their jobs consisted of, or
the extent of their professional responsibilities and influence. Only one
had continued to be very close to a sibling, a twin sister, even though
their lives had taken different directions.

EDUCATION AS AN INFLUENCE ON CAREER CHOICE

Education as well as family played a part in motivating the heads to move
into a working world that differed radically from that of their parents and
siblings. Education potentially provides the structure of opportunities to
support individual aspirations. In the early 1960s, when these heads were
making their career choices, single-sex schools were the norm and the
11+ examination a determining factor in educational opportunity. Only
Susan attended a mixed comprehensive school, the first in the city. Even
here, Susan recalled, the senior mistress worked hard to ensure the girls
remained ladies. Diana's mixed Quaker boarding school had significant
consequences for her ability later to align the different components of her
personal and professional lives. She was used, as a result of boarding,

to compartmentalizing experiences. Barbara went to a girls' secondary school and the other three to girls' grammar schools. All stayed on into the sixth form. They all described themselves, by the age of eleven, as assiduous pupils, hardworking and keen to do well.

They recalled the values represented in the schools they attended and by their teachers as not only acceptable to them but also providing a basis for development of their own later visions of what was important in the ethos of a school. Vanessa ascribed her high standards and feeling that she must be perfect to the culture of her grammar school: 'We were extremely pushed for excellence. I've always had that in mind that everything you do, you should do well.' These values, translated into the different context of primary and secondary comprehensive schools in the 1990s, emphasized high standards in all areas, hard work, consistent support for all in the school. Four had been prefects or form captains during their secondary-school career, though they hesitated in retrospect to identify themselves as leaders. In contrast, Pauline had determined, on entering the school and seeing the headgirl and headteacher, that 'I want to be like you' and succeeded later in becoming headgirl and a headteacher.

All enjoyed their secondary-level schooling and considered they had benefited from it. Of the four who had wanted to be teachers since childhood, three chose to go to teacher-training college at eighteen. Although this was a logical step towards the fulfilment of their teaching ambitions, they had not really considered the possibility of university. In the 1960s the decision to go to a teacher-training college was sometimes seen as inferior to going to university: an easier option for a girl. Their decision, however, was not by default, but demonstrated a single-minded determination to achieve their ambitions. They wanted to teach and for Barbara, Heather and Susan, who all became primary heads, the age of the children they taught was more important than their subject specialism.

Initially the primary motivating factor for the three secondary heads in their career decisions was commitment to teaching their subject, although only Vanessa knew at eighteen what she wanted to do. As a result she chose teacher-training college so she could teach physical education. Diana described herself as 'a conveyor-belt student through university'. She was discouraged from law as unsuitable for a woman by an uncle, and from personnel work by a tutor who considered teaching more suitable for her than the 'rough and tumble' of personnel. Interesting lectures, stimulating teaching practice and thorough enjoyment of the classroom and young people convinced her that education was her right course of action.

Even though it had been a childhood ambition, Pauline also delayed entering teaching and took other jobs on leaving university: 'All my friends at the time told me I would hate teaching and that it was totally alien to my personality and way of life. They thought I was a cut-and-thrust person rather than someone to be involved in a passive service industry.' After 'wilting' on the shopfloor of a department-store management-training scheme she decided to do what she had always wanted 'and felt for the first time I was getting myself together'.

MAKING PERSONAL AND CAREER CHOICES

This discussion of the routes taken by the six women through schooling and higher education, into teaching and then management, raises the question of the sources and nature of the underlying work orientation of managers and leaders in education, particularly schools. The women heads' accounts of family, childhood and educational experiences indicated a conception of their work in schools as one in which commitment to young people's education and to teachers as professionals is fundamental. They differed in how quickly they decided the direction their careers should take, two of the three secondary heads having a period of 'drift' before settling into teaching. Once on the teaching path their commitment to the central purpose of their work never wavered. This appears as a different trajectory from that described in studies of women managers in industry and business, where moving between jobs providing different services or different products is more common. It may also be different from that characterizing the career trajectories of male headteachers, but the research base is skimpy. Acker (1994, p. 79) quotes as her favourite finding in Lortie's (1975) study of teaching 'the small number of male primary teachers in the sample [who] had low commitment and low interest in their work. Nevertheless they all hoped to be principals within five years'. A central theme of this book is the extent to which commitment to the educational goals of the work in which they were involved was a driving force in the women heads' career success and a significant factor in shaping their management styles.

It remains indisputable that the decision to follow through a career path presents greater dilemmas for women than men, while society continues to identify women as having the primary responsibility for care of family members, whatever their age. Acker (1994, p. 82) shows how women teachers are almost invevitably discussed in terms of their marital status and men are not. This chapter perpetuates that focus on the implications of the women heads' decisions about work and family for their career. Not to do so would be to deny the person in the professional. Yet this is commonly the case in studies of education managers that are based on taken-for-granted assumptions about roles and responsibilities. Since managers and leaders are assumed to be men, then it is also assumed that their personal lives are taken care of by a wife at home. This may be far from the truth but, since the questions are never asked, we have no evidence to provide a more accurate picture.

What choices did these six women make as they developed their careers in education towards becoming heads of their own schools? For those heads who at eighteen chose teacher-training colleges, decisions about higher education were closely linked to decisions about whether they intended having a career or not. Implicit in the decision to train as a teacher was the likelihood of continuing to work in that capacity throughout one's life. Teaching offered the possibility of combining work and having children, should that situation arise.

An analysis of the heads' career routes from the ages of twenty-one to their early fifties involves following them through the twists and turns of what Evetts (1990, p. 48) calls the 'labour market' of teaching with relatively high wages, good working conditions, responsibility and control over work in the classroom and employment stability. They resembled the majority of their colleagues (both men and women) in remaining in teaching all that time, with the wages, working conditions and control over work characterizing teaching in the 1970s and 1980s. They resembled a minority of both men and women colleagues in having promoted posts and an even smaller number who reach headship positions, with the opportunities for higher pay, greater variety and control over their own and others' work and the responsibilities that headship involves. Four resembled those women colleagues who take career breaks of varying lengths. They all, as the following accounts will show, shared with other women teachers experiences of the gender inequalities that contribute to differential access to opportunities for career development and promotion. These derived from both their own and others' views of the compatibility for women of career and parenthood; of partner's and own career; of ambition and femininity; of professional and personal goals; of teaching and management; and of management and womanhood. Their working lives showed the constant juggling necessary to reconcile these apparent oppositions, either by refusing to recognize their oppositional characteristics, or reinterpreting or reformulating them to work in harmony.

The constraints on women's career decisions and promotion attempts are well documented both in education and other occupations. They include geographical mobility, continuous service, post-entry qualifications, promotion processes, sponsorship and occupational community. Evetts proposes five types of strategy for accommodating the different demands women experience in managing priorities in respect of career and personal goals. The models incorporate attitudes to promotion (whether and how it is sought), self-image (source and content) and motivation (source and content). Her typology allows for changes in these factors over time. The five types are

1. the accommodated career – self-image wives, mothers, carers, not promoted, and promotion not sought, prefer classroom;
2. the antecedent career – highly committed to career, promoted from beginning, work identity has priority;
3. the two-stage career – promotion negotiated, begins highly committed to all three, may delay one for other;
4. the subsequent career – no clear promotion ambition in early life, family, etc., fundamental to self-image; and
5. the compensatory career – professional promotion to compensate for personal failure. Both family and career equal to start with.

Such typologies acknowledge the possibility of changes in orientation over time. They depend on women identifying retrospectively what had priority at different stages of their lives, in a culture where for a woman to admit work has a higher priority than family or parenthood still evokes disapproval and criticism. Men too may claim family and parenthood as a priority but putting their careers first is justified in the eyes of both men and women by their provider role (Harris, 1995). Women's careers, however, switch back and forth between the options as their personal circumstances change, often to the detriment of their promotion prospects. This was certainly evident in the careers of four of the six women headteachers who confirmed that at some point they had to make decisions about which had priority: family or work. For the other two, things 'just turned out as they did' and decisions about marrying or having children were not, in their view, related to decisions about their careers.

Although each took a different route towards headship, the patterns fitted Evetts' typology, whether they were teaching in primary or secondary schools. The careers of Heather, Barbara and Vanessa could be characterized in terms of Evetts' 'accommodation' type. Having children had equal priority with a career and for Vanessa and Heather came earlier than anticipated. For a while having children took precedence over career, although time out of teaching was kept to a minimum. Heather said:

> At that stage I wasn't worried at the fact this would interrupt any kind of career since I just assumed that I was having a child earlier than anticipated. After three months of post-natal blues I realized I wasn't doing what I wanted to do so I started teaching two afternoons a week in a local primary school doing remedial work. I had a childminder who lived near the school and sometimes, if the school asked me to do more time, I would take my daughter into school. The head, a man with a large family himself, would feed her and change her nappies.

Once a head, she demonstrated the same sympathetic attitude to staff with childcare concerns, although the exigencies of the head's role in the 1990s made it difficult to emulate her own headteacher's role model of practical childcare support! When she followed her husband to another part of England she quickly found a job in a school and stayed for the next twenty years. Initially her preference for staying in the classroom enabled her to continue to accommodate family and work demands. It was still difficult when her daughter was unwell, since it was always she who took the time off although she always made it up and never took it for her own illness: 'I can sympathize with staff now, you never feel you get it right, you either feel guilty because you are at work or you're guilt-ridden because you are at home. It's a strong influence on my behaviour now with staff who have young children.'

Later, when her daughter was in her early teens, her priorities had changed and promotion had become a more attractive proposition. The shift to what Evetts calls a 'subsequent career' began:

> I began to realize there was more to schools than just teaching. I

began to enjoy the management aspect and learned that I quite like organizing people and telling them what to do. There was a point where staff were in conflict with a supply head and I found they had come to depend on me to hold them together, even though I wasn't the deputy.

When the deputy retired, she was asked to take over his role and, within two years, had no doubts about her ability to be a head. With the support of a male pastoral adviser 'who gave me a kick up the backside', she succeeded in getting the second headship she applied for. (The first was in the school where she was already acting head and, because the governors wanted change, she was not appointed.) Her personal life had settled down and she felt ready and confident about taking on a headship.

Vanessa's 'accommodated career' was also precipitated by the early arrival of children. She only stopped teaching for a few months and even then continued part-time teaching in evening classes. A sympathetic woman head arranged that her five free periods in the week were always the last period in the day so she could fetch the children and take them back into school while she took extra-curricular acitivities. With the head's continuing support and an 'au pair' she was able to combine family and full-time work when her sons were older. When time off was necessary for her sons' illnesses, she worked extra hard to make up for her absence.

Although not intent on promotion she soon became head of department and then, having also followed her husband to another part of the country, head of a girls' lower school and senior teacher. She carried with her the seeds of ambition to be a head that had been planted by the same supportive woman head, who one day told her that, in her view, she was the ideal person to become a head: 'I think looking back and I've said it many times, because she said "I think you could do it" I thought I would have a go and I would try to do it. It crystallized the path I might take.'

Her 'subsequent career' began when her children were in their teens and she and her husband separated, a process contributed towards partly by tensions created by her professional success. Her experience as head of a separate lower-school annexe meant that she was in effect doing the job of a head: 'You had total autonomy down there. And you had to get on with it. It was the sort of experience many deputies never have.' The opportunity to apply for a deputy headship in the same school supported her decision, at a turbulent time in her personal life, to continue working and aim for headship. Even though she was not sure she would be successful, she had had no doubts about becoming a head from the moment it was suggested to her.

For Heather and Vanessa, work came to take priority over personal life. They both found considerable support in their early years for combining childcare responsibilities and work. The support came from a generation of heads for whom the concept of emancipatory praxis would have been totally unfamiliar, yet who recognized the conflicting demands of family and job. In the different context of schools in the 1970s, they provided precisely the kind of support needed by working mothers to perform effectively at home and at work. While Vanessa and Heather emphasized accommodating work to family, they took steps to avoid suggestions that they were doing either job less well as a result. The pattern of presenting a 'perfect front', which was apparent in the ways in which all six heads approached their work, emerged for Vanessa and Heather in these 'accommodating' years. There was a connection between the same high standards they set themselves in their personal and working lives and those they expected of others, once they became heads. Vanessa and Heather also tried to reproduce the support they had received as working mothers in their attitudes to colleagues with similar concerns, whether men or women.

Susan also focused on promotion and headship later in her career. Promotions came quickly, but she did not apply for her first deputy headship (which she got) until she was forty-one. Modifying Evetts' 'accommodation' type, she did not seek promotion initially, had some promotion thrust upon her, but delayed the biggest promotion steps until she felt she was ready. Her motivation regarding promotion was less about making choices between personal and professional life, more between different sources for job satisfaction: teaching or management. She combined remaining predominantly in the classroom with work experiences outside the school relating not to management, but curriculum development and teacher training.

At this stage, school management as represented in the heads with whom she had worked (all men) appeared singularly unattractive: 'all buildings and drains which worried me and not budget and curriculum which I enjoyed.' Her choices were less about the personal and the professional and more about whether to remain in teaching or move into management. In her view her career moves had not been planned but dictated the extent to which they felt right. By sustaining her commitment to self-development as a teacher, she strengthened her capacity later to fulfil what Hughes (1985) distinguishes as the 'leading professional' role, one in which teaching expertise is uppermost. She took the acquisition of management responsibilities at a more gradual pace which felt comfortable and which equipped her later for the 'chief executive' function that, with its administrative emphasis, complements the leading professional. Her 'subsequent' career when she had changed her mind about promotion also reflected her decision to seek opportunities for more influence on what went on in the schools where she worked. The critical moment was also a negative one, when she realized that as a deputy she felt responsible for what the school was like, but did not have the power to put wrong things right: 'I had a blinding flash coming out of assembly one day that the job [running a school] would be easier if I was doing it, if I was the head.'

These three heads had in common a career path in which initially home life was as important as or took priority over working life and promotion. They differed from women managers described in other surveys in the continuing centrality of their commitment to teaching as a work activity, whatever happened in the other domains.

This was also true of the other three heads, whose personal and work priorities had been managed in ways reflecting Evetts' 'antecedent career', in which promotion either precedes family or is negotiated alongside other commitments. Determined to have a career, Barbara was comfortable in combining personal and career goals. She became a deputy head when her first child was very young and became a head when her second was one year old:

> I always intended to have and develop my own career above everything else. Even though I got married immediately after leaving college, it never entered my head that I would do anything other than have a career in the same way as it never entered my head that I might leave school at fifteen or not train to be a teacher.

She shared decisions about job moves with her husband, also a teacher. When he chose to work abroad for two years, she accompanied him willingly and took the opportunities it offered to extend her teaching range to include adults. The experience was so successful that 'I ended up being treated like the queen and earned more money than my husband'. At this stage the 'buzz' that she got from teaching, whether children or adults, was more important than making her way up a career ladder. On returning to England, the decision about where to live was based on 'whoever gets the first job, that's where we will go'. He did and, as teaching jobs were scarce, she spent six months with a fill-in job as a hairdresser's receptionist. It seemed at that point as though her father's wishes for her to 'just be a hairdresser like your sister' might have come true. Eight years as a scale-post teacher in an infants school followed, which convinced her, like Susan, that she wanted to become a head and have more control over the way things were run. She had little support from a (woman) head even for going for job interviews elsewhere. The feeling was 'it upset the routine, why couldn't you stick happily where you were'. When her daughter was born she was determined to keep her career going alongside family life. Supported by a childminder and a husband, with whom she shared childcare responsibilities equally, she was able to do so. Her experiences of negotiating career and family in this way provided a baseline for her attitudes as a head to colleagues' parental concerns: 'that's part and parcel of being a human being, you have these babies.'

She had always been opportunistic, a characteristic reflected too in her approach to headship. When two headship jobs were advertised locally it was an opportunity she felt she had to seize: 'If I had not applied I would have been kicking myself for ever more.' Her son was only eleven months and her main concern was coping with a young baby. The job itself was an additional challenge; she wanted to learn, come out of the classroom and do something different: 'National Curriculum, LMS, delegation – it seemed a good time to move. It was completely and utterly uncharted water for so many people.' She succeeded in getting the second of the two jobs for which she was interviewed and plunged into headship, relying on her capacity for being totally organized and thorough preparation to carry her through the challenges ahead.

Diana also postponed having a family until her career was firmly established but, like Vanessa and Pauline, she was convinced from an early stage that she would become a head:

> I had no idea of the kind of school at that stage but just a feeling that it would happen. When I look back I'm amazed how casual I was about the whole thing compared to young people today. I think I was attracted to headship because it would mean I would be better able to make things happen. I always had the feeling that women should be and are as capable of doing and of organizing and running organizations as well as men.

Getting on meant moving out of the traditional grammar school where she was teaching, and where 'promotion in dead men's shoes was the norm'.

When she married in her early thirties, she moved to another part of the country for her husband's job and became a head-of-year in a comprehensive school. Her growing confidence in her capacity as a manager to make things happen was given a seal of approval by a senior colleague's comment: 'You won't be with us long. You'll soon be getting a deputy headship.' Stroking of this kind was welcome but rare. Later she attempted to ensure that her own behaviour to colleagues was positive and encouraging. When she obtained a deputy headship, her husband's job enabled him to follow her. This was also the period in which she had her two children, taking maternity leave each time for as short a period as possible. Her concern was to protect her classes as much as possible as well as meet the very high expectations of the (male) head of his senior management team. It meant making sacrifices to ensure she was on top of the job, not made easier by difficulties with nannies. She felt she had to show that being a woman with children did not affect how she did the job.

Her way of coping with the dual demands of family and job, i.e. by minimizing the visibility of family at work and compartmentalizing the different areas of her life, continued to characterize her lifestyle once a headteacher. Even at interviews for headship 'I know I wanted to convey that I was freestanding as a deputy and as a headteacher, and that was separate from my family life. And governors have very subtle ways of finding out whether you have children'. In setting these standards for herself as a head, she was concerned she might be doing colleagues an injustice in seeming to imply that it was inappropriate to bring domestic concerns to work. While valuing her own self-sufficiency in dealing with conflicts between work and parenthood, she tried to give every support to colleagues faced with similar conflicts. The school's audit of reasons for supply cover revealed 'head's discretionary leave' as the dominant category, i.e. she had been generous in recognizing family responsibilities.

Although Barbara and Diana resembled those heads that Evetts describes as 'career ambitious from the beginning', they were in their late thirties and early forties when they became heads. As I show later, all six women based their decision to apply for headship on a judgement about whether they were ready for what the job entailed, as well as family circumstances and career ambition. In four cases, this decision was made after the Education Reform Act 1988 when a time of turbulent change for schools was anticipated. Vanessa applied in the mid-1980s for internal promotion, so that the decision was propelled by her own head's early retirement.

Pauline was the longest-serving head in the study, having achieved her first headship (of a girls' comprehensive school) in 1983. Her choice of first teaching job was idiosyncratic. Aged twenty-two and on the point of leaving for Canada to teach in Montreal, she recalled saying jokingly to a friend: 'The only job I would stay in this country for would be to teach chemistry in my old school, and I quite literally opened *The Times Ed* and there it was: a chemistry post in my old school.' She got the job and, a year later, promotion to head of department. From then on her career evolved in a way in which, although having children was not excluded, it did not happen: 'Every time I got broody, I was promoted and teaching was such hard work I only just had time to survive.' She found working with young people at all hours totally demanding but also satisfying. In retrospect, she felt she could have fitted in a family and work, 'but then I was not certain enough of my own worth to know that I would probably have made it, even if I had had children. I think it must be quite difficult to have family ties and pulls and have to nurture your baby, which is your school'.

Subsequent decisions about which job to go for next were based partly on the location of her husband's job and partly on the opportunities different posts offered her for career advancement. She took advantage of every training opportunity, usually in her own time and paying for it herself:

> I felt it was important. It was for me and there was no way I could ask anyone else. I did the training both to do my job better and to advance. Also I always liked to have a safety net of something else that I could do. If something goes wrong I always have to have that security of knowing that there is something else. That was partly because of my mother being widowed and I was always very uncertain about the future and what would happen if she died and I always thought I have got to make sure that there is always something else that I could do.

The safety nets continued, even after becoming a head. She developed her skills as a management trainer and when things in school were particularly gruelling, contemplated buying and managing a boutique. Although career ambitious, she never considered moving on until she had mastered the stage she was at. Having learned to be a good teacher, she applied herself to learning to be a good manager. She had the benefit in her early career of a male head who was 'an inspirational head to work with. Even though his style was not mine, he gave me the framework for judging where my own values lay, for knowing how I would want to be as a head'.

When her husband's job required relocation elsewhere, she agreed to give up her first deputy headship and follow him if she could get a job at the same level in a good school. She did and used her six years as deputy to prepare for headship. Unlike her previous experience as a deputy, which had almost put a brake on her developing skills, this post provided the right opportunities for practising at a senior level all the skills she knew she would need as a head:

> I worked ever so hard for that school. I have worked hard for all the schools that I have ever been in and I always knew exactly what I had done and how I had done it. I feel I was able to synthesize all the experiences I had had over the whole range of schools to get some idea of how I would want it to be for me if I ever had the privilege of my own school.

Her competitive spirit was the final trigger to go for headship, since it was assumed in her school that a male deputy colleague would be the first to succeed. Her choices of which headships to apply for were limited by wanting to stay within the area of her husband's work. She applied locally and the first headship she applied for, got the job. Success in that headship was followed by lateral moves into county staff headships and the decision to apply for her current headship. By 1993, after nearly five years in the job and twelve years in headship, she felt that, although not ceasing to be ambitious, she had reached 'the Chinese plateau', a levelling off of the hunger for ambition: 'I was simply hungry to be a head, but I am not hungry about anything now, because I have achieved all that I wanted to, and anything I get now is a bonus.'

FINDING AND CHOOSING ROLE MODELS

One explanation commonly advanced for women's disproportionate representation in management and leadership positions is the absence of role models for girls, thereby limiting their aspirations. Later chapters look at the role models the women heads aimed to provide to others, both colleagues and students. How important were role models in their own path to headship? Who constituted for them positive and negative role models and what characterized the models they provided? The absence of women in senior positions in schools during their own early careers could have made it more difficult for them to visualize promotion. When women did hold senior positions in schools in the 1970s, they were often stereotypical, for example, as the pastoral deputy or senior mistress in charge of girls' concerns. There were more women role models available to women primary teachers than secondary but, as the three primary heads in the study showed, the job their models were observed doing bore little resemblance to the job of headship created by the 1988 changes.

Role models demonstrate the possibility of reaching certain positions (e.g. headship) and a way of doing the job, once it has been achieved. Al-Khalifa (1989) has argued that women teachers' images of headship are based mainly on men in post, thereby contributing to a conception of management as masculine and making it less likely that women will apply. If this is so, what encouraged these six women to seek headship? Hennig and Jardim's (1977) study of women in top jobs argued that, to be successful, women had to model themselves on men and, by implication, become like men. This suggests that, once in posts that carry status and power, women are faced with two options. They can either continue with the 'masculine' behaviour characterizing their male predecessors or use their new authority to reconstruct their role to include their own interpretations, based on their experiences as women, of what is appropriate. The women heads' role models in childhood and during their working lives set some of the parameters for their future style, but none included becoming more like a man. They were all adamant that they had at no stage of their careers sought to imitate men's behaviour in order to progress.

An additional distinction is necessary between the concept of models and mentors. Making career choices that lead to senior positions often depends on getting the right advice and support from people (i.e. mentors) already well established in the system. Women have often felt relatively deprived of mentors, not least as a result of their exclusion from 'old-boy networks'. The women heads exploited the opportunities provided by each career move to expand their range of experience, but their use and membership of networks of any kind was limited. Their progress, like the high flyers described in White et al.'s (1992) study, was achieved by moving between jobs within the same school or moving between key positions in different schools. All reached headships before the formal mentoring schemes, which now characterize initiatives in teachers' continuing professional development, were in place.

Mentors for women seeking promotion can serve two purposes. Both are influenced by the fact that in most organizations (including secondary, and less so, primary schools) the mentor is likely to be a man. First, mentors may act as a guide to an unfamiliar male-dominated organization culture. Secondly, they provide sponsorship and legitimate access to power. None of the successful women in White et al.'s study had been involved in a formal mentoring programme, but over 80 per cent could identify a person who had been influential in their careers and acted as a mentor (ibid., p. 141). In so far as mentors are identified by these 'high flyers' as significant others who have shown faith in their abilities, given opportunities to grow and practical help in advancing their careers, then each woman head also acknowledged at least one formal mentor. Mentors did not, however, necessarily provide role models and it was rare to find both functions embodied in one person. In one case the mentor was a woman head, in another a local authority adviser, but their input was limited.

Single-sex education meant that, for four heads at least, their secondary-schools years were dominated by women teachers as potential role models. Diana's, once embarked on her career, were almost exclusively men. She described her first head, 'a man of considerable stature and considerable tolerance and detachment at a personal level, but certainly not tolerant at a professional level; a man of considerable intellectual prowess, an autocratic figure, but with tremendous compassion'. Many of the qualities she identified in this early role model were apparent in her own interpretation of headship: detachment, personal tolerance, compassion, intellectual drive and high professional standards. She claimed never consciously to have modelled her behaviour on anybody, suggesting that those whom she identified later as influential may have reflected characteristics she valued already. The second major influence on her development, while a deputy, was a new head in his first headship: 'A blast of wind. He was phenomenal in what he changed in a relatively short space of time. I had a tremendous appreciation of his vision, his ability to get things done and his very real concern for children's learning.' The third, whom she described as a tremendous influence on her growth and training, was a male LEA senior adviser who provided her with valuable development opportunities through a year's secondment to the LEA. Although she would have been applying for headships anyway, it gave her greater assurance about her values and intended course of action.

Barbara's role models had been mainly women, at least before she became a head. From a head who refused to delegate and rarely encouraged, she learned what she did not want to do when she became a head herself. Later, when she grew interested in extending her career beyond headship and infant schools, the absence of women role models or mentors to whom she could turn for advice and support was marked. All her 'advisers' were men, as were those responsible for the selection decisions which determined whether she should move to a new post or not. This meant she was reliant on them for a view of the more 'masculine' world of school management that lay beyond the infant-school culture to which she was accustomed. In the new working environment, men were the dominant group, both numerically and in setting a 'political' agenda with which she was at first unfamiliar.

For Heather and Susan, role models were, at different times, either men or women, positive or negative. Susan's first positive role model during her early years of teaching was her deputy head, a woman 'very much of the old school'. Miss Brown resembled Susan's sixth-form teacher at school who taught them to be ladies. Being dignified, in control, polite, considerate were qualities she continued to respect and model herself as a head. Later, having worked with six male heads before becoming a headteacher herself, she recalled how influential they had been as models: 'I always observed my various heads, the different strengths and weaknesses and what they meant for schools.' Weaknesses included not making the pupils and staff first priority, making people feel small, creating fear. Pauline described the powerful role model her head of science provided, when she was a young head of department: 'He was the most wonderful teacher I have ever met in my whole life and I learned at the feet of a master because he had the skill of making every child look wonderfully able.'

Role models for being a manager often represented behaviours in both men and women which the heads chose later not to emulate. One described her previous woman head as 'chaotic and disorganized', only interested in teaching, thus allowing her deputy to take over much of the school's organization. Another's male head had poor personal skills, which meant that she was required to fill the gap and practise at senior level the personal skills which were later to be a key component of her management style.

While the heads described role models for teaching and managing, they never mentioned role models for how they might combine career and family. Yet, to their own staffs, the women heads demonstrated lifestyle choices as well as management and leadership styles that acted as a model for others faced with the same dilemmas. The role models they described were exclusively related to qualities and behaviours associated with being a good professional, whether as teacher or manager. Astin and Leland (1991, p. 47) describe role models and mentors as giving permission to aspire and to act; to be ourselves and to transcend prescribed gender roles; and to try to realize our greatest potential. As we have seen, some men and some women supported the women heads on their path to headship, but their learning was within a framework of taking responsibility for one's own progress and of developing what White and her colleagues refer to as 'a strong internal locus of control' (1992, p. 217). This view suggests that women who enter management, which has been traditionally stereotyped as a male domain, need high self-efficacy beliefs. The successful women in their sample, like the women heads, were reinforced in these beliefs by successful performance. This in turn led them to believe that further success was contingent on behaviour in the job and not external factors such as luck and fate or 'whom they knew'. White et al. conclude that the relative absence of mention of role models by the successful women in their study suggests that vicarious experience is not an important source of efficacy information for successful women. Similarly, although the women heads described role models when prompted, they did not appear to have played a significant part beyond strengthening self-confidence by confirming the rightness of their chosen path and evolving style.

Unlike White et al.'s sample, the women heads defined themselves in terms of career achievement and success in the activity which was at the core of their work: first teaching in, then running, a successful school and, in both cases, contributing to an effective educational experience for young people. Both the women 'high flyers' and women heads took minimal maternity leave but for different reasons. The 'high flyers' aimed to obscure the fact that they were stepping temporarily off 'the fast track'. The women heads were concerned to minimize disruption to the children's education, for which they felt responsible.

SUPPORT FOR PROFESSIONAL DEVELOPMENT AND PROMOTION

Equally important in developing confidence to go for promotion and ultimately headship was the support they received from family and friends. These sources of support indicated a preference on the women's part for self-sufficiency. None belonged to the kinds of groups or networks that characterize many descriptions of the lifestyles of other successful career women or of women combining childcare and a job. Their lives appeared as mainly solo performances, other than the crucial support at different stages of one or two others with a strong interest in their success at work and at home. Generally they interpreted the problem of being a working woman who is also a wife and/or mother or caregiver as their own personal problem, not one to be shared with others. They were concerned to protect others' time, but were also unwilling to admit any need for help themselves.

As they moved through their careers, emotional, moral, childcare and household support came mainly from husband or partner and, where relevant, childminders or nannies. Byrne-Whyte (1987) describes women's attitudes to promotion as being strongly influenced by two sources of support: on the one hand organizational and work cultures which accept or reject women and, on the other, the character of the relationship individual women may have with their male partner or husband. The possibility of a partner who is not male has not been addressed in the management literature and was not an issue for this sample.

In general, the women heads felt supported in their aspirations by the organizational and work cultures of which they were a part. They interpreted barriers as challenges to be surmounted rather than sources for despondency. Usually there was someone (a head, colleague or adviser) with faith in their capabilities and keen to give them opportunities for demonstrating them. Heather described her local authority pastoral adviser (a man) as a prime mover in urging her to apply for headship. Vanessa's encouragement came from the male head in the school where she worked who first supported her when she applied for the deputy headship, questioning even at that stage whether she should not be aiming higher, then encouraging her to go for the headship itself.

There were also key development experiences that contributed to their growing sense of self-efficacy and determination to seek further success. The challenge for one head, when deputy, was working alongside a colleague who, disappointed that he had not got the deputy's job himself, made things very difficult for her:

I think I learned a lot from going through that. I remember going home and saying to my husband on more than one occasion, 'I'm not sure if I'm going to be able to manage this', and feeling I wanted to jack it in. My husband said to me, 'look, you're tougher than that underneath'. But it was a tremendously toughening-up period. Having had to deal with my colleague's approach and look for strategies to minimize his influence means that now, in dealing with colleagues around the school, I aim for prevention.

For another the strengthening experiences came in her personal life, dealing with both her own and her daughter's serious illnesses.

In some instances, hostility to promotion aspirations came from other women who questioned the desirability of a woman combining career and family. Barbara said:

> I've met a lot of prejudice from women in my career because I have had a family and career. Women have openly said to me, 'how can you bring up your children and have a career at the same time?' Or they say things like 'you must have a very good husband', and I find that quite offensive because it's as if I'm some appendage to a man. It's made me quite an aggressive person because I've had to fight these prejudices mainly from women and a little bit from men.

Even though they did not see gender as a constraint once they had achieved headship, it influenced their job interview experiences. They had all had the experience of thinking at final interview that the job was more likely to go to a particular male candidate, who appeared to have qualities they did not. One was told after an unsuccessful interview for a deputy headship that she was considered too attractive for the job. Diana was amazed when she got this job rather than others for which she had applied, as she thought the Chair of Governors had made it clear that she was not the favoured candidate. As a result, she felt she had nothing to lose. Pauline also recollected her astonishment at getting the first headship she applied for. The post, as head of a girls' school, seemed predetermined for the male head of a closing boys' school in the authority 'which meant I relaxed completely in the interview and said exactly what I thought'. In her view, the governors wanted a breath of fresh air (which, among other things, her hobby as an advanced disco dancer suggested she would be!). In both cases, their surprise in getting the job was not because they did not consider themselves ready, but because they thought they did not fit the desired stereotype.

Unlike her secondary colleagues, Vanessa did not feel she had done herself justice at her interviews, not least because, as the internal candidate, arrangements were lax. She knew the Chair of Governors had reservations about her ability as a woman to handle a tough inner-city school, even though he supported her candidature. Her confidence came from knowing she had the staff's support and her determination to be a head: 'I didn't think I'd be successful but I had no doubts about doing it.'

Having failed to get the first headship she applied for (of the school where she was acting head), Heather's first external headship application was successful. In the same way as her own governors had been looking for new blood, her new school sought someone different from the previous male head, someone with experience of special needs, able to move things on but not sweep everything away. She thought that her flexibility, adaptability, humour and caring approach compensated in their eyes for any questions they had about toughness and acceptability to a male-dominated community. At the interview she felt confident and relaxed, but sure that the sharp, astute male candidate who listened and said little – 'a sales rep type, as opposed to me who blabs on' – would get it. The significant difference for her inner state during the interviews was that 'in the first job I was looking for a headship, now I was looking for a school'. Like the other heads, she put considerable thought into how she dressed for the interview and the impact it would make: 'I wanted something conservative with a small "c", but I wanted something a little bit bright so I didn't look dowdy.' She also thought it helped when she mentioned her grandchildren and used her slightly self-deprecating style of humour at the interview. The grandchildren lent her dignity and the humour put everyone at ease.

Generally the women heads did not see organizational and work cultures as insurmountable barriers to promotion. This perhaps explains in part their own attitudes as heads to men and women's respective promotion opportunities. Since they did not experience barriers themselves, they did not see how school cultures on which they had a considerable influence could be anything other than supportive of both women and men's desire to progress. All recognized gender as playing some part in their own career success, but not to the extent of requiring positive discrimination on their part when in a position of authority.

In Byrne-Whyte's typology, the women heads were 'adapters' in extending their work orientation into their responsibilities at home. For the two heads who experienced inconsistency between work and home lives, divorce followed before they became head and a new balance between home and work demands was achieved. Otherwise, the women heads paid testimony to the centrality of continuing support from partners and family to their career success. Their partner was the first person they turned to outside work about difficulties at work. Their careers reinforced the importance of a supportive partner in a stressful job for their relatively non-stressful adaptation to the dual demands of home and work. In the main they continued to see themselves either responsible for domestic tasks or sharing them. They were reluctant to employ outside help and only did so when ill-health made it necessary. Those with children thought that their children had grown accustomed to their working lives, as they had never known anything different. Unlike a man head of my acquaintance, who was perturbed at receiving a present from his five-year-old daughter labelled 'to C.H. – Headmaster', their children took for granted what they did and it was rarely discussed. Vanessa found her sons, once adult and working, showed more interest and concern about the demands the job made on her than they had when young.

It was important to them to feel in control of the home environment in the same way as they aimed to keep control of the school. The knowledge of the battles they had faced in convincing selectors they could manage was an inevitable influence on their judgements of the capacity of other women to take on management responsibilities. If, as later chapters suggest, they appeared in some respects to continue the bias against women seeking promotion by not making allowances for difference circumstances, it was from the standpoint of subjective knowledge and experience.

CONCLUSIONS: WOMEN SEIZE THE DAY

Other studies (e.g. Marshall, 1985) have shown the problems facing women in moving from a 'culturally defined' to 'self-defined' career orientation. Within the cultural definition, it is acceptable for women to be teachers if they put children and male partners' careers first. The women heads' early family experiences mainly confirmed this definition. As they started to challenge the definition (by combining family and work or seeking promotion in schools) they felt it incumbent to keep personal and professional lives separate. They learned gradually how to be assertive and draw attention to their own accomplishments and potential. They also guarded against accepting tasks that would keep them in women's roles. As Marshall points out (*ibid.*, p. 138), women's attempts to disprove stereotypes can also be dysfunctional in that they strengthen the image that they are deviants, that is, that they are not warm, caring women. The women heads' steps towards promotion and moving beyond culturally defined roles were therefore fraught with the need to walk a tightrope between being acceptable as a manager and as a woman.

Marshall describes the 'transitional phase' as one in which would-be women administrators redefine themselves and their organizational roles so that they can be comfortable and competent administrators. However, unlike Marshall's sample in the United States, who were aspiring to be district administrators not school principals, the women heads' accounts were less of battles, more of a growing realization of the desirability and possibility of taking control themselves. They talked less of traumas, more of key developmental experiences which acted as revelations of their own capacities for survival and taking charge.

They reported little organizational resistance to their career progress and considered they had made few personal sacrifices or role adjustments in attaining headship positions. Although all were in their late thirties or early forties on achieving their first headship, the factor holding them back from earlier applications was not anticipated organizational resistance but their own assessment of whether they were ready, willing and able to do the job. Their formal attempts to acquire additional qualifications such as university degrees were primarily determined, in every case, by a commitment to self-development, rather than a judgement about their usefulness for moving to the next stage.

Their careers suggested that, if informal barriers to women's promotion exist, they can be surmounted by other organizational socialization processes in schools that enable some (but not all) women to define and follow their own paths in their own time. Unlike men, who are often driven in their careers by expectations which are equally culturally defined, such as being the main breadwinner, the women heads demonstrated the possibility of an inner path to headship based on self-efficacy and self-actualization; a path that is chosen rather than a response to a demand.

4.

THE MAN IN THE MOON IS A MISS: TAKING OVER A HEADSHIP

Remember her gender
And never offend her
The man in the moon is a miss

(Aunt Mame)

INTRODUCTION

Like the Man in the Moon, the expectation in schools is still that the person in charge will be a man. Even after years in post, the women heads reported parents and others asking to see the headmaster. However successful they proved themselves in the job, they still had the weight of school mythology to contend with. The previous chapter described the heads' inner path to headship and their preparation over the years for assuming leadership of a school. This chapter focuses on their organizational socialization into headship and the choices, constraints and demands influencing their performance in their initial years in the role. Prior to becoming a head, teachers are likely to have had variable opportunities for leadership but never ultimate responsibility. Only Pauline had been a head prior to the headship in which I observed her. For the remaining five, this headship was their first.

Moving into a leadership position means establishing a personal style that is both effective in enabling people to function successfully in their work and is acceptable to the written and unwritten norms of the group of which they have become a part. All the heads had been in post long enough to have worked through the initial challenges of inheriting a school and a position, and long enough to feel confident that they had discovered their personal leadership style. This chapter depends on their and others' recall to explore their early headship years. It presents how they and others perceived their initial impact on the school, the problems they encountered, the strategies they used and the outcomes for the school. It is based mainly on the heads' own accounts of their first years in the school and their strategies for influencing the school's culture.

Interviews with other teachers confirmed much in the heads' accounts, while adding perspectives of which the heads themselves might not have been aware.

This chapter looks first at the issues involved in taking over a headship. It then focuses on a case study of one head, Heather, who moved to another headship during the time of the project. It constructs a picture of what was involved for her in taking over two headships in different contexts and at different stages of her personal and professional development. Her move provided an opportunity to explore whether gender was a constraint on her preferred style when she was first establishing herself as a head, since she succeeded a man in both headships. The chapter concludes by looking at commonalities and differences between the six heads in moving into headship and achieving what Weaver-Hart (1995, p. 107) calls 'endorsed leadership':

> Leader successors are newcomers who must be integrated into existing groups, validated by social processes and granted legitimacy by subordinates and superiors before they can have significant impacts on the actions of others. This need for validation . . . places particular pressure on people who differ substantially from conventional preconceptions about leaders.

She calls such people 'socially incongruent leaders' – that is, they represent a minority group among those who usually take up the role. The women heads were within this category.

On taking over a new school heads have a choice about whether to make a strong impact straightaway or sit back and get to know the culture first. Weaver-Hart's three case studies of women principals ascending to leadership show the more effective strategy to be that which eschews an immediate impact in favour of learning the nature of the existing culture, while striving to effect some changes within it. The hierarchy in schools may have become flatter, but the head is still at the top as the person with formal authority to clarify the school's mission and develop a shared vision among teachers and others. This has to be done within the constraints of existing organizational cultures and structures. Gender is a component of both of these since the takeover in this instance involves a woman (the new head) and a situation with its own history of gender relationships, including the gender of the head's predecessor, senior colleagues and the staff as a whole. The path the head takes will be dictated by her idiosyncratic choices in adapting to the environment and the norms and values of the school. The people with whom she works will have expectations of her as a head that will be influenced by their relations with her predecessor and their experiences of and attitudes to women in leadership positions. Margaret Thatcher's decade or more as prime minister did nothing to enhance the image of women leaders in most teachers' minds. The model she provided was mentioned frequently by both the heads and others as one to be avoided. At the same time it was the one which came to mind when women as leaders was mentioned.

Issues about power emerged in the ways in which the heads established the legitimacy of their authority with different constituencies in the schools and sought to influence those with whom they are working. They assumed that through their symbolic leadership behaviour they could shape the culture towards the values and behaviours that they believed should underpin the work of the school and relations between young people and adults. Years of experience of working in schools told them that this could only happen within the constraints of the existing culture and its many subcultures.

SLAYING DRAGONS: ISSUES INVOLVED IN INHERITING A SCHOOL

In their study of the first years of secondary headship, Weindling and Earley (1987) describe the significance of a new head's arrival in any school's history. They talk of new heads having to establish relationships, build reputations, respond to the historical legacy of previous heads, particularly the style and effectiveness of their immediate predecessor. They do not identify gender as a significant variable. Decisions have to be made about the appropriateness of inherited structures and processes and the fieriness of the dragons to be slain. Most crucially, the new head has to decide how far the culture of the school ('the way we do things here') is indeed the way she wants things to be done in her school. As far as staff are concerned, the departure of a headteacher does not alter the way 'we' are. A new head has to decide how far she is going to become part of the existing 'we' and how far she can transform the culture and win staff's allegiance to a new interpretation of what the school is about.

When other new staff enter a school, induction will be weighted more towards 'fitting' them to the culture, rather than the culture to them. They will often have been selected for the apparent fit between their values and style and the school's ethos. A new head, on the other hand, particularly in the wake of the 1988 education reforms, is more likely to have been appointed for the skills and qualities she brings that are different from her predecessor's, and on which she is expected to draw to take the school in a new direction.

This was true in five of the six headships discussed here. The exception was Vanessa, who was deputy, then acting head in the school to which she was appointed head on the early retirement of her male predecessor. Her appointment reflected a belief that she could continue to develop the existing strengths of the school and add her own vision as a head. In each of the other schools, the advent of a new head was seen as an opportunity to turn the school in new directions and develop new strengths to make it more successful in an increasingly competitive climate. A new head may have the formal power and authority to lead and change the school, but she also has to work within the informal power structure of the school. As Weindling and Earley (*ibid.*, p. 66) point out, 'for those working within the organization, the head's initial period of incumbency is therefore crucial and it is an interesting process of negotiation and impression-management'. Many demands of the job are likely to be similar not only for the six women heads but also for all heads irrespective of gender, as they arise out of current expectations of schools. Constraints will vary according to the type of catchment, community, school history, staff relations and expectations of women in a headship role. Choices are specific to each head and based on her own experiences and the values she brings to leading a school.

Each head went into her new headship with a vision and agenda for the school's future, as well as a set of beliefs about how that future was best secured. Each used the demands created by government reforms as a mandate to implement changes with the support of governors. Each was constrained in her ability to realize personal and professional goals and behaviours by others' expectations, inherited staff (particularly the senior management team – SMT) and the school's problems at the point at which she took over. Research in Britain into others' expectations of school leaders is limited, but Johnston (1986) found that male heads of primary schools were perceived quite differently from female heads. He concludes that this has implications for the female head's choice of style, since to model herself on men is likely to confound expectations, disappoint and frustrate. Whether a similar drop in morale would occur if men heads modelled themselves on women is not discussed. His findings suggest that, in seeking to control and influence, a woman leader must take account of others' expectations of her as a woman in that role.

Regardless of gender there will be issues around the roles and respon-sibilities of the head and deputies and other members of the SMT. These will be influenced by whether any were unsuccessful candidates for the headship, whether inherited or appointed by the new head and the head's conception of how the team should operate. Gender can also be an influence on the definition of role and allocation of responsibilities in the team, the team's gender composition, the dynamics of teamwork and the head's interactions with individual members.

Each head inherited a school at a specific point in her own personal and professional history, in the school's development and in the educational policy context of the late 1980s. The list in Figure 4.1 is not exhaustive but shows the demands and constraints that all described as affecting them at one time or another during the project. Included under demands (which may be external or internal) are factors influencing the choices they made about prioritizing their energies, meeting demands and taking action. Constraints included others' expectations, which may or may not have corresponded to how each head wanted to do the job. Within this framework of demands and constraints they attempted to produce the changes they saw as necessary for a quality education for the children in their charge. While they had many of the choices and demands in common, the constraints varied according to the school's size, situation, staff and history.

A key question is how far gender was one of those constraints. Other

Constraints

- gender and style of the previous head
- gender and style of senior colleagues
- composition and expectations of the governing body
- type and expectations of parents
- quality of head–staff relations on takeover
- characteristics of school culture
- existing structures
- reduction in LEA support
- quality of support staff
- quality of teaching staff
- quality of school site
- relations with unions
- number on roll
- budget size ·

Demands
(Many just emerging when the heads started, others arriving during the next
three years.)

- SATs
- restructuring special needs
- health and safety regulations
- publishing exam results and other information
- staff and own appraisal
- new responsibilities of governing body
- school development plan
- Ofsted inspections
- budgetary control
- parental choice
- religious education
- National Curriculum
- involvement with community education
- Children Act
- LEA's equal opportunities policy
- requirements for written policies
- range of external initiatives
- Records of Achievement and profiling
- pay and conditions of teaching and non-teaching staff
- redundancies
- reorganization of school meals

Figure 4.1   Demands and constraints on new head's behaviour

studies of school leaders describe the constraints of having constantly
to meet the expectations of a multitude of others (e.g. Wolcott, 1973).
Studying each woman head's experiences of moving into a new headship
revealed that gender was a factor complicating still further the myriad
expectations of her in the role. It may have been a factor too for Wolcott's
principal, but the question was not asked.

These issues are now explored through Heather's experiences of
inheriting Edgehill Junior School, then, a year later, Summersby Primary
School. Edgehill was built in the 1930s. It was situated on a site adjacent

to a nursery and infants school, on a large council house estate on the edge of a city. Between 200 and 250 children attended the school between the ages of seven and eleven. Apart from the head and her male deputy, there were eight teaching staff (two men and six women). The remaining staff (secretary, caretaker, general assistants and school-meals assistants) were women, except for a male kitchen manager. Summersby Primary School was built in the 1950s and expanded gradually to accommodate over 300 pupils (aged five to eleven) and a nursery unit with sixty places. Apart from the head and her male deputy, there were fourteen teachers and fourteen non-teaching staff. All but two were women.

A CASE STUDY IN TAKING OVER THE HEADSHIP OF A SCHOOL

When the project began, Heather had been head of Edgehill Junior School for just over three years. Six months into the project she successfully applied for another headship at Summersby Primary School, just five minutes away from Edgehill but serving a very different type of community. In each headship she both succeeded a male head and was the first woman head in the school's history. She told me of her experiences on taking over Edgehill, her first headship after twenty years in another school nearby. Her subsequent move to Summersby provided an opportunity to observe as well as discuss the transition. It came at a point in her own development when she felt she had tried out the style that suited her best and the strategies that benefited the school. The two schools were radically different from each other and from the schools run by the other five heads. Yet the issues that Heather faced and her responses to them reflected the experiences reported by the other heads in taking over their headships.

Heather, more than the other heads, found her first headship exceptionally demanding. Her time at Edgehill had not been easy. The demands of a junior school in a deprived area with high unemployment, many single-parent families and high rates of vandalism and crime were considerable. She described a working week as typically 90 per cent crises and 10 per cent routine. Although she had worked in a similar school for many years, the challenges of the problems assumed a different character when she was the head. After three years she felt she had achieved the targets which had been her brief on appointment. She also felt she was in danger, if she did not move on, of being run into the ground. In spite of this, her intention was to stay at least five years but when another vacancy occurred nearby, she felt she could not miss the opportunity it provided to try out the style with which she had become increasingly confident in a different setting. At the interview for the job she told governors, 'when I took on my first school I was looking for a headship, now I am looking for a school'. Three years previously she had been 'hungry for a headship' and was disappointed not to get the headship of the school where she was acting head. Edgehill was the next one she applied for and got. Now confident about her style, she was looking for a school that offered new challenges.

Four heads, in contrast, were looking forward at the end of three or four years to extending their own school's development rather than moving. Diana, for example, felt that she had evolved into her role. Every year felt different in character and the school's success made predicting the future difficult. There was no question of giving way to complacency or routine. Having increased the intake over the first two years, the challenge of continuing growth was still there and she saw the school as ready for a period of concentration on the quality of life and learning it offered. In the light of positive feedback, the other heads were confident that their schools had moved in hoped-for directions under their leadership. Like Heather, Barbara was seeking fresh horizons, her appetite whetted by a secondment to the LEA in a management development capacity. Heather, therefore, resembled the other heads, when she took over her first headship, in having to find ways of dealing with unfamiliar demands and unwelcome constraints. She differed in experiencing the school's social context as a considerable constraint on how she wanted to be as a head, to the extent of moving on quite quickly. This was in spite of others' acknowledgement of her considerable and positive impact on its structures and processes and on some aspects of its culture, though not as much as she would have liked.

Working with her over the next year as she settled into Summersby, it was clear that for her it was the 'right' school. By this she meant one in which she could be the kind of educational leader she wanted to be. The school was situated in a stable community of mainly owner-occupied housing, with a mixture of parents (factory workers, professionals, tradespeople). She anticipated difficulties but not of the same order as those which characterized Edgehill. She judged her effectiveness to depend on the opportunity the new school offered for being herself both with children and adults. Anticipating the move, she described the differences she envisaged. Edgehill had forced her to behave sometimes in ways with which she was uncomfortable, colder and harsher, to support discipline. In the dining hall, for example, she would talk in an authoritative way as though she didn't expect anyone to disobey her, something she felt the context demanded. She would pull herself up physically, mindful of being a woman. At the end of the first year at Summersby she was confident she had found the school she wanted. Her previous experience had equipped her with the knowledge and skills to avoid pitfalls: 'Also I am more confident. I know I have done it before in a much more difficult situation and I am fairly sure, touch wood, that there is very little that can be thrown at me that I won't cope with.'

The theme of having moved from a situation which 'did not allow me to be me' to one where 'what I am doing is being me' ran through all our discussions of how she was handling the new situation:

That is the good thing. What I am doing is being me. And it's funny, I hadn't realized why, what it is that is making me happier. It's not less hard work, it's more hard work. It's more positive but not without its problems and frustrations like any school, but I'm happier because I am being me. Being allowed my style because it is my natural style and I have the freedom to be that way.

In our earlier discussions she had said that she might be different in a different school. Having moved she discovered that, though the strategies she used varied to meet the different needs of the new context, her style, now fully fledged, was consistent. What had not changed was her commitment to getting the relationships right as a basis for effective leadership:

As much as I go for efficiency and structure and all the other things, I believe that if I get the relationships right then the rest will follow more easily. We will still have to work, I'm not talking about a cosy, cosy situation but at the very heart of the school are the relationships between pupils and pupils, staff and pupils, head and pupils and head and staff.

CHANGING PARTNERS

In taking over a new school a head inherits existing structures and practices as well as a set of relations which they have to decide whether to keep, modify or change. All these have evolved during the previous head's incumbency so that, in inheriting a school, a new head is also potentially inheriting a style which may or may not be different from her own. Heather thought she was 'doomed to follow men with a different style from my own'. Her male predecessors' behaviour combined the values and beliefs they brought to the job and their assessment of what the context of the school required. Having been in post for some time, they had put their stamp on the school. In this way they had set expectations to others about how their successors (men or women) would do the job, including expectations about whether a woman would do it differently (and more or less effectively) because she was a woman.

The previous (male) head at Edgehill had been there sixteen years and had run the school, according to others, 'with almost military precision'. For many it was what the school needed, given the instability of family life in the surrounding community and the behavioural difficulties that children brought into school. Heather knew when she was appointed that 'they would rather have a large man in post'. From the start she was on her mettle physically: 'As I come in I have to physically raise myself up and tell myself I am in charge of the school.' While accepting the appropriateness for that type of school of many of the practices she had inherited, she did not want to compete with her predecessor's style which, according to some staff, was quite theatrical. Like a stage manager he would get the children hyped up, making it more difficult for staff to control them after. At the same time his discipline was stern and loud, sometimes so loud that 'when a child ran out of school the whole school would hear him roar and that meant the others wouldn't do it'. While welcoming the strict discipline, parents were wary of him and he kept them at bay.

Heather felt she had to prove quickly that she could establish the same discipline, without compromising, in her own eyes, the principles that underpinned her leadership style. Staff commented on her ability from the start to build relationships with children's mothers, who came more frequently into the school than fathers, often in distress. Heather felt she was able, as a woman, to empathize with many of their concerns, drawing on traumatic areas of her own personal life so that she could assure them 'I know what you are feeling, I have been there'. Whereas the previous head would bawl children out and send them back to the classroom, Heather would sit them in her armchair, calm them down. The real test in everyone's eyes was whether she could deal with the occasional angry, often abusive father who might come to the school. One teacher described such a father's visit: 'You can't be shy here. A big burly dad came in the other day and threatened to stick his son's report up Heather's arse. It didn't upset her. She's a Londoner and she can cope.' Being a Londoner, with its associated toughness, seemed to compensate for not being a man!

Succeeding a man, as well as someone with a different style, was significant in determining her behaviour, in particular how much of his more 'masculine' behaviour (which was preferred by many in the community) to adopt. When she moved to a new school, the gender of her successor at Edgehill was an issue. Women staff wanted to see another woman; they had been won over by Heather's emphasis on relationships and teamwork. Men staff and some parents remained less convinced and wanted a return to the more autocratic style they associated with men heads.

MOVING IN

Moving to Edgehill, Heather's priority had been to establish her credibility with staff as a basis for setting in motion the menu of reforms with which all schools had been charged. She knew that she had been appointed because of her special needs experience and its relevance in a school where at least half the children were seen to have special needs. She also recognized that while the governors wanted a new style to deal with the new regulations, they did not want a clean sweep. This suited her own interpretation of her first headship as a time to explore what her style should be. She wanted to see what worked in the context of this kind of school. She did not come in with a predetermined vision. She wanted that to evolve, when she had had a chance to make mistakes, read the situation and establish productive relationships.

The governing body gave her three briefs: to open up the curriculum; to forge links with the infant and nursery schools on the same site; and to shape the staff into a team. These demands had to be responded to within the school's constraints, including its difficult catchment and a competent staff 'who too often felt they had their backs to the wall'. They had become used to having someone to fight for the school's survival while they got on with the teaching. From the start Heather involved them in decision-making and generating the new policies and practices necessary to meet the new demands. At the same time, as a head in her first post, she had to work out the most appropriate way of being part of the team, but also leading it. For the first few months she struggled with coping:

> I took over from a head who had a very distinctive style and had been in the school a long time. At first I didn't do anything to establish my credibility. I foolishly thought I had it. I thought I knew about those kids and those sorts of schools. What I had done over there would work here. Then I realized I wasn't being told everything. Two probationers whom I had appointed and with whom I therefore had a different relationship told me and I was hurt because they could but the others couldn't. So I stopped, looked at the school more, made a point of getting into classes more, asking more questions and identifying how this school was different. Now I take things slower. I realize that just because you say something is going to happen it isn't necessarily going to. You have to do a lot of things to make it happen.

The most obvious potential ally or allies for a new head is the *in situ* deputy or SMT. At Edgehill the deputy had not been a candidate for the post, so he was not a disappointed competitor. Other difficulties arose in part from differences in Heather's and his interpretation of management tasks and responsibilities and the deputy's role. She was never sure of his approval for what she was doing and felt she had continually to justify herself and adjust her style to meet his needs so that 'I was active in a way that wasn't me'. Unable to discuss her discomfort with him, she never knew whether her perception of his disapproval was imagined or real. The uncertainty and feeling that they were not talking the same language, in her view, put considerable constraints on their partnership, and the way she would have liked to share running the school. Instead she extended the sharing through the creation of an extended SMT, on to which she invited two potential adversaries, both strong-minded, supportive, outspoken women, with many talents but initially suspicious of her. She also co-opted a man who held an allowance, had been in the school many years and she thought had good qualities of organization. Through creating a team and encouraging a team approach she established a strength of shared purpose to compensate for its absence in her relationship with her deputy.

The infant and nursery school heads with whom she was expected to work closely also appeared to question her more democratic style and its appropriateness for the area: 'They expected me to tell staff what to do.' In contrast, the governors were unresisting and, if anything, too malleable for her liking. She had instant credibility with them. They had, after all, chosen her and looked for confirmation of the rightness of their choice. But she also had the much harder task of getting them to accept the extension of governor responsibilities, for example for budgets and staffing, spelt out in the recent government reforms.

Once the initial obstacles to leading the school forward had been overcome and her relationships with staff were open, consultative, supportive and friendly in the way she wanted, she felt confident enough to move on. 'I have developed from going in and being one of the gang to knowing I've got to be separate and acting like it.' She left a school in which many problems continued but budgeting and curriculum structures were in place, and staff were involved in decision-making in ways they had not been before. According to one colleague, the school would miss

> the warm, friendly relaxed atmosphere that she's brought. There's so much tension in this place, you've got to be able to say what you want. Staff have got to be able to cry in her room. She treats all the staff individually according to their needs. She's everyone's friend but she can also act the boss.

MOVING ON

Four years on and in a new school, Heather's ideas and values had not changed, nor the framework of her personal life which provided so much support for an often stressful job. The difference was in her knowledge about and confidence in the capabilities and qualities that she brought to headship, and their refinement as a result of practice and fine tuning. She also knew how important it was for her to read the new situation carefully and accurately from the start to avoid the pitfalls of inappropriate action. She listened and watched, attending staff meetings before she started as head and talking to people.

Again she was taking over from a male head who had been in the school some time and was well liked by staff. Tradition rather than school context had led to men heads only for the previous twenty years. One teacher recalled that when Heather first arrived the idea that 'at the end of the day a man is better than a woman' still prevailed, to the extent that one woman teacher was ready to hand in her resignation.

This resistance to the fact she was a woman accompanied the resistance any overworked staff is likely to have to a new head. A teacher described it as 'the feeling that here we go again, new changes, another person with new ideas who is going to inundate us'. Unlike Edgehill, the initial resistance was not embedded in gender-based stereotypes of who was better able to control undisciplined children and abusive parents. It arose more from unfamiliarity with a woman in that position, a concern more easily overcome. Additionally, Heather's style resembled more than differed from her predecessor's. They were both described as 'people people', although the previous head and his male deputy were seen as more distant than staff would have liked. One younger woman on the staff testified to the positive impact on her own development of Heather's encouragement and coaching. The previous head had given her little feedback, leaving her uncertain about whether she was doing things right. In contrast, Heather and the new deputy working together contributed to her growing confidence in the job, by expressing their appreciation, treating her as having equal rights and valuing her opinions.

The strength of Heather's partnership with the deputy at Summersby was, in her view, a key factor in her success in the post. The deputy in post on her arrival had already applied for headships elsewhere (though not at Summersby) and moved on soon after her arrival. This provided an opportunity to appoint her own deputy, someone whom she felt in tune with about how the school should be managed. While the decision was officially the governing body's, she used her influence to ensure that the person she thought would best support her in creating the school ethos she wanted got the job. She saw his talents, skills and abilities as complementing her weaknesses and vice versa. She saw him as more dynamic, more proactive, strong on curriculum issues. Others had described him as political without always being politic, a characteristic which she felt her own cautious personality would counterbalance rather than conflict with. Her decision about whom would be best to work with was, therefore, based not on gender but on her assessment of complementary skills. The constraints on communicating with her previous deputy, which she attributed to a combination of different styles and gender factors, played no part in this new relationship where willingness to be an active rather than passive partner was crucial. A sense that the new deputy was someone with whom she could be open was an important criterion.

The strength of the partnership and the different character of the school meant that she felt she did not need to create an SMT to support her actions. The whole staff were the team, supported by herself and the deputy. This time she had a vision for the school and a mandate from the governing body to be a leader from the start. Whereas at Edgehill she had preferred to lead from behind, she sensed that Summersby 'was needing leadership, needing to feel as if they were going somewhere again, needing to feel as if someone was there in the driving seat.' It was important to her that staff should not feel threatened by the changes. Knowing some staff prior to coming to Summersby helped. She decided to be assertive from the start:

> My own head always used to say to me 'start strong', so maybe there's that behind it; but I also wanted them to focus on next year and I wanted them to know what I wanted, and I wanted to reassure them that I would help them get there, I wasn't demanding it of them on their own.

At a staff meeting before she started, she told them the kind of person she was and her style: consultative and democratic and having high expectations. She followed this up by demonstrating the high level of support she intended giving, to individuals, groups and the school as a whole. Although discipline was not a problem, she prepared a behaviour policy straightaway so that the issue of children's behaviour did not undermine the changes in management in the school she wanted to introduce. Similarly, her decision to propose a model for appraisal based on her previous school's policy reflected her judgement about when it was appropriate to lead from the front. Summersby was some way behind with its appraisal schedule and she judged that it would be speedier to suggest a model rather than wait for one to evolve. Had it been unacceptable, she would not have imposed it but, in fact, staff viewed it favourably. At Edgehill, she had had to introduce the National Curriculum and systems for managing the school's budget. At Summersby these were already in place. What was missing, staff told her, were any real foundations for reviewing and developing the curriculum. She saw her job, together with the deputy, as supporting staff in putting in those foundations, reviewing whole-school curriculum planning and bringing the ethos of different curriculum stages more in alignment.

Working with the new governing body and a different group of parents was also a challenge. Unlike her previous governing body, who had been content, in the main, to leave decision-making to her (there were no governor subcommittees, for example), Summersby's governors were keen to be involved and had a flourishing subcommittee structure. One strategy for dealing with challenges to her leadership from governors was to ensure that she always had every bit of information at her fingertips, so that she was ready with a response. The previous head's relationship with the governing body (which she described as 'male dominated', referring to their input rather than numbers) had been described as confrontational. This was not her style and she took care to circumvent clashes. Governors' labelled folders were put out for meetings in such a way that the most confrontational member was with people who did not make him into a power base.

She saw the governing body as dominated by men seeking power and influence. The parent groups were made up of proactive women who, in the deputy's eyes, thought that they would be able to push Heather in the directions they wanted, because she was a woman. He was concerned that they used guile rather than confrontation, but was consoled by the knowledge that they would eventually have to register that Heather was just as tough as her predecessor, even though she was a woman.

In spite of her different strategies at Summersby from Edgehill, comments on how the school had changed under her leadership again referred to a more relaxed atmosphere, people feeling less stressed, staff mixing together socially, which they had never done before. Large-scale curriculum change had been managed through involving people, giving responsibility and building people's confidence. She overcame resistance by showing how the changes would reduce rather than increase individual workloads. Staff knew and shared her vision for the school and Heather was confident in leading the way towards its achievement.

SIMILARITIES AND DIFFERENCES IN TAKING OVER

The main themes identified in this case study are reflected in the other five heads' accounts. Commonalities in experiences in taking over headship far outweighed differences. Players and scenes differed: gender and style of their predecessors and new deputies, the school context flourishing or in decline. Whatever the situation, gender was still an important part of the dynamic of the interplay of demands, constraints and choices determining how they established themselves as women heads, and sought to make their impact on each school. Their choices related to where they wanted the school to go and the ways in which they worked with pupils, staff and others. The constraints included the style, generation and gender of their predecessors and the support available from senior colleagues.

Heather felt constrained in her style by some of the expectations generated by her two male predecessors. Vanessa and Pauline also succeeded men, whereas the other three heads succeeded women. I explored with each head and colleagues how their styles resembled and differed from their predecessors, and the implications of differences for establishing their own styles in the opening stages of their headships. There were differences between the women heads and their women predecessors as well as between the women heads and their male predecessors.

The women heads had in common characteristics which differentiated them from their predecessors and enabled them to deal with the demands of the job in the wake of the 1988 reforms. Generation appeared as a factor in the three cases of women succeeding women since differences in style were less to do with being more 'masculine' or 'feminine', more to do with what they considered appropriate to running a school in the 1990s. Their predecessors had learned to be heads in the previous generation of schools (the 1960s and 1970s), which bore little resemblance to schools in the late 1980s and 1990s. Since the study did not include interviewing previous heads, it was not possible to determine their own perceptions of headship.

When Barbara took over Meadowlane Infants School, she inherited eight teachers and seventeen non-teaching staff, all women. The school was opened in the late 1960s on a grassy site adjacent to the junior school. It catered for 225 children from the ages of four to seven. She also inherited the legacy of her woman predecessor's style and the staff's discomfort with anything that was labelled management. The previous head was described as 'of the old school', very methodical, orderly, keeping to routine, no staff meetings: 'an authoritarian head who had the respect of teachers because she was the headteacher.' Barbara's woman deputy had worked for many years with the previous head and was very comfortable with her style. When she retired early through illness, the deputy was acting head for a year, until Barbara arrived. The deputy had not applied for the headship herself, being content to remain a deputy in a school she liked. In the deputy's view both Barbara and her predecessor were very hardworking, always thoroughly prepared and totally committed to the school. She perceived the main difference to be in Barbara's enthusiasm for applying what she had learned about management to every aspect of the school, teaching children, working with governors, involving parents. This was in contrast to the previous head's and deputy's approach which was always to start with the school situation itself.

At Covington Primary School, Susan took over from a woman head, who retired early in response to the anticipated pressures of all the coming reforms. The school was built in 1906 and consisted of a nursery, infant and junior schools with over 400 children up to the age of eleven. It was situated close to the busy high street of a suburb near the centre of a large city. Apart from Susan and her male deputy there were fifteen teaching staff, all women except two. All the non-teaching staff except the caretaker were also women. In her deputy's eyes, Susan was, from the start, more comfortable in her approach to management and leadership than her predecessor and able to deal with the reforms as they came. The staff were already accustomed to working with a woman head, and parents and governors had no concerns about Susan's ability to handle any problems created by the catchment. She aimed to run a tighter ship than her predecessor had done, but they respected her professionalism and welcomed the high morale that existed when she took over. Initially there was some concern among staff about a new person coming in who 'might rock the boat' and 'issue directives on what to do and not to do'. Her strategy of involving all staff from the beginning eliminated their fears. Five years later the value she placed on tight organization had become part of the school's mythology. She knew staff said, if they wanted to please her, 'put it in a box and label it'. She moved the head's room from an office tucked away at the top of the stairs to a position by the front entrance and opposite the school secretary's office. This made her more accessible and put her at the hub of things. She worked differently from her predecessor with parents and governors. Her greater approachability (described in Chapter 5) meant that they no longer went first to the deputy as they had under the previous head, but directly to her.

Diana's woman predecessor had been head of Heathland Comprehensive for many years. The co-educational school was opened in the 1980s in a post-war suburb of a large city, catering for about a thousand students aged eleven to eighteen. As well as the head and four male senior managers, there were around sixty teaching staff, just under two-thirds of whom were women. Of the seventeen non-teaching staff, six were men. The previous head's style was described as different from Diana's, more traditional, less collegial, more remote. Diana was expected by staff to be different. A relatively ageing staff led to a 50 per cent turnover in staff during her first four years in the school. This included a deputy who had been a candidate for the headship in the school and who took early retirement soon after her arrival. The school was in decline and there had been much redeployment. A colleague commented on differences in responses to Diana's style between those who were in the school when she came and those appointed by her. The amount of change that she introduced to transform Heathland into a 'dynamic forward-looking school' had inevitably engendered some wariness and unease among those who had been there some time. At the same time, they and the governors recognized that the school had stagnated and needed to change. According to one teacher the school had reached a stage before Diana's arrival where professional issues were rarely discussed, meetings few and far between and the staff car-park empty at 3.30. Diana's mission was to work with colleagues to transform Heathland into a school where professional discourse was the norm.

Both Vanessa and Pauline, like Heather, succeeded men. Vanessa recalled feeling that she had to do better than a man in the same job. She had worked in Westrise Comprehensive (co-educational) for eleven years. Built in the 1970s, it occupied a large grassy site near the city centre and was classed as an inner-city school. It had around 800 students aged eleven to eighteen. As well as the head and three deputies (two men and a woman), there was a teaching staff of about fifty, with an equal number of men and women. Of the fourteen non-teaching staff, two were men. Having been in the school for eleven years meant she also had to establish credibility as a leader, after so long as a peer. This included being acceptable as a 'boss' to male colleagues in the SMT, none of whom had been internal candidates for the job although they were ambitious for their own headships. In her view, some staff thought initially she would be 'a softer touch', compared to her male predecessor, so she had to demonstrate that was not the case. She aimed to capitalize on what she saw as her strengths: the good relations she had developed with staff over the years. Her predecessor's strengths had been in oratory and intellect, both of which she admired in him as greater than her own. Her credibility in the eyes of parents of children in the school, drawn from at least six different social and ethnic groups, also had to be established. Even though she described her appointment as 'a safe bet' from the community's point of view, there was some initial suspicion from parents in Muslim households that she might not be sufficiently tough to handle boys used to more patriarchal discipline. She recalled how a male teacher would deal with these situations and be uncomfortable if she involved herself. 'Now if something happens I deal with it myself. I'm the head and that's it.'

At the start of the project Pauline had been head of Broadstone School for nearly four years and acting head for a year before that. Broadstone, an eleven to eighteen co-educational comprehensive school with just under a thousand students, was built in the 1970s in a post-war suburb of mixed private and council-owned housing. Apart from the head and three deputies (two male, one female), there were just over fifty staff, slightly more women than men. There were nearly forty non-teaching staff (full and part time) of whom six were men (caretakers, groundstaff and a technician). Her male predecessor had taken early retirement as soon as he was fifty. Pictures of both him and his male predecessor hung in the school's foyer and their styles were described by staff who had worked with them as 'patriarchal' and 'traditional'. Pauline knew she had been appointed to change the school substantially. Her main constraint was in the preference of two of the deputies to continue the same working partnership that they had had with the previous head and with each other. This conflicted with her own expectations of the kind of SMT she wanted to create in order to share the management of the school.

CHOOSING A DIRECTION

The desire to be in a position 'to make things happen' was a strong impetus for the heads' decisions to apply for a headship. For Pauline, previous experience as a head as well as having been acting head of the school for a year before taking over made it easier to gauge how best to make an initial impact. From the start she felt she had to give 'a reasonable amount of leadership on where we wanted to go to get out of where we were'. She was equally determined that the next stage of working out the vision should be the staff's responsibility as well as her own. Five years as head of a girls' secondary school as well as a brief period as acting head of a mixed comprehensive had given her ample opportunities to practise the leadership and management strategies that made up her style, albeit in different environments. Coming to Broadstone she was confident she had enough technique to make things work and get parents on her side. Her year as acting head at Broadstone gave her time to assess the school's needs but she needed the permanent post to implement the radical changes she deemed necessary. As soon as her permanent appointment was confirmed, she repeated the strategy honed at her previous school and made an enormous number of changes very rapidly. One staff member said 'she came in like a hurricane' and she described herself as making all the major decisions in the first term to get them over and done with. Once in post she worked hard at getting to know staff well, even though she found it easier to make the changes she wanted when colleagues were less familiar. This reflected the problem faced by the heads, and discussed further in Chapter 5, of judging when to be close and when to be more distant; when to have open, easy relations and when to lead from the front.

Making the school a brighter place for students and staff was a key part of her strategy in winning the competition (which she relished) for pupils. Broadstone's 'dull, commonplace, male environment' needed transforming into one which was full of 'life, joy and celebration of children's work'. It was also one of the easiest areas to tackle and led to the appointment of a technician with a part-time responsibility for display. When asked about the changes that had happened since she became head, a senior colleague said: 'A word comes to mind – brightness. The school is brighter and I mean that in all sorts of ways. The actual physical appearance of the place is, the atmosphere, the children seem to be brighter, there was this feeling before of dullness.' Other priorities included revamping the curriculum and pastoral structures from banding and setting to blocks of curriculum areas in which groups of subjects were not always curriculum linked. She sought 'high risk' solutions based on her belief that 'high risk brings high quality'. Her focus was on changes in teaching and learning styles, on loosening them up from the traditional form in which they existed. Extended teaching periods (of 1½ hours) were introduced, with shorter breaks and lunchtimes and an early finish on Wednesdays to create space for other activities. She aimed to create a fast efficient day, with minimum student movement and maximum time for learning. Short daily briefing sessions for all staff were introduced, the only time in the day everyone came together. More important, in her view, was to encourage every curriculum area to have its own space so that people could meet calmly outside the hectic atmosphere of a common staffroom. The changes reflected the values that she brought about the kind of culture she saw as appropriate for a school of which she was head. Some things which she knew contributed to a positive image for the school in parents' eyes, like strong discipline and uniform, were already in place and retained.

Vanessa's insider view of her school was both a help and a hindrance when she moved from being deputy to being the head: 'When you are a deputy you think you know what the head's job is. But it's not until you actually get there that you realize it's both what you expected and different.' She considered herself lucky as a deputy to have had a head who delegated extensively, a practice she continued with her deputies. She saw her main challenge as enhancing the school's already good performance, through changes in the management structures to involve staff more.

Her predecessor had also been consultative and participatory, so it was easier to continue. The main difference in her approach was in making good relations with individual staff central to the process of consulting and involving them in decisions. Initially, she found difficulty in defining the boundaries between using her position as headteacher to initiate ideas and persuade colleagues that they want to move in the same direction, and valuing their ideas and using them to define directions for change. A major change involved initiating, through her SMT, a collaborative management structure in which each SMT member worked with one or two faculties, and governors were members of task groups with staff, rather than in separate committees. She considered it her responsibility to allocate SMT tasks and to devise the appropriate management structures.

Like Pauline, Diana considered change necessary right from the start of her appointment to Heathland School. There was a history of difficult staff relations and 'wounds to be healed'. Her priority was to make staff feel valued, enhance their self-worth, help them feel essential and integral to the school and establish the school as a caring institution. On arrival, she was unhappy with some aspects of staff–student relationships, concerned with the 'second-class citizen' status of some pupils, only coming to the school if they could not get into independent schools. She was also concerned to change how management functioned and was seen in the school. She drew with confidence on the framework of values and management style that she had developed as a deputy and thought right for running a school. Her preferred strategy for winning people over (including a reluctant caretaker) was to 'get alongside them, to try to build from a human level, to try to build a good working relationship with them and involve them'. In her own and others' perceptions, it had worked.

From the start she focused on communication to develop autonomy, encouraging contributions to decision-making in the school, building up the team, making optimal use of colleagues' talents and competencies. She judged the school ready for change. She identified 'the thinking people' who had the expertise to spearhead specific changes of which they took ownership right from the beginning. In her view she did no more than harness the motivation and competence that was already in the school. Where that was not possible, new appointments were made to support change. In the first year she made it a priority to discover what staff had to offer by listening and then talking to people across all the levels, not just senior management. She placed a high value on thorough groundwork ('I spent a lot of time working on individuals') to lower resistance to proposals for change. Her priorities included reorganizing the allocation of curriculum and pastoral responsibilities so that as much of the administration as possible was done by non-teaching staff, to allow both deputies and the senior teacher to have oversight of both, as well as the head of the lower school. The uniform was changed after her arrival so that girls could wear trousers.

Unlike the other heads, Barbara had been less confident about getting this headship as it was her first application. When she came into the job she had to construct it for herself. She could not turn to other people because others had not done it either. On taking over she was less conscious of the changes she wanted to implement, more aware of the demands of educational reforms that she wanted to ensure were effectively implemented to the benefit of the children. 'Vision was always pushed to one side because we were pushed along this route where we had to try to keep up with change and any kind of vision was taken away.' Her enthusiastic adoption of a managerial approach was her strategy for managing the plethora of changes hitting the staff, with which they were less familiar than their secondary colleagues. At this stage her management style was instinctive rather than the result of reflection, although she immediately applied herself to acquiring (through reading, attendance at courses and study) the management knowledge to which she had previously had little access. She inherited little in the way of management structures (apart from changes that the deputy had begun during her year as acting head) and was forced to take the lead in unfamiliar territory with staff and governors. 'Even though I was as innocent as the rest, because it was new and emerging I had to lead and go by my own instincts and feel my way through it.'

She was cautious in the speed with which she took over this leadership role. The deputy recalled Barbara standing back during her first term and watching and listening. Her first significant act as a head was to announce that in future staff would use weekly planning books with their classes. She felt uncomfortable about using her powers as a head in this way: 'I had to be tough and say it's staying but it's not something I did comfortably even though I felt I was justified.' She recalled that it was easy to make changes because everything was pushing schools to change. 'It was easy to talk about the way maths should be taught because the maths document was there. You almost had a clean sweep.'

Changing the culture was a higher though no less difficult priority than formulating a vision. She associated some of her on-going difficulties in getting acceptability for a more managerial approach with the fact that she was a woman working with women. At the same time the staff were easy to work with, concerned mainly with the best interests of the children. Difficulties were associated with trying to involve them more in decisions (something Barbara valued), and avoiding imposing decisions on them. As they became more accustomed to her consultative style, they also demonstrated a greater awareness of their right to be consulted. Expectations changed towards the consultative and collaborative culture she was aiming to create. It was increasingly welcomed rather than viewed with suspicion, and brought with it rights (to participation) as well as responsibilities.

Another priority was strengthening relations with the junior school on the adjacent site. The previous male head's attitude to the infants school had been 'you play with them down there and we'll teach them when you send them up here'. She was determined that the new male head should not continue to harbour the same judgements of the infant school's work, and sought ways of building links among herself, the head and the two staffs. She established a good personal relationship with the head and designed projects that would bring the staffs of the two schools together. The biggest challenge in the first six months was setting up the budget, since she had no prior experience. She worked closely with the school's secretary to learn the necessary skills and, when there was a vacancy, persuaded the (male) bursar of another school to join the governing body so that she could draw on his expertise. She took any opportunity offered for support in the many challenges the job threw up. These included fifteen temporary relief caretakers in the first two years because nobody would take the post.

Susan's intuition told her that the headship of Covington Primary School was right for her and she for the job but, alongside candidates including two heads and the school's acting head, she considered herself the outsider. Estimating the likelihood of her getting the job as low, she was more relaxed, saying what she wanted to say rather than what she should say. 'There wasn't a question where I felt perhaps I shouldn't say that, because I had nothing to lose, did I?' That certainty brought her success at the interview and carried through to the immediate changes she made, once she was head. The advent of the National Curriculum gave the boost she needed to reviewing thoroughly the curriculum, instituting mechanisms for curriculum planning and encouraging the development of the co-ordinator role. She took a back seat while the co-ordinator led INSET sessions, something she was happy to do. In her view she 'gave them power, I empowered them. I think that's what they hoped I could do, and I did, or the National Curriculum did'.

Another priority was to improve the school environment. The school was run down to an extent that enraged her. At the same time, she was concerned to show that she saw the fault lying with the LEA, not the staff. The deputy admitted that staff had got used to a number of things that Susan refused to accept when she took over, including the dilapidation of the classrooms and site as a whole. Unlike her predecessor who was more easily put off by the LEA's procrastinations, Susan continually exerted pressure (phone calls, letters, visits), until something was done. She was prepared to risk making herself unpopular for the sake of the school: 'We didn't have our own budget for eighteen months and in that time I had the playground resurfaced, the junior building removed, the outside painted; and that started it so that staff could see I meant business.'

She was also determined to share her vision from the start and recalls sitting with staff at the end of the first year and saying:

> I've been head for a year and the problem with new heads is they don't always communicate their vision; and so what I would like to do now is sit and say what I want. I made a joke of it and I know I sat and said quite a few things and I heard one member of staff say 'cor, she couldn't want much more could she!'

In Susan's account there appear to have been relatively few constraints on her preferred behaviour as head of Covington School. She was not expected to live up to her predecessor's image, the catchment did not present insurmountable problems and staff were supportive from the start. A high turnover of staff in the five years since her appointment (as a result of promotions, moves and pregnancies) meant that she had been able to reinforce her attempts to implement her 'vision' for the school, by appointing teachers who sympathized with, and were prepared to challenge, her style. Over the years she modified some of her initial aspirations: 'I came into the school with this wonderful idea of wanting to involve everybody in decisions and found as a philosophy it just wasn't practical. Now I will take things by the reins if necessary, though I wonder if staff think I just want control.'

DEMONSTRATING TOUGH LOVE

In their study of the selection of secondary heads, Morgan *et al.* (1983) found that selectors consistently expressed doubts about whether women were tough enough to run a school. But in demonstrating they could be 'tough cookies', women also ran the risk of appearing unfeminine. Similar doubts were expressed initially by staff and governors in three of the schools in the study. The onus was on the heads to show they were unfounded. The doubts were not based on empirical evidence of women heads' inability to handle difficult situations, and the heads were careful not to provide any. In extreme situations they would raise their voice but generally their approach was to be tough on principles and not on people. They sought to praise before they censured, particularly the primary heads who had more immediate contact with children who had misbehaved. The three secondary heads saw themselves mainly as the last port of call and preferred to delegate responsibility for pupils' problem behaviour. This enabled them to strengthen the symbolic impact of their intervention without needing to draw on more physical means. Their response to the expectations that they should be 'tough' where discipline was concerned, was to remain true to their own beliefs about how it was best managed. They shared a view that responsibility for discipline had to lie with each teacher, as an integral part of his or her work with young people.

SUPPORT FROM SENIOR COLLEAGUES

The transition to headship is potentially a lonely process and, as new heads, they looked to their senior colleagues for support. Its type and extent was influenced by whether the senior staff concerned were inherited or appointed by the head. Senior staff (both men and women) who had worked with the previous head had more reservations about the new head than those appointed by the head. As Chapter 8 shows, how disagreements were handled was influenced, among other things, by gender and the head's willingness to be open with her senior colleagues. The impact of gender was therefore on the resolution of differences in preferred management styles than on differences in the styles themselves.

Pauline inherited an SMT of two men and a woman, long-standing members of staff. One of the men deputies had only been appointed to the SMT just before her arrival. The other two had worked closely with the previous male head, whose style they accepted and who gave them a considerable amount of influence. As a result she found them resistant to her style, which conflicted with what they had experienced previously and preferred. The power of their partnership, formed in the previous regime, brought necessary strengths to the school but was also a constraint on her chosen style and strategies. She felt it had strongly influenced how the management of the school had evolved since her arrival and put a brake on its development in the way she hoped. Over the years she had tried different strategies for winning their approval and co-operation, including some which circumvented the effects of their disapproval; for example, working directly with and through middle managers and strengthening team-work throughout the school. Even if her strategies were less successful than she hoped at senior level, she was confident that they worked successfully at other levels (which was confirmed by middle managers interviewed).

At Heathland School one of the male deputies had been acting head for a year before Diana took over. She inherited an SMT of two men deputies and a woman deputy. When the woman deputy retired she was replaced by a man acting deputy and a man senior teacher, to broaden the team's expertise. The team thus continued as a woman head and three senior male colleagues until it was extended to other staff as a result of advertising internally for staff to join them. Then a woman joined the team but withdrew later. While the dominance of men on the team was not seen as an issue by the core group, it was an issue for many women on the wider staff, concerned at their lack of representation at this senior level, even though the head was a woman. Diana knew when she took over the SMT that 'they were not entirely rapturous about all the change and all the work they now found themselves doing. It's much easier managing decline, it is much more leisurely'. She was keenly aware of how much they had had to adjust and work with her to move the school along. In bringing new people into the team she aimed not to encourage the formation of an 'old guard' versus 'the bright young things', by demonstrating a concern to hear all their views.

Vanessa's challenge in working with senior colleagues was in moving from peer to head status in the team, particularly before she was able to make new appointments. 'When you appoint your own deputy you feel closer to them than to colleagues appointed by your predecessors.' She continued the practice of rotating the deputies' major individual responsibilities, even though it created difficulties when colleagues performed better in some areas than others. Later, to her regret, she had to change that policy when problems arose and they refused to change. In contrast, there was little evidence that relations with senior colleagues acted as constraints on Susan and Barbara's early years in post. On the contrary, they provided the support they needed to introduce the changes they considered necessary.

SHARING THE NEW MAP

This description of the heads' early years has been based mainly on their own recollections, supported by others' testimony. Such recollections can present a distorted version of events. A test of the heads' impact lies in the extent to which they and others judge the school to have moved forward since they took over. After five years as head, Pauline was confident that Broadstone resembled closely the vision she had for it. The school had been turned around and was now oversubscribed. There remained goals to be achieved and new directions to explore but in most areas she had achieved what she had set out to do. In her view the choices she had made had been justified, the demands met in ways that benefited the school and most, but not all, of the constraints surmounted. At times the strains had been considerable though concealed from others, but she saw the next stage as challenging and optimistic:

> For the first time since being a head I actually have a total picture and vision and logical pattern for what is going to happen. I have always known what I am doing and why, but I've not perhaps seen it under a bigger umbrella. I feel I have come through an advanced driving course.

In a colleague's view the school had become as it was, almost exclusively because of her presence. 'People feel they have more of a stake in running the school now. Before it was more top heavy. Because of the person at the top the structures have changed.' There was a synergistic effect that had created an atmosphere in which what was good before could flourish.

Similarly, Diana's colleagues thought she had done 'fantastic things for the school'. A recently appointed colleague commented that 'the school's moving forward, popular in its catchment area, a super school to be in, and I think the staff feel very lucky to have appointments here'. Another said 'she's seen as a very competent head who has turned the school around, who'll fight her own way sometimes and give in at others'. Diana attributed the school's current popularity to the community's awareness that changes had taken place, the fact that they have been upfront with their priorities and that parents now knew that there was a genuine concern to give every young person a good education.

Barbara was less certain about how the school had changed since she took over. 'I'd like to go back as a fly on the wall. I get the impression we've moved on but no one ever knows, no one ever tells you.' It had been and was continuing to work well. Her concern had been to manage external demands which threatened its stability and staff's confidence in their ability to cope. It had taken time to develop the confidence to feel she had hold of the reins and be able to say to the governors: 'we must make our own personal statement.' At the end of the project the school was facing a drop in intake to the reception classes with implications for funding and staffing. Although the drop did not reflect how the school was perceived in the community, Barbara expressed, for the first time, her awareness of unwelcome competition from a neighbouring school with a nursery. The other women heads were confident but not complacent about having moved their schools on. Susan's school had increased its intake from nine to fourteen classes plus a nursery. Vanessa was proud that Westrise was seen as something of a showcase, exam results had improved and a community programme was starting to flourish.

CONCLUSIONS

This chapter has looked at issues faced by women in taking over the headship of a school. Many are common to both women and men, such as working with inherited staff, pacing the introduction of innovations so that they fit the school's capacity for change, dealing with differences between their own and their predecessor's style. Some are common to women, in so far as they relate to expectations about gender and leadership; being collaborative when control is deemed a priority; and demonstrating toughness where discipline is concerned. Faced with these issues, what did they commonly do to help their schools move forward?

First, they sought to differentiate themselves from their predecessors' styles by staking out clearly from the start their own parameters. For Heather and Barbara, who were initially less confident about their styles, it meant learning quickly from experience, including mistakes. For the others, it meant appearing sure from the start, even if their assertiveness was only internalized when the rightness of their headship actions was confirmed. They sought allies or influenced appointments so that new-comers were likely to be supportive. The behaviours that characterized their symbolic leadership style (discussed in Chapter 5) were evident from the beginning in their sensitive reading of the situation and culture. All paid careful attention to managing the environment. It was important to them to get the school looking right, partly to compete successfully by making a good visual impact, partly because that was what they felt comfortable with, in their home as well as work environment, and which they considered a necessary foundation for working effectively.

They differed from their men and women predecessors in introducing collaborative work styles and seeking, not always successfully, to reduce hierarchies. Chapters 7 and 8 discuss further whether this represents a more natural way of working for women, as a result of how they see and use power and influence. They sought to transform teaching and learning styles by using government requirements for curriculum review and planning to stimulate staff reflection on practice. They treated the demands of the Education Act 1988 as opportunities for leading the school in the direction of their own vision. At that stage, the vision was their own and not necessarily a shared one, although that was their objective. They consciously drew on their management knowledge, experience and skills in order to implement their leadership objectives. At the same time they recognized the limits to their own expertise and involved colleagues wherever possible. Particularly, they drew on the self-management skills they had developed during their careers, which had contributed to their success in attaining a headship post. These are the focus of the next chapter.

5.

THE SYMBOLIC LEADERSHIP BEHAVIOUR OF WOMEN HEADS

Only those who have fully found themselves in this world can realize their natures. Only those who realize their natures lead other natures to self-realization. Only those who lead other natures to self-realization can realize the nature of things.

(Tzu-Ssu, quoted in Apslund, 1988, p. 91)

INTRODUCTION

Organizational settings in which everyone assumes responsibility for their own development and growth are dependent on leaders who have sought to realize their own potential. The domination of leadership and management by male norms and hierarchical structures leads, Apslund (1988) claims, to constraints on self-insight and the knowledge and expression of individual (both men and women's) natures. This, in her view, accounts in part for the relative absence of women from management. Speaking from her experience as a management researcher and consultant, Apslund (*ibid.*, p. 96) concludes:

Any resolution of the dilemmas of power seems to call for a truly competent and well-integrated personality; respect for other people has to be based on self-respect and a clear sighted sense of one's own integrity. In my experience, people who doubt their own competence are generally those who cling to a formal position and the superficial symbols of power as a basis for authority and prestige, while those whose authority springs from genuine competence have no need to keep to the defence of position and prestige, but can allow and even encourage other people to realize themselves.

Absence of self-knowledge creates organizational cultures characterized by suspicion and fear, in which people feel relatively impotent. Women leaders in particular are expected to change the norms of organizational cultures to create a working environment which respects and uses to the full the talents of all its employees.

Chapters 5–8 look at the kind of practical educational leadership modelled by women heads (see Table 1.1 in Chapter 1). They are linked by their focus on the women heads' symbolic leadership behaviour and use of power. Symbolic leadership behaviour is a central component of a head's management style and of how she behaves as a leader in the everyday reality of the school. It describes how they attempt to manage the meaning of their organizations. Following Sergiovanni (1991), their behaviour can be understood in terms of what they do (substantive) and what it means (symbolic). Actions, language and artifacts may be overt (non-routine) or embedded (routine). For example, they may choose to attend a particular meeting, to add the symbolic weight of their presence to the debate. In this case the symbolic action is overt. They may always include a personal note in verbal exchanges, an example of embedded symbolic language. Reizung and Reeves (1992), using Sergiovanni's definition of symbolic leadership behaviour, suggest a taxonomy of symbolic leadership forms that classifies behaviours, as follows:

- Technical (e.g. planning, co-ordinating, initiating structure).
- Human (e.g. consideration, reinforcement, team building).
- Educational (e.g. coaching teachers in instructional matters, supervision of instruction, professional development).

Within these, symbolic actions may include the way time is spent, location of meetings and visiting classrooms. Symbolic language may include conversation topics, recurring phrases, gestures. Artifacts may include handbooks, memos, displayed objects (*ibid.*, p. 192). Reizung and Reeves's taxonomy thus provided a useful starting-point for investigating the women heads' symbolic leadership behaviour.

Leadership, in turn, can be described as the process of translating intentions into reality. Being a leader means balancing the influence of normative role expectations about how leaders should behave and how women as school leaders should behave. It is also about an individual's own disposition towards and values about leadership. Chapters 5 and 6 describe the symbolic leadership behaviour underlying the strategies the women heads used to lead their schools in desired directions, and to influence an organizational culture they considered appropriate for achieving the school's goals. Chapters 7 and 8 present their interpretations and use of power, particularly in their relations with senior colleagues and governors. These chapters provide a basis for the discussion in Chapter 9 of the relationship between the heads' perceptions of being a woman in an organization and their attitudes to gender and social justice issues in school. They demonstrate how the ways in which the women have learned to manage their own presence as women heads of schools influence their expectations of and the support they provide for both women and men in the organization.

MANAGING SELF, MANAGING OTHERS

Chapter 3 tracked each woman head's journey from childhood to head-ship. Two themes emerged: the importance of self-efficacy and managing their professional identity. Their inner as well as outer journey to headship involved making self-defining choices that allowed them to retain control over their work and career. Job satisfaction and being competent took precedence over career ambitions until the point was reached when the two coincided. The reality of what it means to put oneself forward as a woman manager and leader had to be negotiated without compromising their personal identity.

This chapter explores how the women heads managed themselves, in order to carry out more effectively their responsibilities as managers and leaders. The themes are linked by the significance of being a woman for how they manage themselves and the school. The analysis draws on a small-scale study by Lipham and Francke (1966) of the non-verbal behaviour of administrators, as well as work by Gronn (1984) on how administrators use 'talk' to manage others. Both offer frameworks for reviewing the heads' practical actions and the extent to which they are influenced by their perceptions of others' expectations of how they should behave. Lipham and Francke use the phrase 'what you are speaks so loud that I can't hear a word you say' to capture the impact of non-verbal behaviour on interaction. Similarly, when women leaders interact, the impact of their messages as leaders may be distorted by perceptions of them as women. In other words when women lead organizations, they are responded to both in their formal position and as women. As a result their management behaviour has to take account of the constraints imposed by often conflicting expectations of women in power. Figure 5.1 suggests how, in any interaction, their own and others' behaviour is influenced by norms relating to expectations of them as heads and as women. How they managed their own behaviour reflected its continual adjustment to match their own and others' perceptions of them as women in a leadership role. Their primary concern at work was to be responded to as a head, although they all expressed an awareness of others' responses often being influenced by the fact they were women. In Vanessa's view:

> Even though we have in our subconscious the issue of gender stereotyping and the way you are treated very often by men, I try not to let these show through. I would not want to feel that any man was inhibited in the way he needed to behave simply because he might upset me because I am a woman. But I suspect that many of them are inhibited. If they respect you and care for you, they probably would not want to do something if they risked upsetting you.

At the core of their symbolic leadership behaviour was their commitment to managing self. Nias (1989, p. 79), in her study of primary schoolteachers, shows how the personal concerns of teachers relate to their professional identity. She concludes: 'although teachers can and do develop, they

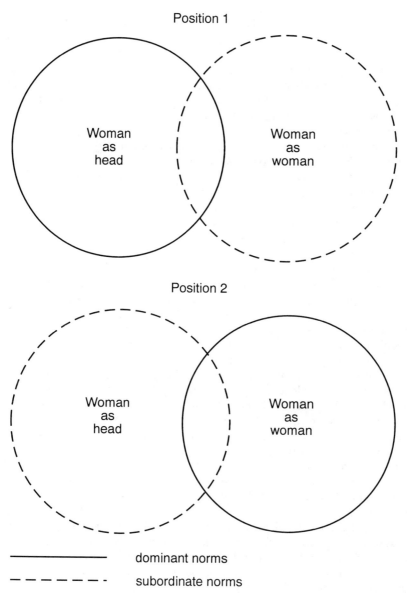

Position 1

Woman as head

Woman as woman

Position 2

Woman as head

Woman as woman

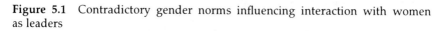

——————— dominant norms

– – – – – – subordinate norms

Figure 5.1 Contradictory gender norms influencing interaction with women as leaders

will not change professionally unless they also change as people. It is, inexorably, the person who takes up and carries out the job – and people . . . are characterized by a stable sense of self, imbued with values and beliefs which are powerfully self-defining.' Her empirical analysis of what it is 'to feel like a teacher' suggests that it is to have learned to feel relaxed, whole, natural in the exercise of one's job. She shows these states in turn to rely on a sense of being in control of self, pupils and their learning, environment and destiny (ibid., p. 201).

Similarly, the women heads' careers described in Chapter 3 demonstrated that they chose to become heads when they felt adequate (had survived), expert (had become competent teachers) and had their own agenda for headship. Once in post, they demonstrated a continuing concern to maintain their self-efficacy as leaders and managers by surviving the initial years in headship, developing management skills and using power and influence wisely. Their concern to link inner and outer worlds, in order to be effective as a leader and manager, emerged as a dominant characteristic of their leadership styles. How they managed themselves was a cameo of how they managed the school. As Heather said, describing her vision for the school: 'I want it to reflect me. There's a personal side that's warm and friendly and supportive but there's also the other side, the ultimate professional who is going to get the job right. So my vision reflects me and if I'm wrong, then the school will be wrong.'

This relationship between inner self and performance is central to understanding their symbolic leadership behaviour. Sergiovanni (1991) argues that symbolic leadership does not require grand dramatic gestures but takes place through simple routines that communicate important messages. These routine behaviours of school leaders derive from the framework of values and beliefs that constitute the head's personal paradigm of headship. Through providing selective attention and modelling to others what is valued in the school, they contribute to defining and strengthening the individual identity of the school's culture. All members of an organization influence its culture, which is made up of the values, beliefs and actions of everyone associated with a school. Headteachers, by virtue of their official position, potentially exert a greater influence through the ways in which they seek to manage the dominant culture, even though they may be excluded from many of the subcultures.

The relationship among conception, verbalization and action in modelling desired behaviour is not easy. A study of mainly men heads found many inconsistencies between how men heads said they behaved and what they were observed to do (Hall et al., 1986). In contrast, in this study, I observed the women heads aiming to 'walk their talk', and acting in ways that matched how they described their interpretation of the job. Like Pedler and Boydell's (1985, p. 8) description of the New Age Manager, they attempted to combine thinking and doing, to take action in full awareness of what they were doing and why, and its consequences for other people and, most importantly, the school. Without having consciously applied themselves to the art of self-management, which is Pedler and

Boydell's primary concern, their behaviour consistently demonstrated a commitment to self-management as a first principle. Carrying out their formal managerial role was based on how they managed themselves and their immediate environment. Managing their inner selves was the basis for managing others and the environment. The capacity for continuous self-reflection was demonstrated in the detailed analyses they provided for the behaviours I observed and questioned them about. For example, one reviewed a meeting I observed with a senior colleague as follows:

> I think the meeting went well but sensed some tension in him, in his tone of voice, but that's not unusual because I'm used to that. There was a bit of speeding up, and I was aware that as I was saying something he was coming slightly forward toward me. He wanted to interrupt but I made sure I finished, and I tried then to lower my voice a bit.

After any observation, she described in similar minute detail her perceptions of others' responses and the ways in which she was adjusting her behaviour accordingly.

The problem with discussions of symbolic behaviour is that what the performer feels the behaviour demonstrates may be interpreted differently by each individual involved in the interaction. Whatever the heads did was symbolic, whether they wanted it to be or not, but they also tried to manipulate the messages conveyed by their behaviour. Figure 5.1 suggested that women leaders' behaviour carries a double burden of symbolism, in that their actions are interpreted in terms of their identity as women and as leaders. The actions of leaders who are men are perceived mainly in terms of their leadership content, rarely in terms of how they are symbolic of their masculinity. Leadership and being a man are synonymous, not contradictory.

This study was not exclusively about symbolic leadership behaviour and it was not possible to collect systematically and extensively the multiple interpretations of others of the meaning of the heads' routine daily actions, language and visual signals. My choice of focus was on the meanings the heads intended their actions to have, with some formal and informal cross-checking with others of their interpretations of the resulting behaviour. This showed how the heads managed their own perceptions of how others might interpret their behaviour as women and leaders, and adjusted their behaviour accordingly. Sometimes the adjustments were in line with others' expectations. At other times, they chose to act contrary to expectations but in line with their self-concept of how they wanted to be as a leader and as a woman.

They knew others were aware of them as women and sometimes allowed that awareness to influence their responses. As a result, their behaviour had to take account of the symbolism that might be attached to it, precisely because they were women. They had to develop strategies that dealt with the potential disturbance they created as women leaders in order to gain organizational acceptance. Marshall's (1984, p. 32) research, for example, suggests that women high in dominance can exert influence and achieve an outcome which suits their social purpose of not appearing deviant by using power differently from that typical of male leaders. Tannen's research into gender and conversational style confirms that men and women have different styles that need to be identified and understood, if communication is to be effective. In her study of linguistics in the workplace (Tannen, 1995), she shows how women aim, through talk, for consensus views, bringing in people as equals, asking for opinions and ideas. What they see as strengths are often perceived by men as weaknesses, and undermine their authority if they are already leaders, or they are obstacles to achieving promotion.

I documented the many ways in which the women heads attempted to structure a domain for discourse in which what women value in communication was as legitimate, if not more so, as what men value. Obstacles to their attempts to construct a different world of school management through different words were not the same in both sectors. In the primary sector there was resistance to the language and techniques of management, but the heads' collaborative styles were accepted. At secondary-school level the language of management was more acceptable but the head's collaborative styles were more open to questioning. I have based these judgements on what I heard others say about the heads' behaviour and the heads' perceptions of obstacles to what they were trying to do.

Their self-management strategies had at least three purposes. First, by keeping control of themselves (their words, behaviour, reactions, movement, dress, time) they felt more able to keep control of the ever-increasing demands of the job. Heather summed up her concern about keeping control:

> I can't control what happens to the children outside school or what the government is doing to this and every other school. I can't control the way parents or staff are. I can't always stop or start things the way I want them. And I'm somebody who'd rather do one job properly than a hundred badly, so it specially goes against my nature. But I can organize and make things happen and help others to do things.

Having control of processes in order to make things happen was a major reason for going into headship. They talked of headteacher colleagues, usually men, who had succumbed to the pressures of the job. They were determined to survive as heads, motivated in part by their determination as women not to be seen to fail.

Secondly, self-management was a necessary precursor of being a good role model to others. They took seriously their responsibilities as role models for others (men and women equally) and tried to reflect in their behaviour how they wanted others to be. They recognized how much they had learned from observing others and wanted to ensure that what others learned from them was positive, rather than negative; that as a result of observing them, others wanted to act in similar ways, particularly in their relationships with colleagues and children.

Thirdly, as we shall see in Chapter 7, their interpretation of power included its potential for empowering others. This meant first of all feeling empowered themselves, that is having the confidence to develop and use their full potential. They attributed their success in gaining a headship to their own and others' conviction that they could do the job well, which gave them confidence and contributed to their sense of self-efficacy.

HOW AM I DOING? LOOKING FOR FEEDBACK

Reflecting constantly on themselves and their performance in the job was their strategy for facing the demands of headship in the 1990s. Chapter 3 showed how they only felt ready to present themselves for headship when they had clarified their personal values and beliefs as a basis for becoming an educational leader. In post, they were often faced with the problem of sustaining self-knowledge in the absence of feedback on their performance. They spoke of the isolation of the head's position, in spite of teamwork, and people's reluctance to give feedback at their level. They would all have welcomed it, although others voiced conflicting views on how receptive their head was to a sympathetic ear or criticism when it was offered. The difficulty for others in giving feedback came from the heads' beliefs about maintaining a distance while at the same time encouraging closeness. They appeared inhibited in talking intimately about problems they were experiencing either in the job or personally which might have an effect on how they were in school. Vanessa recalled that, when female deputy to the previous male headteacher, he would use her as a shoulder to cry on, whereas she would be reluctant to use her own male deputies in the same way. Having a female deputy eased the situation but there were still barriers to sharing, including fearing to appear to favour one team member more than others, as well as finding time to talk. She said: 'I've never really confided in anybody. I've always just got on with it. I've never ever really, even now, got an outlet.' She considered it inappropriate to socialize with other staff and most other secondary heads were men. She knew they saw her as a strong head and she did not want to reveal weakness. The women's reluctance to show weakness meant that both men and women colleagues felt that feedback might not be welcomed and were reluctant to give it, even though they wanted to support the head during what they sensed were more stressful moments.

The secondary heads were less likely than the primary heads to turn to colleague heads for support. This was partly influenced by gender, since they constituted what Kanter (1977) calls a 'skewed group' as a result of their minority representation as women among secondary heads in an LEA. Like Vanessa, Pauline felt male colleagues had been patronizing at times, perceiving as a threat the competitiveness with which she success-fully marketed her school. When she first became a head, the other heads were like gods so marvellous and eloquent. They were in the middle of the ocean and I was still on the shore. Then when I started to meet staff from other schools and saw them through different eyes and heard what they did in their schools, I found it was all a myth. It was mainly men. With women the rhetoric matches the practice. There's a much greater integrity about what they are and what they do, whereas I found a gap between the men and the reality.

Even so, she valued positive feedback from men more than from women. She sought professional approval from two very close male head colleagues and also from her husband. She wondered whether it came from wanting to please her father who set so much store by her success. In her view, it was harder to win men's approval than women's, who were more generous with praise.

The primary heads were not reluctant to seek advice (rather than approval) from their male colleagues. Competition between primary schools was less, there were more women primary heads and they did not see themselves or think others saw them as a threat. They were more likely to attend both sector-specific and cross-sector meetings and to phone men and women colleagues for advice, though not frequently. At one point during the project two of the primary heads were faced with the same problems regarding staff redundancies and took joint action to support each other's predicament.

Talking about problems to male partners was a source of support for the heads since it provided a sounding board of different work experiences against which to set their own. The main difficulty was in finding someone in the school whom they could trust as a confidante and who would not be compromised by the relationship. The head's secretary fulfilled this role in three instances and a general assistant in the fourth. Diana and Pauline, however, held back from identifying anyone in that capacity and sought their support mainly outside the school.

In spite of difficulties in sustaining an accurate self-image, created by absence of feedback, the heads demonstrated considerable consistency in their behaviour across situations and those with whom they interacted. There were few occasions on which they 'let down their guard', a feature confirmed by others with whom they worked. Susan was disappointed in herself on a rare occasion when she failed to be consistent in her usually calm behaviour as a basis for her working relations with others. She lost her patience with the mother of a difficult child and shouted. After she said: 'It was the one and only time I really lost control, and I was ashamed.' It was important to her to keep under control what she saw as her instinctual sharpness.

By being consistent, the heads aimed to give credibility to the role models they provided for others' behaviour in school. There was little difference in the primary and secondary heads' preferences for a working environment for pupils and students that was calm, warm, peaceable, happy, lively, constructive, relaxed; and for a lively, proactive and collaborative staff. They hoped their actions expressed the personal choices they had made about the kind of school they wanted to shape. This meant, in Vanessa's view, 'creating the climate by giving a lot of myself to the place, using my personality to encourage that'.

FROM PERSONAL POWER TO SKILLED ACTION

Sustaining an effective and consistent performance as a head meant developing and using 'personal power'. Cantor and Bernay's (1992) study of women in power in the United States shows personal power and a belief in empowering others as a pivotal feature of what they call 'Woman Power', i.e. power as redefined in the light of women's experiences. They define personal power as a capacity that causes people to do things for you because they know and like you (*ibid.*, p. 42). Using this kind of power implies self-knowledge and self-approval: a strong sense of self to promote deeply held principles. In common with the women in Cantor and Bernay's study, the six heads all made confident use of their personalities in their interactions and were aware of when they were doing so.

Developing personal power as a basis for managing themselves in the job meant making choices about

* self-presentation (visibility, role modelling);
* self-organization (managing time, space, avoiding stress, accessibility); and
* self-development (reflection, career choices, continuing education).

They saw the legitimacy of their claim to be in charge of the school as valid only in so far as they demonstrated self-control. They aimed for an inner strength that would provide security against the demands of headship in the 1990s. Working alongside this principle was their attempt in each of these areas of self-management to achieve a balance between personal and professional needs so that one did not compromise the other. Presenting a publicly unflawed persona (immaculate dress, smiling, hard working, sensitive, concerned, authoritative, collegial) required much effort and anxiety backstage. Their aim was skilled action, that is action that displayed control and confidence and contributed to the well-being of others and getting things done. For them, skilled action came from skilful self-management leading to skilled management of other people.

Like all recipes for success, positive outcomes could not be guaranteed. Constraints on achieving skilful performance included conflicting values about, for example, being open and protecting privacy, knowing but not probing, being authentic but not revealing weaknesses. Marshall (1984) points out that women may fall back on the male principle when their way of working leaves them exposed. They may choose, for example, not to talk about their families or health problems. The women heads saw themselves as striving for 'authentic' behaviour by which they meant a congruence between what they fundamentally believed about how they wanted to be and how they actually behaved. In so doing, they continuously faced obstacles, many of their own making, of being perfect, being in control, being professional, being a woman.

The desire to be authentic potentially clashed with not wanting to feel exposed. In this respect, they did resemble Marshall's women managers by obscuring aspects of their lives. Being authentic potentially includes having and showing imperfections, not always being in control, acting impulsively. Being consistently authentic could conflict with 'being consistent', if consistent behaviour includes concealing weaknesses. Heather gained satisfaction in her new job from the opportunities it gave 'to be the real me' but that did not include warts and all. Many features of the heads' preferred management and leadership styles left them exposed. The values they held about being perfect clashed with their values about admitting when they were wrong; those about being readily available clashed with their preference for not making decisions on the hoof. They aimed always to be thoroughly prepared, however many additional hours of work it took. It has become a commonplace that a woman needs to be better than a man if she is to be acknowledged as successful. Where women believe this to be true, they are likely to strive for a perfection in their performance in the job that leaves little room for faults to be found, unless self-confessed. However confident they appeared on the surface, all spoke of occasional self-doubts. The level of self-control they sought to demonstrate required superhuman efforts on their part, both in front of and behind the scenes. The constraints placed by this interpretation of their role on their people-centred, relational approach were considerable. It was demonstrated through which tasks they did, where and when, the length of their working day, how they used weekends and holidays, the extent to which they used others for support, how much they revealed about their personal lives, their usually frustrated desire for honest feedback, their continuous reflections on their performance and their commitment to on-going self-development.

Like ballet dancers rehearsing at the bar, they held up mirrors to their own performance. Symbolic leadership behaviour is manifested in numerous ways, including language, structuring interaction and structuring the environment. The heads had thought long and hard about the messages communicated by how they spoke, looked and moved, as well as what they did, with whom and to what effect. Their sensitivity to how others might interpret their language and behaviour provided a mirror for their own action. This predilection for reflection on performance has its roots in the ways girls are socialized in societies where a premium is placed on pleasing others (particularly men) through looks and behaviour. Their accounts of childhood revealed the importance of winning a father's approval. Concern about others' opinions becomes ingrained early in a girl's life, and remains for many a dominant characteristic throughout adulthood. The profiles of the women heads suggest that the same sensitivity to others' responses, that trap some women into passivity and subordination, can be transformed in women who seek leadership positions into an ability to assess expectations and situations, and shape them through their own assertive behaviour. Sensitivity to others' perceptions includes understanding where they are coming from, a powerful tool for managers looking to motivate others towards desired goals. This sensitivity to others, combined with an awareness of personal values, potentially creates 'wise politicians', that is managers who are aware of what is happening within the school, able to read the situation and act on the basis of that knowledge (Baddeley and James, 1987). It is reinforced by the value placed by women on listening skills which take account of both verbal and non-verbal clues, fact and emotion.

I referred earlier to Sergiovanni's (1991, p. 107) distinction between the 'substantive' component of symbolic leadership (i.e. what the leader does) and the 'symbolic' or 'semantics' component (i.e. what the leader's actions represent to others). If, as he suggests, focusing on the symbolic helps in understanding that very often it is 'the little things that count', then the women heads in the study were empowered by their sensitivity to semantics. This included their concern for the semantics of self as head, as evidenced in their attention to self-presentation, self-organization and self-development. Their strategies for 'structuring self' were manifest in how they dressed, moved and organized their day. Throughout their working day, their priority was to show that they were in control of the situation and of themselves, each word, gesture and action. They aimed to both be and be seen to be thoroughly prepared. To be able to demonstrate this command of, first, the situation, then themselves within it, they worked hard to ensure that self-control was a reality and not a charade. This involved organizing their working days in a way that allowed time and space away from work to reconstruct daily their public persona as headteacher. Diana's inner strength depended, in her view, on not being blown around in the gale: 'I don't very often feel downhearted but if I did I would just go off the site. Things are always different next day. Detaching myself, whether in distance or mentally, brings clarity and judgement.' In common with the others, she needed the quiet time set aside each evening to prepare herself for the rigours of the next day:

> It's important for two reasons. For preparation in terms of doing your homework, so you are well informed and you pre-empt problems the next day. Second, I think there's a need to prepare yourself in terms of rest and relaxation. You're more composed because you've built up your inner resources while resting and reflecting. It's necessary to be composed through rest, through giving oneself space, withdrawing from interaction so you have space to give yourself fully the next day. I couldn't have a hectic social life and do this job.

The quiet periods took a different form for each head, depending on their home circumstances, but all considered them essential for successful performance in the job. As a result they gave little time to activities other than those associated with family and work. They described hobbies and interests (including amateur dramatics, badminton, collecting first editions of books) but confessed that they were rarely able to indulge in these activities on a regular basis. Work was the priority. The exception was Vanessa, who enjoyed her additional work as a magistrate, as well as her involvement in activities arising from her interest in education and business.

DRESSING TO LEAD

Lipham and Francke (1966) suggest that, in managing self, interaction and the environment, administrators seek to produce greater compatibility between their personal values and what others in the social system to which they belong expect of them. The heads aimed to model in all their words and actions the behaviour they expected of others in the school environment. Stress arises, according to Lipham and Francke, when role requirements conflict with the administrator's conception of how she wants to be. As I noted earlier, women heads valued being authentic or true to themselves, but authenticity for women who are also leaders is constrained by role expectations derived from masculine definitions of gender and leadership.

This was no more evident than in handling visibility, a challenge for all leaders. Men, too, are on display when they become leaders, particularly of schools and, for both men and women, visibility brings vulnerability. For women, school leadership is not just about being a head on display but also about being a woman on show. Heather felt she was scrutinized from the moment she entered school each day. There was always the strain to present well, which meant being acceptable as the head and as a woman. Women managers are doubly on display and doubly vulnerable, since their authority is not automatically established through their position. It has to be reinforced through the sensitive manipulation of dress, speech and behaviour so that they appear in charge but not controlling, strong but not threatening. In her study of women managers, Sheppard (1992) describes one woman manager buying an expensive business suit to wear when she did not want anyone to be reminded that she was a woman. Sheppard (ibid., p. 148) concludes, 'The area of appearance seems to be the one where women feel they can most easily exert some control over how they will be responded to' – something girls learn in childhood. This was true for both primary and secondary heads, although they permitted different dress codes for other staff in each sector. The heads were tolerant of more informal dress in primary schools although it was still liable to be questioned by parents and governors. The primary heads were also more conscious of the distinction between their dress and that of female colleagues in the classroom, whose work they considered required more informal attire but from whom they did not want to be too differentiated.

The challenge to the heads was to dress in a way that established their authority, was acceptable to their different audiences but did not prevent others from hearing what they said. Women at work, particularly in managerial positions, are also faced with what they see as the problem of dressing to desexualize and remaining feminine. The women heads considered that smart dress sent a message to others that they were in control of themselves and, where the outside world was concerned, of the school as a whole. Within this framework, they claimed they dressed for themselves as much as for others. Each tried, in her dress, to avoid conforming to the 'conventional' stereotype of a woman head. That such stereotypes abound for teachers (and can be confounded) is amply borne out in Weber and Mitchell's (1995) study of teacher images and identity in popular culture. The cover of their book shows a woman (a teacher?) with loose, blonde hair in an open red négligé, sprawling seductively. It challenges teachers' own and others' preconceptions of teachers which otherwise come through the images used to portray them. A myth prevails which ends up influencing their practice:

> This type of myth emanates from a traditional conception of teachers as superhuman role models who exist in a separate dimension from the everyday world. According to this model, teachers live in the classroom, and never have to do ordinary things like go to the bathroom, or buy groceries, or show emotion. They certainly never lie languorously on the floor wrapped in silk.
>
> (*Ibid.*, p. 3)

To some extent, the women heads bought into the myth of appropriate dress codes, but manipulated them to express their interpretation of being 'at the top'. They felt most comfortable at work in dress that expressed self-control but not rigidity, adventurousness but not flamboyance. Each managed dress in ways that suited her desire to express her individuality, her conception of her role as head, and the occasion. Gray (1993, p. 113) reports on his experience, as a headteacher trainer, of men's tendency to dress in a similar way all the time, thereby restricting their capacity to express themselves as freely as women, who varied clothes according to how they felt and the day's activities.

Heather was not alone in knowing precisely the values and beliefs she was intending to convey in how she dressed for work. For example, when she knew she had to inform staff of impending redundancies, she chose a more casual outfit (woollen cardigan rather than jacket) than usual because 'I thought it would be tactless today when people in the school are thinking about losing their jobs'. It was a day when she was also attending a heads' meeting and 'normally I would have been dressed in a smart suit, to compete with the men!' She had learned the importance of smart dress from her father, a tailor, who claimed: 'If somebody can't dress and look after themselves as far as clothes are concerned, how are they going to look after the job?' Her lecturer at training college had impressed on her to dress smartly 'to give you confidence, to give other people confidence in you and, if you fall flat on your face at least you'll look good doing it'. When she literally fell on her face, when she tripped down the platform during assembly, the message was thoroughly reinforced.

Barbara, with an all-female staff, was just as concerned to use dress asexually at work as her colleagues who had a greater proportion of men staff. She was equally concerned not to look like her conception of the media image of the woman headteacher, 'ruffles, silk blouses and suits'. Diana had always worn suits as a teacher since she had always thought it important to dress well. Even so, she questioned whether her clothes said anything about her self-conception as a head since 'when I go to buy a suit I'm not thinking about the audience, I'm thinking about something I like the look of personally and feel comfortable wearing'. Both Vanessa and Susan were conscious of their headteacher image when they bought clothes, both investing at times more money than they intended in trying to live up to it. Susan described the five suits she bought when she first became a head 'all still hanging in the wardrobe because I think at primary level, if we are going to muck in, dress isn't important'. Even so, she would 'power dress if required', such as for the official opening of the nursery and a member of parliament's visit, when she wore 'a very expensive suit indeed'. Vanessa's smartness of dress was part of the school's mythology. One male member of staff even went around for a while with upmarket dress-shop labels sewn on each arm of his tracksuit.

Their dress and demeanour out of school were in sharp contrast, highlighting the sometimes contradictory relationship between their front and backstage performances. Pauline, always immaculate at work, liked nothing better at the weekend than to get thoroughly dirty gardening and emerge 'chrysalis-like, immaculate and ready for Monday morning's performance'. The heads themselves acknowledged that dress was a way of differentiating themselves from staff, not to underline hierarchy, but to provide support by being easily identifiable (particularly to outsiders) as the person 'in charge'. Dress, too, has a specific set of meanings in education where staff behaviour is seen potentially as a model for children's behaviour. Debates about school uniform reflect the myriad associations among class, gender and educational values and outcomes. Working in schools where children were predominantly from families with low incomes, Vanessa and Heather took a more relaxed attitude to colleagues' dress than the other heads. At the same time, they did not relax their own dress codes.

MOVING LIKE A WOMAN

Dress is only one aspect of self-presentation. How the heads used body language was another. Giddens (1991, p. 63) has described the 'chronic monitoring of the body and bodily gestures' involved in being a 'man' or a 'woman'. The heads reflected others' observations of women's greater awareness of body language than men, and greater ability to bring these observations to a conscious level. To support this claim, Stechert (1986) describes the example of a research anthropologist teaching university classes in non-verbal communication. When students were asked to write down all their observations of non-verbal signals given by others over a period of time, women brought back full notebooks and men the excuse 'I didn't see anything' (ibid., p. 32).

The heads aimed to use gender-correct body language which conveyed self-control and leadership but did not contravene expectations of how women should sit, stand, walk or relate physically to others. Susan contrasted her posture at work, where she strove always to appear dignified, with home where she would put on jeans and 'fall in a chair, legs under me'. These changes in dress and posture symbolized the relationship between gender and context. In the public domain, the women heads mainly followed the rules of gender-correct body language: sitting neatly not sprawling, knees together or crossed not open wide, hands in lap or arms crossed, not behind the head.

They smiled a lot 'to make people feel good', used touch but with caution in case it appeared patronizing. Both smiling and touching are ambiguous signals at work and easily open to misinterpretation. Stechert reports research documenting that women smile 17 per cent of the time when they are listening; men less than 8 per cent of the time. She concludes that, 'because women smile easily and men less often, women can be confused. Even though there is no indication that men are necessarily feeling less friendly or attentive, they seem to be, to a woman' (1986, p. 43). Similarly, women are disconcerted if other women do not smile during interaction. One teacher reported the staff's view that the head was moody 'because her demeanour as she walks down the corridor sometimes appears grim, and yet I'll talk to her minutes later and realize there is no problem'.

Smiling is often a gesture of appeasement or submission and can therefore convey inappropriate messages if the person smiling is also a leader. Touching, too, can communicate unintended messages. Stechert suggests that touching privileges are part of the dominance hierarchy; the higher the status of a person, the more touching privileges he or she has. The heads' awareness of its potential to affect the power balance, by enhancing the power of the toucher and diminishing that of the recipient, meant they used it judiciously. It was more common for the primary heads to use touch (with both men and women) than the secondary heads.

Their continuing attention to the impact of non-verbal communication could have inhibited their movements. There was a potential contradiction between their desire to use gender-correct body behaviour and using behaviour appropriate to their leadership status. Typical high-status, power gestures show relaxation and aggressiveness simultaneously, yet, as we have seen, relaxing physically at work was not part of the heads' repertoires, since it was in conflict with their attempts to appear in control.

This is not to say that they never appeared physically relaxed, but the form it took (smiling, being humorous, touching) differed from that normally associated with men (sprawling, legs open, hands behind the head, telling jokes). As with other aspects of their behaviour their emphasis was on control, in this case of their body language, so that it sent the signals they wanted it to send. Susan, for example, valued appearing dignified as she walked around the building because 'left to myself, I would run. But I'm also a teamworker who likes to muck in and get dirty'. Modelling continual dignity and calm was easier for the secondary heads than the primary heads whose preferred behaviour was constrained by the ever-close proximity of children, as a result of the much smaller size of primary schools and different conventions for the head's approachability. Heather, for example, had two comfortable armchairs outside her room, where ill, unhappy or naughty children as well as children waiting to be heard reading or be congratulated would often be found as she entered and left her room. The primary heads had to be able to change their demeanour more radically from moment to moment, without compromising their image of being in control. When faced with threatening behaviour, for example from angry parents, their strategy was to draw themselves up physically and demonstrate calm self-confidence, whatever they were feeling. Generally, their body language in most situations (including disciplining children) demonstrated their preference for more affiliative behaviour, conveying warmth and expressiveness rather than status and dominance.

MANAGING TIME TO KEEP AHEAD OF SELF, OTHERS AND EVENTS

The value they attached to balancing the personal and the professional, through efficient self-organization, was reflected in how they managed their time to keep ahead. Typical days for them were no different from those identified in other studies of primary and secondary heads at work (Hall et al., 1986; Southworth, 1995). They combined relatively permanent points (leading staff briefings, assemblies, SMT meetings) with unanticipated contacts and events with a range of people and a variety of purposes. There were some differences in the routines of the primary and secondary heads. More of the secondary heads' meetings took place in their offices with the door closed and the meetings often went on later into the evenings. They all, however, spent long days at work from around 7.30 to 8 often until 10 in the evening. Diana and Vanessa chose to have a small timetabled teaching commitment. The primary heads spent more time teaching but often to provide cover for staff to do other things. All the heads spent some part of every week out of school (at heads' meetings, LEA-organized events, pursuing particular interests such as training other heads, mentoring or developing education–industry links). Their working days were fragmented, people-centred and continuously demanding. They rarely took time in the school day to do paperwork, but carried it home and brought it back completed next morning. They valued (and usually achieved) starting each day with a clear desk. They toured the school at different points of each day, though the primary heads went more frequently unannounced into classrooms. The tours provided opportunities for discussing teachers and pupils' work and for picking up problematic situations. They spent some part of each week, if not each day, dealing with immediate crises or critical incidents with longer-term implications for the school.

Their days can therefore be summarized as resembling those of other heads described in the research literature. What does not emerge elsewhere but was central to their need to keep control of events were their strategies for dealing with contingencies by which they might otherwise be swamped. Leithwood *et al.* (1992) identify 'cognitive flexibility' as a characteristic of expert school leadership dealing with 'problem-solving in the swamp'. They define cognitive flexibility as including 'controlling one's negative moods and approaching problem situations with an air of calm confidence' (*ibid.*, p. 92). The women heads' systems for managing time were a protection against being overtaken by events and losing control of their mood. Their pleasure in creating order from chaos, whether at home or work, was reflected in how they approached gardening and housework. For Pauline it meant 'getting mucky, then unmucky, making immaculate a disordered room'. For Susan: 'The way I run my house is the way I run my school. It's using something creative in me which satisfies me in my job as well as in my home.' For Heather, growing things was an antidote to things not growing at work. Both house and office had to be pristine, if she was to feel on top of everything. The desire for control of the environment as well as self might appear inflexible rather than flexible, but it was always accompanied by an enjoyment of the challenge of what Leithwood *et al.* (1992) call 'swampy problems' as long as the 'high ground' remained in sight.

The desire to do things properly strengthened their ability to accept the administrative requirements for greater accountability, through systematic planning and feedback that other heads with more *ad hoc* styles have found antipathetic. To meet the continuous pressures of work and their own high standards required high energy levels, as well as enjoyment of the adrenalin buzz the pace of the work stimulated. Holidays were limited to going away for one or two weeks in the year but were otherwise spent with family and friends, interspersed with planning tasks for the term ahead. Their long hours inhibited regular commitment to activities out of school, leisure or otherwise. Their preferred way of relaxing was over a meal with friends, partners and their own or others' children.

DESIGNING AND USING THE SET

How they organized their office environment reflected the values they held about keeping control of the work and at the same time creating space and a setting conducive to the kind of interaction they wanted with others. Each had an office which represented an ordered environment, in which everything had its place and she knew where everything was. Each spent the first fifteen minutes of the day emptying her briefcase, distributing and filing the papers dealt with the night before, so that she began with a clear desk.

Their offices were bright, well organized and reflected the considerable thought each had put into her working environment's efficiency and symbolic impact. They adorned their rooms with objects to convey messages they considered important: gifts from overseas visitors; coffee-making facilities and biscuits; photos of children and grandchildren; ornamental gifts from staff; and changing displays of pupils' artwork. Nothing about their offices was taken for granted, including their location in relation to senior colleagues, and the school as a whole. The primary heads had smaller offices, barely holding more than three people at a time. Even within this constraint, they resembled the offices of their secondary colleagues in distinguishing the more formal deskwork area from a comfortable sitting area. I never observed any of the heads remain behind their desk during interactions. They all consciously used different parts of their room according to their perception of the formality or purpose of the interaction.

Their offices provided the framework for structuring interaction either on a one-to-one basis or in meetings. They mainly got up and went to greet someone coming to their room rather than remaining seated at or behind their desks. The primary heads' doors were usually open as they had fewer prearranged meetings during the day. Sometimes others, such as the deputy or general assistant, would use the room. Even when they were on the phone, anyone entering was acknowledged verbally and invited to wait. This pattern for welcoming staff and pupils and other visitors and for terminating interaction (by standing up and seeing people out) was also demonstrated by Lipham and Francke's (1966) sample of effective administrators. The women heads would always position themselves for maximum eye contact and usually at a minimum distance, often sitting side by side at the table.

While they used their own room as a primary location for prearranged meetings, they would go elsewhere if they considered it appropriate to the purpose. Implicit in their choices of location for interaction was their acknowledgement that using their own room, i.e. on their own territory, underlined their formal power. They used decor and seating arrangements to defuse their formal authority and relax visitors. When a situation required them to act in a more authoritarian manner (e.g. in disciplining a child or dealing with an angry parent) they would express it through tone of voice (colder), posture (stiffer), distance (standing instead of sitting), facial expression (not smiling). The performance in this context was always in marked contrast to their normal demeanour.

Elsewhere they were keenly aware of being on others' territory. When that happened it was because they wanted the other person or people to feel in control. When Pauline, for example, was interviewing individual staff in order to collect information for the deputies' appraisals, she went to the staff concerned rather than asking them to come to her. She respected the value of departmental bases around the school and encouraged their continuation, recalling how important her own departmental base had been to her as a teacher and head of department. Diana, on the other hand, was not prepared to let others' perceptions of her position as head interfere with her preference for keeping her finger on the pulse by going into the classrooms (sometimes unannounced) and staffrooms frequently. She also used corridors and other public spaces more than her room for informal contacts. This was part of her policy of picking up on issues as they occurred, listening as she toured and storing up information for processing and acting upon later. Like the others, she was keen to protect herself from making decisions on the hoof, but this did not prevent her from, as it were, listening on the hoof.

In contrast, the other heads visited the staffroom judiciously, weighing the value they placed on a culture of collegiality in their schools against their acknowledgement of the impact of hierarchy on their interactions with colleagues, however much they tried not to let it interfere. When Heather first went as a new head to Hillview she would take her lunch into the staffroom. Her confidante (the school secretary) told her that staff at that stage wanted some distance while they weighed her up. The previous head had never joined them in the staffroom, so Heather too refrained from doing so. By her second headship, she felt she had learned her lesson and only went in to the staffroom once she had established she was welcome. Similarly, Susan always planned carefully her visits to the staffroom to give staff time to let off steam uninhibited by her presence. She respected it as 'their place'.

All their self-management actions involved balancing distance and closeness. The distance was part of their self-image as heads which included standing out from the rest when appropriate. At the same time their interpersonal leadership style encouraged closeness and a certain intimacy, since it was based on the primacy of good relationships. Being available to others when needed was something they valued. It kept them in touch with people and events and forestalled problems by enabling support at the right time. It fulfilled their view of themselves as heads who listened, were sensitive and related directly to individuals rather than through others.

Keeping in touch enabled them to be available to deal with issues as they emerged rather than when they had developed into problems. The following cameo of Susan's working day illustrates how she moved in and out of different situations to be receptive to and influence expectations about how the school should operate:

She arrives every day at 7.30, is first in the school and leaves her door open. Her room is by the school's front entrance so that people constantly come and go throughout the day. At 7.55 Pam puts her head round the door and reports on the outcome of yesterday's incident in the playground. Susan tells her she visited Tim (a sick pupil) in hospital yesterday and reports his good recovery. She asks how Pam's situation at home is working out. While she talks, she touches Pam's arm frequently and comments after: 'That particular lady likes contact. I see one of my tasks as a leader is to get to know teachers individually, that's why I know her personal circumstances. I know what upsets different people and what doesn't because I know quite a lot about them.' At 8.05 she goes to the staffroom to make coffee and chats to Jill about the Staff Fund, again touches her on the arm as they joke about how the money could be spent. At 8.30 she goes to a classroom to catch Rachel, before her class arrives. She tells her about the new music appointment, and they congratulate each other on having opted for the same strategy to deal with a problem. Further along, Jill shows her some rotting window frames and Susan promises to get them replaced. She moves on to other classrooms, greeting teachers and pupils, passing on information, listening and sharing news. Pat is clearly unwell, but says she'll try and see the day out. Susan worries later whether she should have told her to go home and, at break time, suggests it to her. By 9.00 she has been on the move for over an hour, trying to catch staff before they teach and parents and children as they arrive in the school. She knows all the parents' names and their children's, and prides herself on having a good knowledge of their personal circumstances. She continuously urges teachers to keep her informed of any difficulties with a child so that she is always ready, if a crisis occurs or a parent arrives suddenly in the school. She uses assembly, which she takes three times a week, to keep in touch with the children, give the staff non-contact time and remind children of what the school values in their work and behaviour. The bonding with teachers that started the day is now transformed into bonding with the children, using the assembly as her way of saying 'aren't we good'. She stands at the front of the hall, while they file in, and tries to reflect in her own stance (being still rather than having a conversation) the opportunity assembly provides as a quiet moment in the day, a chance to give the children space and silence. She is aware that many have not had this before coming into school. She tells them of Tim's progress and reminds them that money they raised at the craft fair means 'we have all worked hard, now we can buy a PE trolley'. At the end of the day, she crosses the playground on her way to the Infant Block. The infants are all going home, mothers congregated outside the door from where they collect their children. As she walks through the playground she says 'hello' to lots of the mums, using their names, comments on their children, both those in the school and the babies they have with them and others who have been through the school and left; talks to one mother about whether she's coming to the PTA disco on Friday night, and communicates the information that the mother gives her (she's going into hospital) later to her senior colleagues at an after-school meeting so that any implications for the child in the school are taken care of.

(Extract from field-notes)

Where self-presentation is concerned, being available also means being approachable and having a personal manner that encourages interaction. It was important to each to be seen as someone whom others felt able to talk to, confide in, whom they trusted would listen and respect confidentiality. They aimed to be sensitive to the personal in the professional, rather than limiting conversations to work-related matters or neutral events. Vanessa's exchanges, as she moved around corridors, staffrooms, play-grounds, invariably began with a personal exchange (about family, health, etc.) followed by professional matters. The heads prided themselves on knowing well the personal circumstances of colleagues so that they could take account of these in their interactions. Knowing others in this personal way was a two-edged sword, since it implied power over others unless personal knowledge was shared and the heads were self-revealing too. The primary heads found this easier than the secondary heads, although all shared confidences with me as a researcher that they had not shared with colleagues.

They used their senior colleagues to provide information or feedback on how others were thinking or feeling, although they preferred direct contact, in order to form their own judgements. Vanessa felt her deputies brought more gossipy information to her than was necessary or desirable. She suspected this was because 'as a woman they think I want to know'. In her view, it was the deputies' job to look after the staffroom and give her just enough information for her to keep in touch, intervening only when it was absolutely necessary. She did not want to be influenced in her judgements of people by the deputies' sometimes jaundiced views 'because at the end of the day I'm accountable for getting everyone to do their best here'.

Maintaining the boundaries was easier for the primary than the second-ary heads, who sometimes faced greater scepticism about their attempts to be 'friendly' and, simultaneously, greater criticism of what some perceived as their aloofness. While differences in perceptions of their approachability might have been the outcome of their different person-alities, other staff in the secondary schools reported pockets of cynicism about actions that appear to challenge hierarchical expectations. For the 'cynics', 'friendliness' was potentially just another managerial ploy. Consultation was either a smoke-screen for predetermined actions or a spurious way of involving others. It was not possible to judge how widespread this resistance to the heads' interpersonal strategies was, but the same suspicions were less evident in discussions with the primary heads' colleagues.

MAKING MEANING THROUGH TALK

How they managed their appearance, presence, movement, environment were all part of their strategies for staying in control and conveying messages about their interpretation of the job. How they talked with colleagues was part of that same set of strategies for achieving intended purposes. Gronn (1984) argues that talk is a key resource for control, particularly of staff relations. His detailed analyses of administrators' daily talk reveals how they use words to cloak their power. It is a resource used by managers to get others to act. It might therefore be expected that the women heads' talk reflected the kind of power or control that they felt would encourage others to act in desired ways. If, as I suggested earlier, they rejected management as masculine and (in this context at least) the language of management as a man-made language (Spender, 1980), were they using 'woman-made' language, as far as being a manager was concerned? Did their 'talk' vary from men's, as a result of their preferences for other ways of using power?

Some part of every observation period was spent recording the precise words used by the heads and others in controlling the meaning of the event. It represented an initial attempt to understand what women were saying about their subjective understanding of school life through their speech. Gronn calls it understanding the architecture and territory of talk by scrutinizing how speakers listen, react to immediately preceding speakers, make do, let things pass, improvise, etc. For example, Gronn noted how the principal's talk changed as he changed territory. His own office, as opposed to corridors, represented his personal domain, allowing privacy and giving rise to confidences. This change in register for talk was not evident with the women heads, whose talk remained relatively consistent across the different environments. The main exception was that the primary heads talked differently to children from adults, the secondary heads did not. The other notable difference between primary and secondary heads was a greater tendency for the secondary heads' informal exchanges with staff to focus on what was happening outside the school and its implications for the school. They saw their role as including a cosmopolitan function of broadening staff's horizons, at the same time encouraging staff to share with others their own professional experiences outside the school. In the primary schools, exchanges related more to immediate issues around teaching. Listening to conversations in classrooms and corridors, I perceived secondary-school grapevines often to be inter-institutional, primary-school grapevines more intra-institutional. This difference may reflect the pressures on secondary schools to see themselves in competition with others, thereby creating a more external orientation, which is, in turn, reflected in the head's behaviour. Primary schools remain more inward looking, with mainly the head holding the wider view and protecting colleagues from its more burdensome messages.

Corson (1992) provides a possible explanation for women's consistent use of language across different domains, compared to men's. Drawing on Shakeshaft's (1989) review of research, he suggests that women have a rarely satisfied need to work in an environment that resembles the one in which they would choose to live. The need is rarely satisfied since they are rarely in positions to shape the work environment. In other words, if women had a choice, the divide between the personal and the professional, home and work, might be less marked for them than it is for men. Drawing on research relating to women's different conversational styles, Corson (1992, p. 249) concludes:

In short, women prefer to share themselves with others in the same way as they have learned to share themselves while growing up and in their childhood socialization, although often men do not learn to share themselves in this way. But this means that, as teachers and administrators, women prefer an interactive and collaborative environment in organizations that allows their acquired cultural interests and discourse norms free expression.

Shakeshaft (1989) concludes that women's preferences for a consensual managerial style that is motivating, not directing, leads them to verbal and non-verbal behaviour that is persuasive rather than coercive, includes humanized feedback and other threat-reducing strategies, has less imperatives ('give me', 'do this'), more qualifiers ('possibly', 'what if') and uses descriptive not evaluative judgements. A close examination of the women heads' talk reflected most of the characteristics summarized by Shakeshaft from the research. These included enunciating clearly (to ensure others heard accurately); not interrupting (to show they were listening); asking questions or for suggestions (to encourage contributions); using humour (often self-deprecating, to defuse tension); and using inclusive 'we' statements.

The quotes used throughout this book as illustrations demonstrate many of what Shakeshaft has identified as the 'female' characteristics of talk. I was not comparing men with women but concentrated on what I heard women to do when using language. Some characteristics noted by Shakeshaft were less evident, e.g. high voice, gossip and emotional speech. To have used these would have conflicted with the heads' values about control and discretion. The heads' use of language and speech rarely included any of the characteristics that Shakeshaft associates with men's talk, e.g. demanding voice, boastful speech, using swear words, showing anger rather than concern, interrupting. The exceptions, where they did resemble men's talk as defined in Shakeshaft, were in using speech to express humour and reflecting a concern for a balance between fact and feeling.

SELF-DEVELOPING HEADS

As Chapter 3 showed, the heads applied for headship when they felt they were ready, but had varying degrees of confidence about whether they had been adequately prepared to do the job. New reforms meant new demands. In spite of their inner core of self-certainty, they were conscious of immediate development needs to be met (e.g. for managing the school budget) as well as longer-term needs. The development activities in which they engaged reflected a dual purpose: to perform better in the job and provide insurance policies for future employment, should they decide or be forced by ill-health to take early retirement. They varied in the extent to which they felt ready or willing to move on to another job. Three had been actively reviewing other possibilities for work after headship, although were not optimistic about opportunities available once they reached fifty.

All had recently been engaged in some kind of professional development activity. Barbara and Vanessa were completing masters programmes in education, embarked upon to boost their self-image by acquiring appropriate qualifications. Neither found it easy to sustain motivation for academic studies in the face of the demands of running the school, but they were determined to complete. Diana and Pauline already had masters degrees and were involved in other training opportunities, either with the LEA or through professional associations. Diana tried, through her personal reading at night, to broaden her understanding of education issues, so that she had some knowledge in all areas. Susan, Pauline, Vanessa and Barbara had recently undergone training as Ofsted inspectors, an experience which they found both threatening and challenging. Given the heads' discomfort if they were not in control of a situation, Ofsted training was potentially destabilizing since it put heads and others through rigorous testing, which they could fail. Undertaking it was both a personal challenge and brought benefits to the school, which could expect a visit from Ofsted inspectors every few years. Susan's experience was not uncommon. In her view, the programme seemed to represent the 'survival of the fittest' with people leaving at the end of each day who could not take it any more. The pressure on participants came from being tested, being put back in an exam situation without feedback and knowing failure was possible. She wished she had not told anyone she was doing it, in case she failed. Going through this kind of development experience had meant putting her reputation as a head on the line. After feeling initially totally deskilled, she ended the week loving every moment and took pleasure in having passed its rigorous assessment programme.

Pauline was more circumspect about who knew she was undertaking Ofsted training. She chose to do it in her 'personal time', justifying the fact it was paid for from the school budget by the money she had brought into the school from training she had delivered elsewhere. It also meant the school would know what to expect when faced with its own Ofsted inspection. She too hated at first what appeared a clinical, judgemental process, with no dialogue or time for reflection: 'It's the course I think I've enjoyed least in my life.'

Whatever their formal attempts at continuing professional development, the main arena for its expression was in their continual reflection on their performance in the job. Chapter 2 described their decision to participate in the research as based on the possibilities it offered for dialogue and feedback, that were otherwise so difficult as a head to obtain. Feedback on their performance in the job was more important to them than formal training, whether it came from individuals or from their assessment of how the school was doing. It was noted earlier that perceptions of hierarchy meant colleagues were not very forthcoming with feedback. When it came, it was mainly from advisers or parents and seized on eagerly as confirmation that they were doing the right thing. Their 'inner locus of control' made them determined not to compromise their own principles and actions based on them. They did not act in order to please others but to benefit the school. At the same time, they needed to see themselves in a positive light in others' eyes. Their own commitment to giving others constructive criticism and praise reflected the value they placed on it as a motivating strategy.

All were delighted when advisers gave feedback on the successful management of their schools. Vanessa's indicators for being successful in the job included awards won by the school, improved exam results, positive comments from parents, advisers and governors. She had commissioned a management review from the local authority which had praised leadership in the school: 'Another measure of my success is that I haven't gone under yet, suffering from stress, and I seem to be able to keep on top of the job.'

Heather's self-development as a head had come mainly through the job, first in one school, then another. To survive in headship she knew she had to learn how to be a leader, learning from failures, going home and 'thinking and thinking and thinking about the job'. Often, when I met her at the start of the school day we would discuss the strategies for a particular problem she had been thinking over the previous evening, how she would put them into action and, after implementation, how they had worked out and what she had learned from them.

As we shall see in Chapter 9, their reflection on their performance appeared to be mainly on their role rather than the convictions underpinning it, about which they had developed a measure of certainty. While they did not waver in their people-centredness, their response to external training initiatives or developmental opportunities were in terms of what benefits they would bring the school and how they would improve their ability to do the job. Barbara seized opportunities to be involved with the LEA's management development programme to enhance her own skills and career progression potential. Pauline took part in Investors in People training for the opportunity it provided to use with colleagues a rational planning approach to reviewing the school's purposes and strategies for achieving them. They used external demands as opportunities to strengthen the school's capacity to meet its educational goals, as well as their own capacity to meet personal goals.

CONCLUSIONS

The picture that emerged of the women heads' symbolic leadership behaviour confirms many of the features described in Reizung and Reeves's portrait of Mr Sage. In their view, he was a 'superprincipal', the most outstanding they had encountered, whose 'ethical' leadership supported the efficacy of overt symbolic leadership and its more subtle forms. This chapter (and Chapter 6) shows how the women heads combined management and leadership, expressed through the symbolic messages conveyed as they fulfilled their management duties. A notable difference from Mr Sage was in the high priority they gave to less overt symbolic leadership forms, arising from what I have described as their acute sensitivity to the nuances of situations.

6.

WALKING THEIR TALK: WOMEN AND HUMAN RESOURCE MANAGEMENT

INTRODUCTION

Symbolic leadership behaviour extends beyond how heads manage them-selves and their interactions in order to influence others. It is manifest too in how they approach the different tasks making up their overall management responsibility. In particular, I was interested in how they handled the core human resource management (HRM) tasks of selecting staff, motivating and developing staff and reviewing staff performance. Was there a congruence between the values they demonstrated through their behaviour and those they claimed guided their action? How far did they in fact 'walk their talk'? Earlier chapters referred to the heads' concerns to be 'authentic' within a framework of collegiality and good interpersonal relations. It might be anticipated that their approach to HRM would resemble those models which see employees as 'resourceful humans' rather than 'human resources' (Bottery, 1992). At the same time, in common with others heads, they had to work within the parameters set by government directives that emphasized the expendability of staff to maintain cost-effective budgets; and the superiority of accountability over developmental processes as a basis for effective school management. This chapter describes how the heads went about some central HRM activities, drawing not only on their own accounts and observed behaviour but also on staff's perceptions. In education, HRM is an integral part of teachers and headteachers' management responsibilities. In other sectors, it is often seen as a separate function, done by specialists. The Education Reform Act 1988 transferred many of the HRM tasks previously done by LEAs to schools, including selection and staff development. Heads and governing bodies are still working out the implications of these new HRM respon-sibilities, so this chapter focuses on the heads' behaviour rather than the structures they are still developing to support their HRM strategies.

There was little that I observed the heads do that contradicted what they claimed were their intentions. However, talking to people after an interac-tion with the head sometimes (though not often) revealed differences in others' interpretation from the head's intention. For example, one male deputy described being 'told off' for writing a note to staff explaining in full detail why a female colleague was away. From his point of view, it was part of being open and 'avoiding whispers' and people thinking 'what is the real problem?' The head, however, wanted to protect her woman colleague from others being too familiar with her health problems. In this instance, the head was working within a norm about 'what we don't normally reveal' and the deputy within what he understood also to be the cultural norm, 'we're all very open and one big family'. All the heads relied on at least one other person to tell them if they had trodden on anyone's toes, though this was easier for the primary than the secondary heads. One colleague felt her head sometimes intervened in problem situations too quickly, which made her very cautious about raising issues. Generally, in all the schools, these difficulties arising from what some perceived as the heads' inappropriate responses were seen as just 'minor upsets' in otherwise skilled performances. A middle manager commented typically:

> The head is seen as someone who cares very much about management. She doesn't really put a foot wrong, so staff will swallow these minor upsets. It just creates an unhappy few days and those of us in the middle position spend a lot of time saying 'Yes, I know, but . . .' I know she's somebody who thinks about everything so much, has all the right aims and I wonder why the situations happen. I know I'm learning from her.

Within any phenomenological accounts of organizations, different interpretations of the same actions will emerge. The fact that the heads sometimes unintentionally upset others does not detract from the integrity with which I observed them work with the range of people associated with the school. The integrity came from the framework of authenticity and consistency that was part of their self-concept (as discussed in Chapter 5) and within which there were sometimes contradictory values.

BELIEFS ABOUT TEACHERS AS PROFESSIONALS

Central to each head's role as a human resource manager is the goal of achieving the policy objectives and vision for pupils and pupil learning that is at the heart of her school's activity. Their approach to this task is guided by the beliefs they have about teachers as professionals and about the extent to which power should be shared. Inevitably this study's focus on the head emphasizes her centrality in determining the pattern of staff relations in the school, however committed she is to power sharing. As we saw in Chapter 5, the women heads aimed to model through their own behaviour how they wanted staff to behave and interact. Selecting, motivating, developing and reviewing performance were all management tasks which presented opportunities to model desired behaviour and move staff in desired directions. By not holding on to decision-taking roles themselves their intention was to empower staff through and by collaboration and close interaction with and between colleagues central to managing the school's purpose.

Their beliefs about teachers as professionals combined assumptions of teacher autonomy and the importance of career orientation (Hoyle, 1974) with what Nias (1989) has called 'bounded professionality'. Nias uses this concept to describe teachers who have 'whole-school perspectives and an interest in collaboration and collegiality but are largely atheoretical and school-bounded in their approach to other educational issues' (ibid., p. 167). 'Bounded professionality' is Nias's challenge to Hoyle's concept of extended professionality and arose from responses from her sample of primary schoolteachers, the majority of whom were women. She uses the concept to describe how some teachers see themselves. It appeared that the women heads also saw some colleagues as bounded professionals, which acted as a constraint on preferred action, both in primary and secondary schools. This perception was reflected in their dual concern for individual men and women's career ambitions as well as others' preferences for staying in the classroom. Having themselves made the transition from successful classroom teaching to school management, they were keen to support others in doing so if they wanted. They were constrained in their preferred actions by the fact that promotion in schools is mainly limited to moving out of the classroom. None welcomed the government's proposals for performance-related pay which, in common with most of their teacher colleagues, they saw as divisive. On the other hand their lives were made easier when senior colleagues did seek career advancement, since this meant they were thinking about and prepared to practise being managers as well as teachers. In all but the infant head's view, both men and women teachers could be bounded professionals or career ambitious. Barbara, however, associated the desire to remain in the classroom with women teachers in infant schools. The others responded to both men and women colleagues' potential for development in the light of individual teachers' expressed preferences for one direction or another. Their keenness not to appear in any way discriminatory meant that they did not feel a need to respond to what others suggest are the different career development needs of women teachers (e.g. Al-Khalifa and Migniuolo, 1990).

THE CONTEXT FOR HRM IN SCHOOLS

Although the concept of HRM is becoming more common in the school management literature (e.g. Riches and Morgan, 1989; Bush and West-Burnham, 1994), it has some way to go before becoming an acceptable title to describe managing people in education. Even where it is used, HRM's most notable aspect – that it is strategic and central to the business aims of the organization – is often ignored. In the past five years, schools in Britain have been forced by central government reforms towards more strategic approaches but the process is slow. The teaching profession remains sceptical of the political nature of imposed strategic objectives and the values underpinning them. Actions based on viewing staff as resources to be managed alongside other material resources are likely to be abhorred by educators who see themselves as valuing people. However, arguments rejecting HRM run the danger of throwing the baby out with the bathwater. By focusing on what, in some HRM approaches, is potentially detrimental for people in education (since they appear to reduce people to disposable objects), the possibility is lost of recognizing HRM's strategic capacity for effectively harnessing 'people power' to achieve educational goals to which the profession itself subscribes. Observing how the women heads behaved as human resource managers revealed the gradual emergence of strategic approaches that tried to balance the present and future needs of the school with recognition of the needs of individual employees. Neither their decisions to work strategically nor the successes and failures that were the outcomes could be associated directly with gender, but were part of the repertoire of the entrepreneurial head in the 1990s that the women represented. They did, however, make a choice about the kinds of HRM strategies they favoured.

Storey (1987) has provided a framework for characterizing the different HRM approaches according to the values and philosophies underpinning action in managing people. He distinguishes the 'hard' dimension which emphasizes the resource element of HRM from the 'soft' which concentrates on the human side of HRM. In the rational, bureaucratic approach which characterizes the 'hard' version, the efficient utilization of staff takes precedence over their involvement through communication, motivation, development and teamwork characteristic of the 'soft' version. This rational approach clearly resembles that implied by descriptions of management as masculine and school management as increasingly technocratic. An association of management as masculine with the 'hard' version of HRM suggests that women managers who reject the 'management as masculine' label might also reject 'hard' HRM, in favour of Storey's 'soft' version, with its emphasis on development and treating employees as valued assets. The educational objectives of schools, with their emphasis on human growth and development, are congruent with school leaders' commitment, irrespective of gender, to 'resourceful humans', in spite of external pressures to act otherwise. A problem with Storey's choices of 'hard' and 'soft' as descriptors are the words' cultural associations with masculine and feminine. 'Soft' can be misleading, particularly when what it describes is either intentionally or viewed by others as the iron fist in the velvet glove. Strategies such as Total Quality Management and Investors in People, which schools are being encouraged to adopt, may claim to have a concern for people at their core, but they can also be seen as aiming to win individual hearts and minds for the benefit of the organization. Potentially, they are as antipathetic to the concept of teacher as autonomous professional as other more manifestly 'hard' approaches such as appraisal for accountability not development.

In the following account of women heads' HRM practices, their behaviour is seen to reflect the principles that are associated with the 'soft' approach. Legge (1995, p. 35) summarizes these as treating employees as valued assets and a source of competitive advantage through their commitment, adaptability and high quality; as proactive rather than passive inputs into productive processes; as capable of development, worthy of trust and collaboration. They also involve using communication, motivation and leadership to generate commitment and producing human resource policies to deliver 'resourceful' humans.

In common with most other heads of schools after 1988, the women heads were feeling their way towards strategic approaches to managing a school, as defined in the management and government literature, as well as according to their own value frameworks. Their challenge was to marry the strategic demands of running a school with the strategies they had developed and fine tuned over the years for getting the best out of people. They recognized the need for strategy but not for treating people as resources. Through their actions, they sought to influence morale by providing continual opportunities for individual and group development. Astuto and Clark (1986) have argued that effective education managers concentrate on developing their ability to work with culture rather than attempting to create it. This was echoed in Chapter 4, in the account of the heads' strategies for taking over a school and the wisdom of understanding the culture first, before seeking to change some of its characteristics. In so far as the women heads sought continuously to read the school's culture accurately and respond appropriately, they could be said to be working with it. In so far as they modelled and encouraged alternative behaviours, they demonstrated a commitment to changing it. Their colleagues testified to their willingness to adopt a different approach, if they were convinced it would work better. In a staff meeting, one head's response to an opinion that was contrary to her own was to comment that it was a good suggestion. She wrote it down and followed it up later. Another head sought her co-ordinator's views on class groupings and, although the suggestion meant a radical departure from tradition, she agreed to the change.

There were limits, as we shall see, to the extent to which their practical educational leadership or 'praxis' was also emancipatory, particularly where staff selection and development were concerned. In their own perception, they were emancipatory in that they felt they treated and supported everyone equally, child or adult, man or woman. Their support for teaching and learning in the school, in that it extended across all subject areas and all abilities and backgrounds, showed emancipatory practice to be more prevalent in relation to children than adults.

Although the dominant mode of their HRM style was 'soft', they were capable of, though uncomfortable with, the need to be 'hard', for example in issues of redundancy or unacceptable staff behaviour. Even then, they pursued every option before coming to a final decision that was a negative outcome for someone else. Disappointment about the heads' abilities to take a 'hard' or 'critical' line on some issues were relatively rare and heard more in the secondary-school context. Specific examples included challenging sexist behaviour on the part of men staff (the head's response was too slow) and dealing with a teacher's unacceptable behaviour (the head's response was too fast). The slow responses left staff wondering if they were properly supported, although, from the head's point of view, it was necessary to collect all the facts first. The speedy responses made staff cautious about mentioning some concerns, in case they were transformed into issues for unnecessary action. Although the heads worked hard to read situations accurately in order to judge appropriate interventions, it was not possible always to get it right.

GETTING SELECTION RIGHT

A strategic approach to recruiting and selecting staff involves judging the potential contribution of applicants, in terms of their skills, expertise and educational values. As in all staffing issues, it was crucial to the head to get it right. Pauline had her fingers burned when she went against her own principle of 'if in doubt, don't'. Impressed by 'a young, fresh-faced, delightful young man' with a first-class honours from Oxbridge, she over-rode the Head of Department's doubts about his ability to control children. When this turned out to be the case (and he resigned to do other things), she regretted, as she always did on the rare occasions it happened, using her instinct as a basis for judgement. A conflict between one head's values and staff perceptions of her actions occurred when the head wanted, in an appointment, to bring someone new into the school 'with fresh ideas and approaches', and staff expected an internal appointment in recognition of individual achievement. In these situations, the head's values about what was in the best interests of the school clashed with their values about rewarding appropriately. She resolved the situation by 'trading off' one appointment (of her favoured external candidate) for another (others' favoured internal candidate). She only felt justified in doing this because of the high quality of the internal candidate.

The interview, which continues to be the key event in most schools for selecting staff, provided the head and colleagues with an opportunity to assess how the candidate would 'fit' the school's needs as well as convey to the candidate what the school valued. The heads were less concerned to put round pegs in round holes, more to find new staff who would be creative, exercise choice and demonstrate the professional autonomy which they valued. They were interested in what the candidates had to offer, as well as whether they fitted. At the same time, given the priority they placed on collaborative styles of working, it was important that successful candidates were not so creative or individualistic that they would be unable to integrate into the staff as a team.

With one eye on the strategic function of selection (i.e. ensuring new appointments contributed to the school's longer-term development plan), they demonstrated a more immediate concern with both the competencies and personal qualities of applicants. Their own judgements about a candidate's suitability were constrained by the extent to which they considered it important and appropriate to take account of the views of others, who were either involved in the selection process or immediately affected by its outcomes. There was a tension between their desire to control the process so that the 'right' person (in their view) was appointed and their belief in sharing rather than imposing selection decisions. In so far as their school's culture was moving towards but had not fully reached the destination they hoped for, they were keen to appoint people who would support them in the journey. By virtue of their authority as heads, they could choose to exert a major influence on appointment decisions, particularly where they were concerned about someone's suitability. Exercising this choice could, however, bring into question the authenticity of their espoused commitment to collegiality, if it became apparent that their opinions took precedence.

The need to manage judiciously their contributions to selection decision-making was more apparent with the secondary than the primary heads, who appeared less anxious about being seen to lead. Southworth (1987) has argued the appropriateness of collegial approaches to selection in primary schools, given the encouragement of teachers to work collaboratively to implement whole-school policies. His case study reveals the value to the selection outcome of the head encouraging discussion and actively listening to everyone's views. Even though a climate of open con-sultation was a dominant characteristic of the three primary schools, in the appointments observed, the heads still had the main respon-sibility for determining both the kind of person and which person they wanted. Seeking constantly not to compromise her own profes-sionalism, Susan went to great pains with applicants to ensure that they were in tune with her style. She was aiming to build a team of like-minded people and had the major influence on judging whether someone fitted the bill and fulfilled her policy of bringing young blood on to the staff. In order to ensure fairness, she brought in the LEA adviser when there was an internal candidate. The higher the grade of the post, the more formal the selection process 'because it's a big decision. It always hangs over me, if you get the wrong one'. Gov-ernors were invited to look at applications and shortlists but more as a protection if things went wrong, since they tended to follow her lead anyway. Similarly she might discuss applications with other colleagues but not as a matter of course. Her role was pivotal. Appointing to a B-allowance post, she spent a lot of time showing applicants round the school, talking to them all the time. She felt she could sense when some were thinking 'I couldn't work here, the expecta-tions aren't mine'. As she walked around with one young woman applicant (later appointed) she told her: 'What I want is someone who can accept me as I am, very organized, but I don't expect you to be like that, but I need someone who won't say that's a load of rub-bish and I don't like that system.' From the applicant's point of view this gave her the right opportunity to decide if she could work with her:

> It was great because just being honest like that, saying I don't want someone like this, but I want you to be yourself as long as you can work with how I am. And it seemed to me she was very proud of the school. I felt I could fit in and I could learn from her.

Although the formal selection processes in Susan's school provided all the usual checks and balances on unfair selection, the dynamic between the head and candidates was a crucial influence on the decision.

The primary heads' emphasis on appointing someone who would 'fit' the school's culture, complement their own style and, at the same time, bring something new to the school was reflected in the secondary heads' approaches but set within a context in which they felt they had to be more sensitive to the politics of selection decisions. The successful candidate for a post in Pauline's school used almost exactly the same words as Susan's candidate to describe Pauline's impact on her decision to continue with her application:

> This was a critical career move for me. It was not one I was going to make for the sake of it. She was a big factor in my decision to go for it. I told her at the interview I wanted to be part of a school that was going somewhere. I didn't mind where they were starting from but I felt she was someone who had a vision. I felt she knew where she wanted the school to be. I'd never had a head before at interview state their principles up front as much and I was also attracted by the idea of working with a successful woman.

Negotiation and bargaining in arriving at a consensual decision about the right person for the job happened in both sectors, but it was more straightforward for the primary heads to express their preferences. The secondary heads trod a more delicate line in seeking to influence without determining the outcome of the selection process. I observed how Diana, during selection interviews, held back from suggesting what she wanted to know about candidates until the other selectors had stated their interests. She encouraged the deputy to lead the discussion of what was being sought in a new appointment as deputy head of faculty. Her role emerged as legitimating the decisions towards which the other selectors were moving. At the same time, through the judicious injection of questions, she provided an undeclared framework for their discussion. At the point at which she had decided her own preference, she encouraged the others to raise their concerns so that they could be clarified and doubts removed, if necessary. Her strategy was to give the others responsibility for decisions about who should go through to the final round, and only intervene if she thought the decisions were not 'reliable' ones. Only when they had expressed all their doubts did she express her own. Her questions at the final-stage interviews reflected her particular concern to reveal the candidate as the person behind the façade. She was reassured when she saw one candidate in the staffroom more relaxed and not performing, because I then saw someone who was nervous, a little uncertain and very different from the poised, confident young lady we had in the formal interview. It's good to see that because you realize here's someone who is vulnerable, who is a human being and young and probably someone who will be moulded by the ethos of the organization.

At the same time she wanted someone who could take the department forward, make changes but take colleagues along with him or her. At the final decision-making stage, she continued to manage the direction of the debate through questions rather than statements, e.g. 'Which of the two would take colleagues along in achieving goals?' Then, at the final point, she came down in favour of one and the others agreed. In these ways she led, without distorting the discussion. As the successful applicant, the young woman concerned later confirmed her own sense of the rightness of the appointment. It brought Diana the support and commitment she needed, and which was not always as obviously forthcoming from the staff she had inherited.

Selecting new staff provided the heads with opportunities to use their power and influence to shape the culture by choosing like-minded yet creative people. They did not use it as an opportunity to remedy any imbalance in the overall staff profile, as far as gender was concerned. On the contrary, it was important to all of them, in particular the secondary heads, not to use positive discrimination in favour of either women or men. The three primary heads expressed a desire at times to have more men on the staff, but in connection with classroom teaching rather than a post with specific responsibilities. Each perceived the problem with men applicants for teaching posts as their relatively low calibre so that they were not usually even in the running. In Pauline's school, they had moved from a predominantly male middle management to mainly women year heads and mainly men curriculum team leaders but the emphasis was on 'balanced' shortlists. Two of the secondary heads also expressed disappointment at the calibre of many men applicants, though they would still aim for 'balance'. Vanessa claimed with pride that, since she became the head, the balance of managerial posts had shifted from predominantly men to being shared equally between men and women. She attributed the change to her own presence as demonstrating that women could succeed as managers, rather than to selection procedures aiming for a greater balance. Even so, she knew some male colleagues saw themselves as less favoured than their women colleagues, in spite of her attempts not to be seen to use positive discrimination.

It appeared that the women heads had a conception of equity in appointments which did not see women as disadvantaged and in need of preferential consideration. Having experienced little gender discrimination themselves in their careers, they were not convinced of the problem it might present to women colleagues seeking promotion, particularly in schools where men were involved. They reflected the general preference in education for not making all the criteria for a promotional post explicit (Morgan *et al.*, 1983), even though by so doing they might deflect some of the male preferment that otherwise operates in selection. In their case, it was less a question of preference for one or other gender, more a determination not to be seen to have preferences in the first place. Equity meant treating women candidates the same as men, not discriminating in favour of them or against them. Unlike other selectors, they were prepared to assume that a woman candidate's domestic responsibilities were no more relevant to her application than a man's. In two instances where race and age, not gender, were at issue, the heads concerned took uncompromising stances: positive discrimination was declared as being as irrelevant to teachers from ethnic minorities as it was to women; and the decision not to appoint a former head of department (a woman in her forties) to a post was supported in terms of the discomfort the candidate would feel as a result of reduced status. Yet there were no teachers from ethnic minorities on the staff in the first example; and the woman candidate concerned was prepared to accept reduced status to get restarted on her career.

BRINGING OUT THE BEST IN TEACHERS

Shakeshaft (1989) shifted thinking on what motivates women school administrators by showing how the most popularly used theories of motivation, namely those of Herzberg and Maslow, failed to take account of the specificity of women's experience. Aspiration and motivation have only been defined using a male lens and male experience. Shakeshaft points out how Maslow's theory of motivation and self-actualization is problematic for women, particularly in emphasizing achievement, adequacy and becoming competent. It positions women either as woman in woman's place (inferior) or woman in man's world. In this model, women have to go beyond their femaleness to become self-actualizing, whereas men's route to self-actualization does not include going beyond their maleness. Shakeshaft (*ibid.*, p. 158) concludes that Maslow's implication is that 'excellence in humanity is, therefore, excellence in masculinity'. Self-actualization is solely a public-sphere activity and women's place is in the private sphere.

Heads used their own behaviour and what motivated them as a touchstone for motivating others. They combined care and control. The 'care' was manifest in actions that were supportive and nurturing, aimed at making someone feel good about what he or she was doing, as well as securing his or her support, commitment and trust. I observed them, during most interactions with teaching and non-teaching staff, find opportunities for praise of some aspect of the other person's performance. Being able to praise meant that they could also demonstrate they knew what people were doing, that they were taking an interest. In the same way as they held a mirror up to their own performance, so they held to others mirrors that were intended to flatter not distort. One male teacher commented on his head: 'She is pleasantly lavish with praise at times but I don't feel aware always of how she sees my performance. I would like her, if she has criticisms, to say them.' They secured support by listening and making people feel their ideas were valued, and secured their trust by not betraying confidences and demonstrating their distance from coalitions and interest groups in the school. They showed they recognized people's strengths by drawing on them when appropriate, for example in meetings where they would defer to others' expertise or by not putting forward their schemes until they had heard others'. The 'control' was in finding ways to shape behaviour to desired ends, by targeting on what served each individual's need, i.e. by appealing to their self-interest. Although they did not favour performance-related pay for teachers or managers, they acknowledged their own salaries as attractive rewards for the job they did. They sought opportunities to reward other's performance, through support for promotion either in or beyond the school or by allocating special responsibilities with an allowance attached. This backfired for two heads when they, in their view, provided development opportunities through extended job responsibilities but without additional pay. While the strategy was acceptable to some, others suspected it as a managerial ploy to get more work without extra money, and were resentful. The heads' actions and their different interpretations are common to both women and men heads, but there appeared to be an expectation (from some women) that a woman head would behave differently. When she did not, even though her motives were directed towards supporting others, individual disappointment could be high.

Blase and Kirby (1992) identify the following strategies used by effective principals to bring out the best in teachers: the power of praise, influencing by expecting and by involving, granting professional autonomy, leading by standing behind, gentle nudging, positive use of formal authority, providing mirrors to the possible. All these characterized the women heads' espoused and actual behaviour in motivating colleagues to perform well. Chapter 4 showed the importance they attached to modelling through their own behaviour their expectations for teacher performance. Strongly self-motivated themselves from childhood on, they saw the opportunities headship offered to support others in their work through positive feedback as a privilege.

What were teachers' perceptions of the strategies the heads used to influence them and how congruent were they with the heads' own intentions? The heads were conscious, for example, of the problems their own high standards potentially created for colleagues, whose circumstances or purposes were different. This was confirmed by others' comments on the heads as role models, working excessively hard and setting personal standards that were sometimes hard for others to reach. One teacher commented: 'I work very long hours but you feel quite pleased with yourself if you leave after the head.' Another attributed the very long hours worked by staff in the school to the head always arriving first in the morning and being last to leave. The head, in turn, was conscious that the absence of childcare responsibilities made this pattern easier for her. Sometimes the heads' comments revealed that as women managers they were as much prey to stereotyped versions of what motivates men and women at work, as some men can be. Susan, for example, expressed a particular concern about the careers of her two senior male colleagues because they had families to support. This did not, however, diminish the whole-hearted support she gave to women colleagues in their career aspirations and, as with the other heads, to women whom they knew to be the main breadwinners.

There was a considerable difference in how the heads were perceived in terms of the support they gave for family and other responsibilities outside work. None of the primary teachers interviewed questioned its strength where their heads were concerned. Comparisons were made with previous heads who were unsympathetic when a teacher's own children were ill, whether men or women. In contrast the primary heads in the study were described as sympathetic, considerate and responsive to family and other demands outside school, whether they had children themselves or not. The all-female staff at Barbara's school were initially concerned at how she would combine headship with having two very young children. Her strategy for dealing with any conflicts that situation presented, combined with her support for others' caring responsibilities, quickly assuaged the doubts. If she was likely to be later than usual, everyone would be informed. If she had to bring her children in, they (and any other teacher's children) would join a class only if the class teacher was totally happy. Otherwise they would spend time in her office. Similarly Heather's women colleagues appreciated her openness about her own life experiences as a basis for responding sympathetically to any problems they were experiencing. It was important to them that she did not conceal her family priorities but demonstrated that it was possible to meet them and do a good job at the same time.

Two of the secondary heads were viewed more critically as not always appearing to recognize the impact of teachers' lives outside work on their performance in the job. As far as the heads were concerned, they made every effort to keep up to date with events in teachers' personal as well as professional lives. It was part of their strategy for reading situations sensitively as a basis for taking appropriate action. At the same time, their own total commitment of time and energy to the job sometimes made women colleagues (though not men) cautious about mentioning other commitments, particularly where they conflicted with school demands. This, combined with the heads' desires not to antagonize the men who made up 50 per cent or more of the staff, meant that they were seen by some as more private, self-contained and unresponsive to domestic demands than their primary colleagues. While the men interviewed tended to approve of the head's preference for not favouring women, their women colleagues were more critical. The basis of the criticism was that a climate existed in the school in which it did not seem appropriate to ask for support, even though it was usually forthcoming when they did. This was reinforced by what both the men and women interviewed described as women's concerns (not men's) about gender among staff as a whole. For women, these related to whether they had to modify their behaviour as women, either as a result of the head's attitudes or of other staff's.

Two women teachers interviewed in different schools described their unease about mentioning family issues, as it might be held against them as women by male staff. They both felt this accounted for their heads' own reluctance to bring such concerns to the surface, in case it undermined women teachers' position in the school. From their point of view, the failure to address it publicly was in itself undermining. The 'professional' line taken by both their women heads had the unintended consequence of appearing to 'warn' women teachers of future difficulties for their careers of taking maternity leave. From the heads' perspectives, they would have been failing their responsibilities as women and professionals if they did not talk through the implications of a career break. When a young woman teacher on Diana's staff decided not to continue to combine full-time work and two very young children, Diana advised her that it would be in her long-term interest to keep her permanent contract for security. At the same time she reviewed with her and found opportunities to support her continuing professional development while working part time. The warning was intended to be supportive and was accompanied by proposals about how such leave was best managed. In spite of this, secondary women teachers still found it as difficult to inform a woman head of their pregnancy as they would a man head, even when the head had children herself.

Chapter 3 described the importance of approval and praise in motivating the heads in childhood towards achievement. At the same time they demonstrated an early independence, particularly in relation to future goals, that carried them through when it was absent. This same combination of motivating through praise yet respecting individual autonomy characterized the support they gave to colleagues at work. Some (usually men) viewed the head's use of praise sceptically, wondering whether it was just lip-service. More positively, the heads felt they were able to trade on people's perceptions of them as someone whose approval was worth winning. The strategy of praise first in any interaction was followed through in all except the most extreme of discipline situations, such as a staff member making racist remarks. Then the tone was cool, firmly conveying that it should not be repeated and indicating sanctions, should it happen again. Even when children were sent to them, as the ultimate sanction, praise usually preceded blame. When the football association asked one head to tick off a boy who had behaved badly on the pitch, her manner was friendly, sharing with him the association's concerns rather than telling him off. She told him: 'I've had a most distressing letter, I nearly fell over' – and read out its contents. She asked for his account, listening carefully, standing close, keeping eye contact. Throughout what was a disciplining interaction, she sustained a positive note, 'we've always been very proud of you'. The heads were concerned that their praise-giving should neither be nor be seen to be manipulative. They recognized giving praise as a power strategy but preferred to see it as 'power for' rather than 'power over' (see Chapter 7). Giving praise emerged as an integral part of working with others, rather than a strategy to be adopted or abandoned at will. It was part of their repertoire of management strategies that, as a result of its effectiveness in improving their own performance, they used often and successfully to support others' performance. Its use was conscious but informed by a principle of demonstrating caring as well as the aim of getting better results.

The almost superhuman qualities that the heads were often described as possessing and to which they aspired could potentially have been demotivating for others. This negative effect has already been noted in their relations with deputies who questioned as a result their own aspirations to headship even though the heads gave them full support and encouragement. It was important to staff that the heads were able to admit mistakes, a seemingly easier course of action for the primary heads. Similarly staff appreciated the heads' attempts to protect them from overload so that they could do their jobs more effectively. The three primary heads would often take over a class when they sensed a particularly stressful situation and staff under pressure.

DEVELOPING STAFF

Drawing on psychological theories of adult development, Levine (1989) asks about the degree to which a principal's own developmental level influences his or her ability to lead and support others. She hypothesizes a relationship between high ego level and the capacity to create a supportive and nurturant environment. In order to be effective in a helping role, leaders need to be at a point in their own development which she characterizes as 'Autonomous':

> Autonomous adults are able to transcend concerns for their own immediate experiences, becoming more realistic and objective about themselves and others. This last tendency is especially useful in helping [a principal] understand teachers' needs and concerns independent of [her] own. The fact that individuals at the Autonomous stage can be both intimate and independent affords them the capacity to identify and empathize with others as well as maintain a sense of distance and personal integrity.
>
> (*Ibid.*, p. 193)

Reaching this level of autonomy is not gender specific, although Levine notes the relationship shown by research between effective leadership and individuals who demonstrate this high level of awareness, as well as an ability to integrate masculine and feminine tendencies (*ibid.*, p. 192). Her case study of one male headteacher, Peter Samson, demonstrates the part he plays through his actions in creating a quality workplace that allows teachers to teach effectively. He resembles the women heads in many ways: he is consistent, accessible, provides positive feedback, listens. His beliefs are mirrored in his behaviours and, for many younger staff, he is a mentor. Describing the different kinds of support he offers different people, Levine highlights the skill of effective leadership in judging what kind of support is appropriate for whom and when, if ever, it is best withheld. Judging accurately depends on listening carefully, something the women heads tried to do most of the time, with only occasional lapses. To do this required constant attention to body language and demonstrating that what they had heard would be acted on. After a meeting with the head to put right a male member of staff's concern that he was not listened to enough, he told me that he did not always know if he was being heard when he was listened to. When I asked the head how, as a 'listening' head, she remembered all the things she heard, she considered her memory was good enough to remember to follow things up, without writing them down. She was concerned that others might have questioned the consistency of her behaviour in following through what she had heard. Colleagues commented on another head's ability to absorb facts amazingly well through acute listening. She claimed she needed only to be told anything once, and staff (and myself as researcher) found that to be true. The difficult decision for heads is in how far to push and how far to create space or leave alone. The heads' preferences were for strategies that supported staff in being independent, rather than 'pushing' towards desired behaviour. At the same time, the high priority the women heads gave to modelling appropriate behaviour, together with continual use of positive reinforcement, meant they were seeking to shape if not push others in directions they had identified. This was their form of control.

Their commitment to their own personal and professional development extended to a commitment to supporting the development of all those working in and with the school. Their reasons for valuing development derived from their views of teaching and non-teaching staff and others as 'resourceful humans'. While new appointments provided opportunities to recruit the 'right' people, they had inherited many of those with whom they worked and who did not always subscribe to the teaching, learning and managing approaches that the heads were modelling. At the same time they were keen to support good people in moving on to jobs in other schools even though it meant that person was lost as a resource to their own school. Their attempts to support individual teachers' development were constrained by changes in funding for continuing professional development that had increasingly shifted the goals from meeting individual to meeting institutional needs. While this potentially served the schools' strategic purposes and the heads' paramount concern for the schools' good reputations, it also clashed with the heads' preferred view of colleagues as professionals wanting to develop, not employees only requiring new or improved skills. They tried to combine humanistic commitment to every individual's right to development (demonstrated through the style of their interaction with teaching and non-teaching staff) with a strategic approach to teacher development and educational change that would promote organizational effectiveness. This was demonstrated through their use of resources to support different development initiatives, mainly for teaching staff. They did not distinguish between men and women's development needs. Nor was there evidence that they were concerned at the specific consequences for women of the changed emphasis in INSET resourcing, which Al-Khalifa and Migniuolo (1990) describe as detrimental to women teachers' development, since it is individual not school focused.

Their conception of the professional, which was at the heart of their support for teacher development, was based on a respect for colleagues' professional knowledge and expertise and an acknowledgement of the unprecedented demands made by recent reforms on their teaching and management skills. The three primary heads all considered themselves novices when they were appointed to implement the new reforms, at the same time needing to be at least one jump ahead of their colleagues. They welcomed others' expertise and drew on it wherever possible. A visiting multicultural adviser brought 'enormous development' for Susan as well as for the school, while Barbara and Heather had no reservations about turning to others for advice if necessary whether on curriculum issues (subject co-ordinators), handing difficult personnel situations (LEA officers) or managing the budget (the school secretary). Even though the secondary heads considered themselves skilled managers on taking up post, they still valued others' expertise as often superior to their own. Often when talking to colleagues, they would refer to their naivety compared to the colleague's expertise. This was not false modesty but an acknowledgement of what they recognized as weaknesses as well as strengths. Pauline said: 'I am very sensitive to what I can't do well and what I am lacking in. That may well be a gender thing.' When identifying SMT members' responsibilities for individual faculties, Diana deliberately chose mathematics, about which she knew little, so she could learn more. It would have been less time-consuming to choose a more familiar subject.

The strength of the heads' approaches to using and developing expertise lay in recognizing where it was located and how it could be used most effectively. Their aim was to be facilitators, not charismatic leaders. The heads' schools were no different from other primary and secondary schools in having formal mechanisms for INSET and staff development which provided an overlay for the daily developmental experiences that the school as workplace offered. Although all six heads had formally delegated staff development to a colleague, they saw themselves as having a continuing responsibility for supporting individual develop-ment, to which they contributed in a variety of ways. Their exchanges in classrooms, corridors and formal meetings always had, as part of their agenda, how the interaction might contribute to enhancing others' and their own performance.

They were not always comfortable with the manipulation of others this implied. Susan, sometimes, put one person's good practice as a model for someone having difficulties but felt uncomfortable about the pressure that put on the recipient. It was her way of indicating that the person concerned should ask for help and she would give it, but she was hesitant to offer it openly. At the same time, she did not want to be manipulative because, as Chapter 7 shows, she did not want it to be part of her 'power' relationship with others.

The effectiveness of a strategy of using interactions to support development depended on individual staff's willingness to be 'coached' in this way, where they were aware that was happening. On separate occasions, I observed Vanessa counsel first a woman, then a man head of department about difficult members of their departments, as part of regular staff-development interviews. She used these hour-long interviews (which were separate from the formal appraisal process) to review how things were going and give individual staff an opportunity to feed back any concerns and triumphs. She considered it important that they should have the opportunity to talk directly with her as the head. Although her intention was collegial, she recognized that she was lending symbolic weight to the discussion because it took place with her as head. There was a marked contrast in the atmosphere of the two interviews. With Sally, they sat opposite each other, lots of eye contact, both leaning forward. Vanessa explored Sally's problem with her, encouraging her to be assertive, even though Sally wanted to hold out an olive branch to the recalcitrant team member. She helped Sally articulate what her colleague might be feeling, then reassured her that she had to be tough to be accountable. Through Vanessa sympathizing, reassuring, explaining and making proposals for strategies, Sally declared herself more confident to deal with the issue. Vanessa concluded the interview by giving Sally a chance to describe some recent triumphs in the department. To the observer, Bob's interview appeared very different. Even though they were seated in the same chairs as Vanessa's interview with Sally, Bob did not lean forward. In spite of her suggestion that they began with what was going well, he started with his problems of not sleeping well at nights and feeling generally over-worked. His main professional problem was the same as Sally's: as a head of department, should he make someone do something or do it himself? Vanessa's response was the same. Having sympathized with his sleeplessness and suggested a pad and pencil by the bed, she reassured him and advocated strategies, but Bob's response did not indicate that he had registered what she said. He was more concerned to describe and justify what he was doing. She ended the interview with praise for work recently done in his department but afterwards felt she had probably had very little impact on his perception of the problem.

These examples illustrate the delicate line the heads trod between supportive development (in this case through sharing problems) and proposing solutions. It appeared in this and other examples that the attempts at joint problem-solving were less easy with men than women, although this was not always the case. Shakeshaft (1993) suggests gender as an explanatory variable in successful supervision, given what is known about men and women's different conversational styles, their different priorities (facts or feelings) and discomfort in communicating with a member of the opposite sex. She says (*ibid*, p. 54):

> Certainly we know that male teachers exhibit more hostility in dealing with female administrators than do female teachers. We also know that women have to work harder to get male teachers to 'hear' them.

Many of the heads' interactions with men and women staff provided evidence to support these claims. It would, however, be misleading to generalize. Whatever the responses of men and women, the heads remained consistent in their own behaviour, only revealing to me after what they had really been thinking and feeling. Their determination to treat men and women the same meant that women teachers were less likely to suffer the negative effects of the reluctance to confront them with misgivings and dissatisfaction, that Shakeshaft associates with male administrators during appraisal interviews. Turner and Clift (1988) also found evidence of gender stereotyping in appraisal. Men were more likely than women to be encouraged to assert themselves and further their careers. The women appraised by the six women heads in the study, however, benefited from the same 'tough love' that the women heads demonstrated to both men and women. On the other hand, we saw earlier how a male colleague would have preferred more of the 'tough' and less of the 'love', both for himself and others.

Committed as they were to self-development and being reflective practitioners themselves, they sought to encourage similar qualities in others. They drew often on their own learning experiences as a source for supporting others' learning. Susan's activities to develop herself had always been out of school and of her own choice but not for career development purposes. 'I always went on courses and always paid for myself because I enjoyed going and meeting others. I went because I wanted to learn and I would always ask questions.' Recognizing that not everyone shared their commitment to lifelong learning, they looked continuously for situations that would provide collaborative opportunities for professional development, as part of the school's daily activities. They were talent-spotters and talent-users based on their knowledge and judgement of what individuals had to offer.

All staff interviewed commented on their head's support for their own and others' development, using their strengths, working with the middle managers to identify where staff were achieving and underachieving. None of the women interviewed considered the heads had done anything less than give them full support for their developmental goals and agreed with the heads that positive discrimination would be inappropriate. One young woman teacher with a number of additional responsibilities commented: 'They are responsibilities I've been given recently and as an individual it's made me feel so much more valued. None of them were thrown at me. I was always asked whether I wanted them and being asked is flattering.'

Heather's male deputy also attributed his upward learning curve to her ability to see the areas he was good at and to offer help in those where he was weakest. His willingness to accept her support came partly from the respect he knew she had for his greater expertise and curriculum knowledge as a classroom practitioner. Diana's support for individual teacher development was the outcome of the strategy she used for most tasks. By keeping her ear to the ground, she could intervene sensitively through the faculty heads, before someone felt a failure, for example, for not being able to manage his or her class.

Their strategies for supporting others' development were no different from those advocated in any prescriptions for effective school management, e.g. giving responsibility for projects, sharing practice, leading meetings, drafting policies. The notable characteristic they shared as six women heads was in their commitment to and practice of 'managing development not just delivering INSET' (Oldroyd and Hall, 1991). Realizing the vision depends on providing the right conditions for staff and school development, including demonstrating a commitment from senior management through daily actions, policies and resources in the ways I have described the women heads as doing.

REVIEWING TEACHER PERFORMANCE

The introduction into schools in England and Wales of a national appraisal scheme provided primary and secondary heads with a formal mechanism for reviewing teacher performance. The value they attached to reviewing others' performance reflected the value they attached to having their own performance reviewed, as well as reflecting on it themselves. They welcomed their own appraisal by other heads and LEA advisers as an opportunity to discuss what they were doing but it was often a disappointing experience. Their own appraisers failed usually to use the occasion to give candid feedback, be critical and suggest further developmental steps. Instead they were treated gently, by both men or women, in the same way as they themselves trod carefully when appraising headteacher colleagues. Shakeshaft (1993) suggests that gentle feedback is a characteristic of men to women, whereas, in the context of headteachers appraisal, it reflects a cultural expectation of not criticizing colleagues, men or women. As a result, the experience was 'lovely' or 'warming' but not necessarily extending. Yet again they were frustrated by the absence of feedback to confirm how far they were on the right lines in how they did the job. They could provide their own mirrors and mirrors for others but others failed to provide mirrors for them. The appraisal process was ritualistic rather than real, although when they were appraising other heads they thought they tried to make the dialogue more meaningful by providing constructive criticism. Even so, they were conscious of being inhibited not only by their appraisees being peers but also, in three instances where they were appraising men heads, by a gender element in their own and others' responses to the situation.

One was conscious that the head's SMT only had one woman and the directive pitch of their language ('we're going to do this, we're going to say that') was unfamiliar to her ears, after her own experience of a team with three women and two men. In another school with a male head and what she described as a 'macho' culture, she felt she had first to establish her credibility with the teachers she was going to interview. She did this by drawing publicly on her own experience of running a 'tough' school.

They had more control over the appraisal process in their own schools and used the opportunity it provided to review individual development needs. In the secondary schools, the formal mechanisms for appraisal were the outcome of consultation working-party recommendations and LEA guidelines. The heads demonstrated considerable sensitivity in the appraisals they carried out themselves, as well as in preparing others in their appraiser or appraisee roles. Vanessa tried to avoid nominating appraisers for people where she knew there would be problems. She told appraisees who their appraiser would be via a note in their pigeon-hole, so that she could not see their reaction and they would be able to request a change, if her choice was wrong. Pauline did not distribute questions beforehand to those she was interviewing about an appraisee. She weighed up the pressure this would put on their time with the advantages of interviewees having had a chance to reflect. She decided protecting staff time was more important.

Hoyle (1989) has pointed out a paradox in these kinds of participative appraisal models. While participative appraisal is conducive to professionalism, because it is co-terminous with professional development, its emphasis on collaboration and collegiality means, in his view, that it runs counter to professional autonomy. The women heads were similarly ambivalent about their actions to promote collaborative professionalism and desire to respect teacher autonomy. It was particularly evident in how they monitored teachers' performance, especially in the classroom. Pauline and Vanessa were more reluctant than their primary colleagues to go into classrooms and relied on other mechanisms such as staff records, books, informal conversations and walking about to keep in touch with teachers' performance. They explained their reluctance in terms of teachers feeling threatened, although Vanessa had overcome some of her reservations by being informal, talking with students when she visited classrooms, so that 'it's accepted and expected'.

Diana was the least reticent of the secondary heads about going into classrooms, sometimes unannounced. Some colleagues perceived it as threatening, particularly when she arrived without approaching them first, so that they were uncertain whether to continue or not. Most accepted it as her right but were concerned her judgement should not be based on an isolated snapshot. She did not see the visits in this way. They were part of her overall picture but it was not always easy to convey that. Going frequently into classrooms enabled her to spot difficulties before they became problems and offer the necessary support, as part of the considerable professional autonomy she and the SMT gave colleagues in the school. It also gave her opportunities for speaking with students.

The mismatch between the head's intention and others' interpretation was more noticeable for the secondary than the primary heads. As a researcher, I was privy to the heads' thoughts as they went about their activities and knew what they intended their behaviour to convey. There are at least two possible explanations for why it appears harder for secondary than for primary heads to be interpreted accurately by those with whom they interact. The first relates to the different cultures of primary and secondary schools, which means that common messages in each sector may be perceived differently. In the primary schools, heads popped in and out of classrooms frequently, often to deliver messages at the same time as taking the opportunity to observe what was happening. The frequency and their informal manner diminished the threat and teachers welcomed the support it provided. One teacher compared Susan to her previous head, who rarely came near the classroom so that staff found it difficult when she did. When Susan saw someone doing something she did not like, she did not say anything in front of the children but sat down with the teacher concerned for a quiet chat after, beginning with praise then moving to constructive criticism. When Heather went into classrooms she often commented on how bright and cheerful they looked. She worked unobtrusively with the children, helping out rather than formally observing. Like Susan, she took up matters after, if she observed anything with which she was uncomfortable. Barbara overcame her initial inhibitions about going into classrooms by making the visits as unthreatening as possible, while at the same time ensuring nothing escaped her attention. 'These children are only here for a short amount of time, they've only got one chance and you can't let it slip.'

In secondary schools, as this study has shown, the distance between 'leader' and 'followers' is greater, however hard the heads try to diminish it. In Chapter 5 I suggested that, in order to know others, the women heads sought first to know themselves. An additional imperative appeared to be necessary for secondary headship: help others to know you. This prescription emerges from observing women heads, but it applies to both men and women although the reasons for finding self-revelation uncomfortable may differ. For men, it may be associated with difficulties in talking personally or they may see it as politically inappropriate to be self-revealing. For women, as we have seen, the discomfort derives from the desire not to reveal weaknesses, but this ignores the impact of this stance on actions like monitoring, where others are anxious about their own weaknesses becoming apparent. Concealing self is as much about using power with others as is asking others to be self-revealing.

However they were monitored, all the teachers interviewed thought that their head had a very detailed knowledge of what was happening in most parts of the school, either through direct contract or through other people. This was comparable with the heads' expressed need to know everything that was going on, so that they could intervene if necessary. In this way they fulfilled their perception of themselves as having the ultimate responsibility for teaching and learning, even though they delegated many aspects of the leading professional role.

CONCLUSIONS

This chapter has addressed two themes relating to women as school leaders: the extent and ways in which how they acted reflected their values about educational leadership and the kind of HRM strategies they adopted. Some contrasting stances to HRM were proposed, including 'hard' and 'soft', 'tough love' and 'care and control'. A simplistic association of gender and management might assume women to be associated with the 'soft', 'love' and 'care' end of each continuum. What I have tried to show in this chapter is that they were both hard and soft, tough and loving, controlling and caring. They claimed to have qualities and beliefs reflecting these contrasts, which they demonstrated through their actions. Their own interpretations of how they wanted to be in the job included doing whatever was required for the school to succeed. This included being hard if necessary, e.g. disciplining staff or identifying for redundancy, but within a framework of 'soft' HRM practices that emphasized human growth and development. Toughness came from sticking firmly to principles about how they believed they should relate to people and people to each other, but within a 'loving' framework that sought to make people feel good. They 'cared' for others but as managers they could not escape (and were aware of) the fact that their caring was a form of control, to ensure that everyone gave of his or her best. In the end, they were using their personal and professional resources to secure what they wanted for the school.

Writers like Blackmore (Blackmore and Kenway, 1993) attack the fashionable advocacy of corporate management based on teamwork and interactive and communicative skills as spurious representation and participation. In her view it merely uses participative rhetoric for managerial ends (*ibid.*, p. 43). One interpretation of what the women heads said and did would thus see them as perpetuators of an essentially disempowering form of corporate culture which failed to challenge inequality. Yet Blackmore also ascribes to this new breed of corporate manager the need for a lack of personal commitment to or experience in the field of activity, since ethical questions can then be avoided. This chapter has shown that the heads' behaviour as human resource managers is underpinned by two principles, which disassociate their practices from those which Blackmore criticizes. First, they aimed to and succeeded mainly in 'walking their talk', inspired to do so by a self-concept which found the alternative strategy of duplicity unacceptable. Secondly, they were driven in their attempts to achieve and sustain personal success by their commitment to the ethical aims of education.

7.

FOLLOW MY LEAD: WOMEN AND POWER

INTRODUCTION

In Chapters 5 and 6 I looked at the ways in which the heads used symbolic leadership behaviour to make their impact on the culture of their schools. Culture, however, provides only a partial explanation of some of the heads' interactions. The ways in which they were using power to develop the shared approach to leadership that characterized their management style was another key feature. The ambiguities of power as a concept are confirmed by the many definitions to be found in the literature. Writers who have focused on women in 'power' have generally sought to discover whether women's interpretation and use of power differs from men in similar positions (Astin and Leland, 1991; Cantor and Bernay, 1992). This chapter looks first at how the women heads described their attitudes to power, leadership and management and relates their perspectives to other discussions of women and power. The empirical examples for the claims the chapter makes for women's reformulation of power and rejection of certain forms of political behaviour are in Chapters 5, 6 and 8. The chapter extends the model proposed in Chapter 5 which suggests the contradictory norms influencing interactions, and adds those relating to gender and power. It describes their views of power and the ways these inform their actions to lead the school.

BEING POWERFUL OR POWERLESS

Kanter's (1977) now classic survey of *Men and Women of the Corporation* discusses women and power in organizations in terms of their 'power-lessness'. She provides her own definition of power as a contrast to those definitions that see it as 'zero-sum' or as embodying dominance or hierarchy: as defined here, power is the ability to get things done, to mobilize resources, to get and use whatever it is that a person needs for the goals he or she is attempting to meet (*ibid.*, p. 166). She distinguishes between organizations where a few have a monopoly on power, thereby preventing the majority from acting effectively, and those in which more people are empowered (i.e. allowed to have control over the conditions that make their actions possible) so that more gets done. For her, power in organizations is synonymous with autonomy and freedom of action. It is also, she argues, associated mainly with men, based on a general cultural attitude that men make better leaders. She deduces this preference for men as leaders from studies which showed men and women as more reluctant to work for a woman, even though they did not distinguish significantly between their leadership styles. She concludes that 'as in the old cliche, everyone loves a winner . . . Perhaps a preference for male managers reflects a "bet" that men are more likely to emerge as winners and powerholders than women' (ibid., p. 200).

The significance of her discussion for a study of women heads is in its identification of the values and beliefs influencing perceptions of who should have power in the organization and how they should behave. When women have the power, as in the case of women heads, these values and beliefs about women as leaders do not disappear but are there as undercurrents in every interaction. The force of these undercurrents becomes still greater when Giddens' conception of power as 'transformative capacity' is applied (Giddens, 1984). By this he means the use of resources to secure desired outcomes, so that any interaction is simultaneously the expression of both the shared values of a culture or a clash in values between cultures, and the differential use of power to realize particular interests. His definition is used in this chapter to provide a means of analysing the ways in which the 'power' of women as heads to realize particular interests is mediated through cultural expectations of men and women in hierarchical relationships. Giddens refers to a multidirectional 'dialectic of control' which, in effect, means that individuals are continuously tussling for control as they interact to achive desired outcomes. As leaders, the women heads required others' willingness to follow. While no leader can take a willing followership for granted, women assume that their relative absence from leadership positions means that they will have to work even harder than men to cultivate it. This inability to take followership for granted, as a result of gender, may constitute another dimension of women managers' repertoires that distinguishes them from men. Men who are given formal positions of power may make the culturally justified assumption that others will follow. The surprise when they do not is potentially all the greater and, to the men at least, incomprehensible.

Much of the literature by women on women in management focuses on why women are not where the power is (Coleman, 1991) or why 'where women are, power is not' (White et al., 1992, p. 14). Most discussions of power in the management literature are written by men and based on analyses of men's leadership behaviour. Writers like Bacharach and Lawler (1980) and Hoyle (1986) are the backbone of education management training programmes, and likely to be absorbed as much by women administrators as men, in their search for theoretical legitimations of preferred action. As we saw, women's accounts of power exist but, in the United Kingdom, the debate is embryonic and research evidence scanty. Even these studies, whatever their genesis, are based mainly on what leaders say about power rather than how they use it. Studies by Webster (1990), Young (1990) and Genovese (1993), provide an interesting contrast since they focus on the behaviour of women leaders (at a national level) to arrive at their conclusions about women and power.

The purpose of this chapter, then, is to look at women heads' interpretation of power and how it was manifest in their interactions. Purely cultural analyses of school management (for example Nias, 1989) can ignore how the distribution of power between men and women in society generally, as well as their different interests and goals, has an impact on how they behave in schools. Interaction between men and women staff, who are also in a formal hierarchical relationship, is influenced by the expression of contradictory norms based on contradictory interests that were described in Chapter 5 in relation to the symbolic leadership behaviour of women heads. Even if it can be shown that gender expectations do play a part in men and women's interactions with men heads, as a small-scale study by Johnston (1986) suggests, there is not the same contradiction between power in the role and power in society generally, as is the case for women leaders.

Figure 7.1 is a variation of Figure 5.1 and includes the concepts of gender, leaders and followers as dimensions within interactions. It suggests how woman as leader in an organization, i.e. in a superior position to men and women and woman as woman (i.e. in a subordinate position to men and equal with other women), can influence interaction. My contention is that both sets of norms are operating in any interaction involving a woman head and men or women teachers, other staff, parents, governors, pupils. It is a hypothesis which is not easy to support empirically in a study which focused almost exclusively on the heads' interpretations. After each observation I asked whether the head was aware of any point of being a woman in the interaction. Usually they answered in the negative. This was not surprising since, as we saw in Chapter 5, their self-concept included making an impact as a person not a woman. From their own responses they generally operated within a definition of the situation portrayed in Position 1. They acted within their definition of leadership as though they had a right to leadership by virtue of their position, though this did not necessarily mean acting in a dominant fashion.

Occasionally they allowed the dominant norms to be those that related to them as women (Position 2). I observed such occasions when they were with a peer group of heads, predominantly male. Then, they made choices about going along with the sexist jokes, innuendo and a sense of not being taken seriously on the basis that the important part of their identity was back in school – accepting, albeit uncomfortably, others' sexist behaviour is part of most women managers' repertoires. Relatively few challenge it.

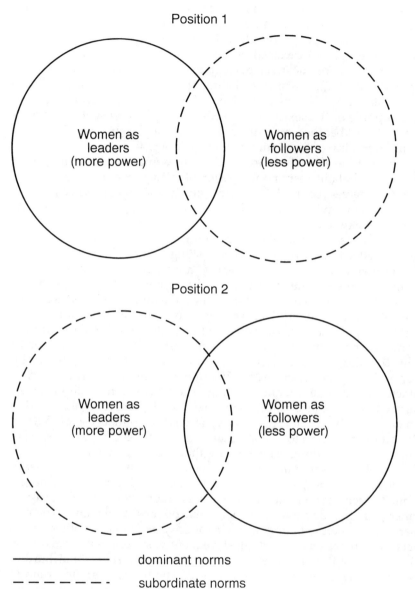

Figure 7.1   Contradictory gender and power norms influencing interaction with women as leaders

Within school, where they had more control of interaction, they chose to think that their actions as leaders were judged mainly on norms relating to leadership with power (Position 1), even though they sometimes (as other chapters show) revealed an awareness of the operation of norms based first and foremost on perceptions of them as women without power (Position 2). Outsiders visiting the school (e.g. male builders, some male LEA advisers and union officials) was given as the most overt example of the sexism they encountered. Otherwise it was mainly latent not least because, at a surface level in schools, lip-service is paid to the undesirability of discrimination. Outsiders who come into the school environment have not been exposed to the same socialization and are less inhibited about responding in stereotypical ways to gender, as the heads themselves reported. Comments like 'We didn't have headmasters like you in our day' were typical.

The difficulty of establishing empirically the operation of these contra-dictory norms arises from the subtle and not so subtle ways that gender is expressed within school cultures. Asking others after an interaction whether they were aware of the head as a woman would elicit the same negative response as the women themselves gave. Generally these norms are operating not only at a 'black-box' level (i.e. in people's heads but not apparent in their actions) but also at a black-box level which is, for many in education, tightly sealed. The potential for conflict between the contradic-tory norms shown in Figure 7.1 was ever present and some of the women heads' 'political' energies were directed towards establishing the legiti-macy of their authority as heads without damaging their acceptability as women. This double intention distinguishes them from male managers who need only be concerned with the first: their legitimacy as leaders. The women heads' behaviour, particularly in relation to their use of 'power', reflected their concern to win allegiance as people, as well as a desire not to make others uncomfortable because they were women leaders.

It is likely that some men will find working with women in superior positions problematic, since the majority of senior and middle managers are men. Men's experience of women is mainly in their capacity as mothers, sisters, daughters, lovers, subordinates or equals. Women's experience of men is mainly in their capacity as fathers, brothers, sons, lovers, sometimes equals and, most frequently, superiors in terms of job hierarchies. Both men and women, therefore, have substantial hurdles to surmount when positions are reversed. The heads were uncertain in these instances whether it was their womanhood or their management style that constituted the problem and men are unlikely to admit to a woman researcher that their interaction is influenced by gender. In my earlier study of heads and their deputies (Hall, 1990), responses to questions about gender were usually in terms of stereotypical comments or anecdotes about domineering women that might or might not have reflected what they really thought. Even so, jokes about gender and sexist innuendo were often present during my observations, as a not very deep second stratum to political correctness.

I do not intend to suggest that norms relating to gender were the only ones to influence the use of power. There were also those relating, for example, to equality and hierarchy in teams, as Wallace and Hall (1994) showed in their study of secondary-school SMT. As Ball (1987, p. 104) points out: 'Heads and their followers are trapped in this sealed political dialectic of colleagueship and hierarchy, professional and employee.' Women as school leaders face all the same challenges as men in the same position including how to balance leadership and followership in a team. There were many situations in which the relative balance of contradictory norms influenced interaction, without gender being a feature, as the discussion in Chapter 8 of their relations with senior colleagues shows.

TALKING ABOUT POWER

So far I have suggested a framework for understanding the women heads' use of power as including power as transformative capacity within interactions in which contradictory norms relating to gender and hierarchy play a significant part. I was interested in the relationship between the rhetoric (what they said they did) and the reality (what they actually did). It is a variable relationship, particularly in education where ideals are often explicit and the constraints on reaching them manifold. The women heads' claim that their schools were about people and consideration for people was at the heart of their management style did not come as a surprise in the people-centred world of schools. The question is, what did their prioritization of that concern look like in action? Wallace and Hall (1994) report that heads frequently described themselves as using a team approach when empirical evidence testified to the contrary. As with gender, the culture of education requires at least lip-service to collegiality and equity; flatter hierarchies and teamwork are the current desiderata. Even more, an expressed concern for people represents the acceptable face of school management. Headteachers, like other senior professionals, are skilled with rhetoric and their statements are not always an accurate guide to belief or action. The researcher's task is to uncover the reality that lies behind.

The headteachers in Bolam et al.'s (1993) study preferred not to describe themselves as leaders. In contrast, the women heads were not shy about acknowledging their leadership status. It was central to their conception of their role. As Chapter 6 showed, they attempted to 'walk their talk', so that what they said about leadership, management and using power was reflected in their behaviour. Of course there were constraints on their attempts to practise what they preached. These included the age, gender, status and values of followers as well as the conflicting demands made on them as leader by different groups. Most notable, where power was concerned, were the effects of others' resistance to their preferred collaborative style on their ability to sustain the approach to which they were committed. This was most apparent in the secondary heads' relations with their SMTs and the primary heads' with their deputies, described in Chapter 8.

We saw in Chapter 5 how the heads' conceptions of empowering others derived from their continual attention to self-empowerment. For them, being empowered meant feeling they had control over their own survival. This sense of empowerment was represented in their successful careers, in that they had achieved what they wanted: satisfaction in managing effective schools and, for some, victory over considerable personal odds. It meant having and being committed to an underlying purpose that provided the meaning for their leadership ambitions. Their work with individuals was based on their belief in nurturing others' power by becoming a role model of how they wanted them to work with others and by providing the structures, policies and practices to support that way of working, as well as opportunities for continual development. Their approach to working with groups such as governors and senior colleagues, which are the primary focus of the next chapter, derived from their expressed commitment to collaboration and power sharing as the most effective strategy for securing the school's goals. Before we look at how far their interpretation of power and leadership fits with other discussions of women and power, it is appropriate to hear what they say about power, about leading and managing and about politics.

There are difficulties in representing how the heads talked about 'power' since, within the Giddens definition used earlier (as transformative capacity within interaction) they may not always have recognized when and how they were using it. Asking a question about power elicits responses in which it is externalized, simultaneously intangible and material, to be coveted or rejected. Like Molière's *bourgeois gentilhomme* who discovers he has been speaking prose all his life, people use power all the time without realizing they are doing so. The primary and secondary heads mainly shared their implicit definitions of power but it had more negative and illegitimate connotations for the primary heads. The shared perceptions reflect other literature about women and power which shows them to prefer 'power for' rather than 'power over'. This supports a relationship between gender and power. More research is needed which addresses gender as a possible influence on perceptions of power, since it is possible that some men heads also prefer 'power for'. Ball (1987) suggests this may be the case but his empirical base is limited. It may also suggest a relationship between educational cultures and power, in that power as control and manipulation may be less acceptable among education professionals who see themselves more as autonomous and as peers. However, there are too many examples of autocratic heads and teachers in everyone's folk memory to give much support to this possibility.

It would appear, then, that when talking about power the heads' dominant concerns about its possible abuse may be associated with their different conception of power as women. The women heads both relished and feared the power of their position to make things happen, as well as acknowledging the ultimate responsibility it implied. For Vanessa it was 'power in order to do something, power to empower'. At the same time, it was something which, if she used it, would leave her isolated and lonely. Pauline's priority was 'working with people on the affinity side rather than being the powerful head'. Both expressed a commitment to collaboration demonstrated, as Chapter 8 shows, in their support for teamwork throughout the school, as well as at senior management level. Others in their schools testified to their collaborative approaches but pointed out the times when they expressed strong leadership in a way that appeared to contradict their expressed commitment to collaboration and teamwork. In the heads' view, this negatively perceived directive behaviour was a last resort, when others did not respond appropriately, in spite of their efforts to 'empower'.

Bolin (1989, p. 83) defines empowerment as 'investing in teachers the right to participate in the determination of school goals and policies and the right to exercise professional judgement about the content of the curriculum and means of instruction'. The constraints on the heads' 'empowering' strategies were not the outcome of an unexpressed preference for more autocratic approaches rather than those encapsulated in Bolin's definition, but their impatience with what they saw as others' reluctance to move forward, in spite of support. In these instances, the 'dialectic of control' referred to earlier manifested itself in their decision to use less valued behaviours in order to secure valued outcomes. In both cases, they were 'driven' to writing for them at least one other colleague's job description when they would have preferred to have worked together on its construction.

Both these heads had been told that they were seen as 'tough' leaders by other heads (predominantly male) in the authority. They attributed the label to the success in a competitive situation that their style seemed to achieve. They had trained themselves to be unconcerned with these reactions which they associated with the 'wheeler-dealer' approach to headship of some men colleagues. Pauline said:

> I've decided it's what you do and the way that you do it that decrees the success of your school. I know I've got to use power to protect the interests of the school but I don't want to be involved in little-boy games. They are not what determines a school's success. At the end of the day it is how every child is treated.

Like Vanessa and Pauline, Diana also saw many of her male colleagues as being good at impression management while 'I just want to get on with it'. For her power was fluid and heads had enormous possibilities for influencing and shaping without being 'political'. As I show later, the heads commonly associated 'being political' with illegitimate behaviour. Diana's determination to forestall conflict and the 'misuse of power'

in the school came from her experiences elsewhere of the effects of
'negative power bases, communication blockages and the unfortunate
use of charisma'. She used her position to support collaboration and
teamwork throughout the school (by providing resources and structures
to make them happen). She was also ever vigilant for the emergence
of cliques and power bases, deliberately influencing groupings so these
would not crystallize. She considered these negative aspects of power as
a distraction from the school's proper purpose 'to get on with the things
that count'.

The primary heads' responses to questions about power portrayed it
more as an enemy to be grappled with than a friend to be welcomed. They
described, apologetically, incidents where they had had to intervene in
what they saw as an authoritative way. Barbara recalled her insistence on
a policy for keeping evidence of children's work. When two staff refused
to keep the required records

> I stepped in there in a quite authoritative way, but after I had qualms of
> guilt because I was using my power as a headteacher. I had to be tough
> and say it's staying, but it's not something I did comfortably, even though
> I felt I was justified. I see myself as an equal and don't want to set myself
> apart on something different because I'm a headteacher.

She wanted control but thought of it in negative terms 'maybe because
I'm a woman'. She felt uncomfortable with having power 'because it can
mean getting your own way through unjustified means'. She associated
it with suppressing others, being thought 'a nasty person', 'being bigger
than someone physically'. At the same time she welcomed the power
of her position to make an impact and strove to act in ways that were
acceptable both to her own conscience and others' well-being.

Susan was similarly concerned about abusing power, while appreci-
ating the opportunities her position gave her to take the school forward:
'I am aware of the power I have and I really do try not to use it, but
I have to know I have got it for good or bad.' In common with the
other heads, she ascribed her determination not to use 'power over' to
observing other heads abuse it and, as a result, make people miserable.
In a long drawn-out situation with a member of staff having difficulties
in the classroom she was determined not to resort to using her power to
criticize and sanction 'even though I am sometimes tempted to'.

Heather, too, expressed guilt about having power even though she
wanted control. She assuaged her guilt by 'getting in and under'
and moving from within. Like the others, she enjoyed the possibilities it brought for action but was wary of using it in dominant
ways:

> I use all sorts of other methods to get people to do what I want them
> to do. I suppose that's power too but not of the Maggie Thatcher type.
> Maybe with her I'm thinking, why is a woman behaving like that. I seem
> to be rejecting the sort of power that I associate with men, as being
> unwomanly and also not always effective. I haven't liked it when I've

worked in situations where someone has come down heavily on me, so I wouldn't do it for other people.

RESOLVING CONTRADICTIONS

How they talk about power, even to a woman researcher, suggests that some of the contradictory norms reflected in Figure 7.1 were operating, particularly for the primary heads. Their discomfort with and need to apologize for power as a concept suggested that their own expectations of themselves as women (Position 2) dominated at times their perception of themselves as leaders. While it was acceptable for the male head in Southworth's (1995) study to be both domineering and considerate, consideration in the three primary heads' view had to (and did) take precedence over domination. This was not just because they know consideration to be more acceptable in a woman than domination, but because consideration was a key part of their leadership repertoire and domination was not. Their belief in power as negative contributed to their attempts to reformulate and enact it as something positive. In this case, contradictory norms created an inner tension which they sought to resolve. They had enough confidence in their own beliefs and values to use power in the ways they wanted. This confidence enabled them to reject 'management as masculine' and power as inevitably 'political'. Whatever differences existed between primary and secondary heads in how they talked about power, there was little variation in how they used it in each sector. The examples of interaction given in Chapters 5 and 6 showed it is possible that organizational resistance to dominating women, reinforced by the women heads' preference for shared rather than autocratic power, may create more favourable conditions than men heads can achieve for challenging hierarchical authority. The same contradictory norms that complicate women leaders' interactions with their followers may provide choices for rather than constraints on other alternative strategies as they seek to establish their legitimacy.

The heads' descriptions of what power meant to them were often in terms of what it was not. Power was not about being censorious, belittling or destructive, or taking arbitrary decisions, being hierarchical or confrontational. It meant being able to make things happen by distributing the resources, interacting in ways that left others confident in their actions, enabling others to do things, being thoroughly organized and prepared, having a vision and shaping a culture. All this took place, in their view, within a framework of accountability, power sharing (with governors), having authority and having status. They felt politically efficacious in so far as they felt their actions did or could have an impact on process.

In their research into what successful principals do to empower teachers, Blase and Kirby (1992, p. 5) claim that teacher empowerment requires at minimum educational leaders who consider their school's readiness, their personal philosophy and their leadership behaviour. We saw in Chapter 4 how the women heads demonstrated from the start, in their professional behaviours and daily work patterns and relationships, their preference for shared leadership and decision-making in their schools. Had their schools not had a reasonable number of staff 'ready' to move forward, their styles might have been less effective and the alternatives unacceptable. Chapter 5 showed how their confidence in enacting facilitative leadership, which empowerment requires, came from their own sense of empowerment, of being in control of their own survival, having an underlying purpose and a commitment to achieving that purpose. They believed that by giving up some control, encouraging self-expression and modelling commitment, others might be empowered too. In so doing they demonstrated a choice in how they used power that reflected a broader definition of power than they perceived many men (but not all) to use.

The extent to which they were successful in empowering others could only be judged by further research with all staff in their schools to explore their assessment of the quality of how they were 'managed'. The testimony from those interviewed during the research mainly supported the heads' claims that they worked in this way. In each case, one or two examples were identified where the heads were perceived to have contravened their usual patterns of behaviour, but they were seen as exceptions rather than the rule. For example:

> She probably isn't as open as she thinks she is but that is a human trait.

> She is very communicative but there are certain quite fixed points which staff are not always aware of.

Below are some statements from those interviewed which demonstrate the heads' 'empowering' behaviour:

> She has a vision for the school and she's done her most to share it and make it a joint vision.

> She has built structures into the school so you'd have to be an ostrich not to know what's going on.

> She's created openness by showing that people's ideas will be listened to, changing structures so they are fully involved.

> Every head I've worked for has said he has had principles but you'd have to use gunpowder to shift her from some of the principles on which this school is based.

> Staff want to please her, they really want her approval and people respect her for all the hard work she puts in.

> She makes a tremendous effort to get to know staff.

> She's very astute, she sees every area of the school functioning, takes an interest in everything. She has a very clear perception of everyone's job in the school and how they are working and departments and faculties are functioning.

She carefully guards and watches over everything in the school.

The heads' attitudes to power and their emphasis on empowerment emerged as strong driving forces of their leadership and management styles.

LEADING THE DANCE: MAKING IT HAPPEN, MAKING IT WORK, GETTING IT RIGHT

I suggested in Chapter 1 that although leading and managing are not synonymous, they are inextricably linked. This was true for all six heads for whom the concepts of leading and managing were inseparable. One informed and made possible the other. In their view, leadership was about having a vision, knowing where they wanted the school to go. It lay in the inspiration, the 'let's go for it' attitude, setting the excitement and the pace. Managing was the means for making it happen, making it work and getting it right. It involved using resources effectively, getting the right people in the right jobs, making sure they were trained appropriately, fulfilling their needs, facilitating all the things they were doing. As heads, they saw themselves responsible for having a managerial overview within a framework of values about professionality, development and equity for staff and pupils. Their leadership and management styles reflected the values they expressed about the use and abuse of power, the virtues of collaboration and the minimization of conflict.

As practical educational leaders they reflected continuously on how they behaved and the appropriateness of the structures and roles they had instituted to achieve desired goals. One teacher commented about her head: 'Challenges for the school were personal challenges too, including the constant challenges of raising standards and keeping ahead.' It took Pauline four years to reach the point where she could feel her vision was a shared vision. To do this, she involved the school in the Investors in People initiative, having judged that staff were ready for the demands it would make on their willingness to collaborate and share decision-making. Vanessa's attempts to introduce the same programme into her own school were not successful because she misjudged staff's readiness. In both cases the impetus for the initiative came from the heads themselves, as a resource to support their own 'vision' of how they wanted the school to develop. In Pauline's view: 'You can't develop people towards the aims of an organization until you know what you want that organization to be.'

Her grand plan also recognized that, in the early stages at least, the leadership thrust would come from her, with carefully selected support from other staff. By the end of the project, when many features of this particular grand plan were in place, she was working hard on handing over to staff as a whole responsibility for defining and implementing the directions in which the plan was taking the school. Making staff less dependent on her input was not an easy task, even though staff had played a central role in devising the programme:

At the end of the day, what we've got out of it I couldn't have got if you'd sat me down with a typewriter and left me there for 2,000 years on my own. The chimpanzee writing the first line of Shakespeare syndrome. I don't think some of them realize how important their contribution has been in setting all that in motion. Now I've got to work at showing them it's a living vision. It's something we can use in all manner of respects to get the things we want.

Although committed to sharing power their leadership visions were individualistic, acknowledging the accountability they felt came from their positions, including salaries, that distinguished them from their colleagues. Being a leader included making sure they fully deserved or earned the money they were paid. Part of their responsibility in having a vision was in knowing what they wanted and in thinking up to five years ahead, in contrast with their staff whom they saw as inevitably caught up with the here and now.

While they managed their school in ways that gave them opportunities to be part of a team and engage jointly in teamwork, in the end their behaviour was shaped by their recognition of the fact that 'the buck stops here'. They walked a constant tightrope between wanting to consult and share decision-making and being expected to 'tell' or 'sell' (Hersey and Blanchard, 1988). Sometimes they feared being pulled, as a result of their collaborative approach, into decisions with which they might feel unhappy. Other times they felt they had to work hard at pulling others along with them. In these instances, the conflicting norms were not about gender (see Figure 7.1) but about hierarchy and equality. In every case, their concerns that the contributions of other senior managers in the school should be maximized led them to take unilateral action at some point on defining the parameters of colleagues' jobs for them, when they delayed taking responsibility themselves. They distinguished themselves from colleagues by their sense of responsibility for having a vision and their prioritization of the school and its pupils in decision-making. Susan had no hesitation in saying to staff 'I'm the head of the school and the pupils come first and staff second'. When she shared this with other heads at a conference 'they were furious'. Unlike her two primary colleagues, she had a vision from the start. Heather and Barbara needed time for it to evolve, even though they had no hesitation in acknowledging their ultimate responsibility.

Like Susan, the secondary heads had a clear idea, based on their values and beliefs about educating young people and getting the best from staff, of where they wanted the school to go. Having a vision and taking steps to implement it is not, of course, gender related. Nor are the stated components of the vision, which resembled those likely to be found across any range of heads (both men and women) and schools. A distinctive feature was the women heads' awareness of what they needed to know about themselves and others, if they were to contribute to making the vision a reality. Hodgkinson (1991, p. 139) suggests that leaders have to do two things: 'analyze and continue to monitor the level of affect in the followership . . . and analyze and monitor his or her own affect.'. For the women heads, this included knowing and understanding how they used power and its impact on others. As I suggested earlier, the fact that women and power is not a taken-for-granted combination may lead women to be more sensitive to its components and their consequences.

FINDING A LEADERSHIP STYLE

All the heads had reached a stage in the development of their leadership style where they felt comfortable and confident in what it had become. Not yet complacent that their schools were congruent with the aspirations they had for them, they had reached that middle stage of headship that Mortimore and Mortimore (1988) associate with the implementation of more effective management strategies. At the same time, a significant feature of their styles was their ability to recognize the complexities and contradictions of choosing appropriate management approaches. The conflicts came from a belief in the style they should and wanted to have, as a result of reflection on their own and others' experiences, and that which came more spontaneously. One deputy commented on her head's need to push down her natural spontaneous, vivacious style in order to be more detached and managerial. There were many occasions when, reviewing how they had behaved after an event, they described their consciousness of keeping guard over their own behaviour so that it resembled the model to which they aspired and which they offered others. It would appear that although their personal identity informed choices they made about their preferred leadership style they were also constrained by it at times. Vanessa captured the ambivalence she felt:

> I tend to have an unconscious feeling of a rather traditional style, of leading by example. That's done through hard work, being on top of the job, knowing what's going on although I hope I delegate. I like to have informal, easy, good working relationships with everybody. It's up to me to set out to have high standards and high expectations of everybody. Because of that I don't want to be seen as distant and autocratic. So the essence of my style is friendly, professional, confident and as near perfection as possible.

The potential for conflict in the different beliefs that guided her actions was considerable. Critical incidents often related to situations where her expectations (e.g. of others' professionalism, of support for decisions) were disappointed. Within the dialectic of control, her strategies based on these beliefs did not always work as others (men and women) brought different beliefs into play. Chapter 8 provides some examples.

Like Russian dolls that nestle one within the other, the heads' different 'personae' in their headship role were revealed, as they told their stories. Unlike Russian dolls, the identities they revealed were not identical. At the centre was each head as a person: her values, beliefs, ingrained responses that had developed over the years. Then there was the kind of head she thought she should be, some aspects of which were in conflict with how she was as a person. Finally, there was the head she was allowed to be, in the context of the school. In each case, their leadership style, manifest in their behaviour as heads, reflected the constant dynamic between these three personae, in which one or other would dominate until it was challenged, or the context changed. Having led two very different schools, Heather could identify consistencies in her style, as a result of always having to put on an act of appearing confident and positive, even when she did not feel it. For her, going to a new and different school did not change her intrinsic personality: 'I joke when appropriate, I can be serious when it's right to be and I am able to be upfront with staff when necessary.' The difference lay in the extent to which the supportive context of the new school allowed her to be herself and follow her 'natural style'.

As Chapter 5 showed, 'knowing self' and 'being oneself' were important to them. They sought an authenticity in leadership that in their view would have been compromised by using power over, being political or being deliberately insensitive to others. There are at least two problems with the kind of 'authentic' leadership their style suggests. First it can appear inflexible, unable to respond appropriately to contingencies in the ways contingency approaches to leadership advocate (Fiedler, 1967). Secondly, authenticity and the strength it gives to leadership action can only be judged by the values on which it was based. Hitler and Attila the Hun were both true to themselves (i.e. their behaviour was authentic) but the consequences for others were devastating. Authenticity can come at a price. Since the women heads, who valued authenticity, were also judged as effective educational leaders, the positive impact of their management style can be seen to derive from the values that underpinned it.

An outcome of their belief in striving for authenticity was a rejection of behaviours with which they felt uncomfortable. These included those they associated with masculine approaches to management ('old-boy networks', 'wheeler-dealering') and 'politics'. Rejecting 'masculine' management behaviours did not mean that they saw management as masculine. Younger women teachers testified to the alternative management model represented by their women heads that convinced them that they too could, and should, aim for headship. Ironically it was the heads' male colleagues who expressed reservations about their own capacity to do the job, if it required the total commitment they saw in their headteacher. In some cases their admiration for the head's approach to dealing with the job's demands led them to question whether they had the same qualities.

In rejecting 'management as masculine', the heads resembled what Marshall (1984) describes as 'creative individualists', that is women managers who have integrated their femininity into their sense of identity and learned how to combine individual power with structural constraints. As the title of this book suggests, they enjoyed dancing on the ceiling to their own tune and their own steps, as long as they were successful (which they mainly were) in persuading others to dance with them. The heads welcomed management and the framework of most of the reforms emanating from the Education Act 1988, as providing them with the tools and opportunities to move the school in the directions they wanted, in consultation with others.

Herein appears to lie a contradiction since, as Chapter 1 discussed, some writers associate success in implementing recent government reforms in education with the new entrepreneurialism which is 'masculine' in origin. An alternative, more positive picture of the new entrepreneur emerges from Kanter's (1990) *When Giants Learn to Dance*. Her advocacy of affirmative action as a basis for organizational success runs alongside her belief in what she calls a 'post-entrepreneurial management' model that has education and training, continuing education and retraining as top priorities (*ibid.*, p. 365). For her, 'post-entrepreneurial' approaches are about challenging the old managerial assumptions, loosening structures and experimenting with new practices. She acknowledges that post-entrepreneurial principles have both an upside and a downside. This too was the response of the heads to recent education reforms, unlike some colleagues who saw them as entirely negative or critics who see anything less than a challenge as a sell-out. For them, the upside was the opportunities the changes brought to give people a chance to develop ideas, pursue exciting projects, experiment with new structures and ways of working. The downside lay in the threat they posed to job security, professional autonomy and teaching quality. In accepting rather than rejecting the entrepreneurial model, the women heads showed, as Kanter (*ibid.*, p. 355) points out, that 'It is not the strategies themselves but their execution that make the difference in whether the consequences for people are expanded entrepreneurial opportunity or anxiety, insecurity and loss of motivation to produce'.

A starting-point for the 'management is masculine' argument, in the context of education, is that teaching allows women to remain within the boundaries of femininity and affectivity, albeit in a public sphere (Al-Khalifa, 1989). Management, according to this argument, is different in requiring people to be more technicist and, by implication, masculine. The arrival of management in education has thus shaped a feminine world into a masculine one. When I discussed this argument with the women heads, only Barbara agreed with the distinction between teaching as a feminine enterprise and management as more masculine. She may have been influenced by the almost exclusively woman's world of infant-school teaching, where the deviants are the tiny proportion of men who become infant-school heads. Her accounts of her attempts to gain credibility as a manager in the school, as well as recognition of the role management had to play in the children's education, reflected difficulties that none of the other heads reported encountering in the same degree. However, the transition for her from teaching to managing was not a deterrent but a challenge to develop new behaviours which would support her goals for children's education. For the others, the transition had been gradual. None recalled having modified her behaviour, as they assumed more management responsibilities, in ways with which they felt uncomfortable.

The heads' responses showed the limitations of the 'management is masculine' argument as it applies to education, since it implicitly divorces management from leadership. While the concept may reflect what happens in other employment sectors (Rothwell, 1985), management in schools has a different quality, for two reasons. Every teacher is both a leader and manager in the context of the children for whom she is responsible. Working with other adults may appear different from working with children, but they both have their roots (from the educationalist's perspective) in successful educational outcomes for children. This is not to deny the effects of recent government attempts to transform schools into profitable mini-businesses with measurable outputs. Such attacks on educational values generate resistance. What is evident in the women heads' responses to the need to 'manage' the school is an interpretation of management that includes leadership and the assurance that management acts can have a moral base. Their negative experiences of others' managerial behaviour earlier in their careers mainly related to others' failure to integrate management and leadership for the good of the children. The women heads resembled those in Grace's (1995, p. 183) study, who were sensitive to the distancing effect which managerial preoccupations could have on their educational and social relations with pupils and teachers and classrooms. The sensitivity did not, however, lead to antipathy to management or being a manager.

In having the confidence to reinterpret management in ways with which they were comfortable and which worked for them, the heads had overcome some of the internal barriers that Leithwood et al.'s research (1992) identifies as continuing to block women's career progress in education. There they claim:

> Even when gender groups perform equally, evidence suggests that males are much more confident about such abilities [to perform well]. Because formal school leadership roles have traditionally been dominated by men, results of our studies may be indicating a lack of self confidence, on the part of women, unrelated to actual administrative ability.
>
> (Ibid., p. 165)

In other words, for reasons relating to their own formative experiences, the women heads in the study developed the confidence to enact their own interpretation of management and leadership, based on character- istics that are neither exclusively masculine or feminine. This was in keeping with androgynous approaches to management which, according to Sargent (1983), demonstrate a mainly comfortable integration of both masculine and feminine qualities (as commonly defined). Schein's (1989) critique of androgyny theories suggests they are based on innate or ingrained socialized differences between males and females. For her, the danger of advocating androgyny is that: 'The same sex role stereotyping that often excludes women from managerial positions can now be used to enhance their opportunities. Florence Nightingale meets John Wayne and together they lead us into the sunset of greater leadership effectiveness' (ibid., p. 155). It is clearly not a partnership she finds attractive. It also misses the point. Identifying management as androgynous can open up possibilities for both Florence Nightingale and John Wayne to extend or discover new dimensions of their repertoires.

FACING THE COMPETITION: THREAT OR OPPORTUNITY?

Changes resulting from the Education Act 1988 meant that all the heads considered their schools in competition with others though this was a greater pressure on the secondary schools. Women's preference for collaboration might be assumed to make them less keen to be competitive, a trait usually associated with men and their childhood socialization into team games. The assumption ignores the fact that not all men are competitive and that many women of the generation represented by these heads had ample opportunities, in girls' schools particularly, to participate in team games, including cricket, hockey and netball. It is true that competition was less of an issue for the primary heads. They resembled the women heads in Grace's (1995, p. 183) study, who differed from the men in that 'the potential "cut and thrust" of the market place was not celebrated in these accounts and the notion of "winning" did not feature as an important concern'. Recruitment of children to Susan's school was more than buoyant and she expressed discomfort that some parents were choosing her school in preference to neighbouring schools. At the same time she was pleased that it confirmed for her the good reputation for which she and colleagues were striving. Heather and Barbara had to deal with the repercussions of a temporary fall in numbers but saw it reflecting demographic changes rather than how their schools were being judged. They did not see themselves in competition or use language reflecting market values to describe their relations with other schools. Barbara was adamant that she would never use the need to compete as a means of motivating staff.

The secondary heads, on the other hand, were very conscious of the competitive ethos that surrounded recruitment to their schools. Pauline and Vanessa had no reservations about joining in the 'cut and thrust', and drawing on the vocabulary and strategies of the market to ensure their school's secure position. They did not see their willingness to embrace competition as contradicting their preference for collaboration, since their strategy was to collaborate within the school in order to compete successfully with other schools. Diana also acknowledged the need to compete in the market but questioned the effects this might have on educational values. Pauline and Vanessa had no hesitation about drawing on models from industry and commerce, if it would help the school's progress. Their schools had successfully implemented schemes such as Investors in People and Education–Industry Partnerships which had their origins outside education. Vanessa considered her activities with education and business links central to her conception of her role, and spent many hours building the relevant networks and organizing partnership events. Having been in the school for nearly twenty years, developing the links provided a mechanism for extending her own horizons, as well as bringing the outside world into the school for the benefit of the students. Pauline also welcomed lessons from other employment sectors which she used 'like a magpie', taking ideas from other people and making them suitable for the school. Through her husband, she used the business world as a reference group, to offset too much managerial idealism on her part:

> I do try to modulate my thoughts within what would happen in a business organization, schools being essentially pillars of goodwill and low wages. We are moving into a different kind of set-up where you have got to have value for money, a concept that is not particularly familiar to me but is to business colleagues. I am more uncomfortable than them with the fact that staffing, for example, has got to be treated now on a more business basis. Your product is people and when each day you are dealing with millions of emotions, communications and interactions, it isn't the same as running something that is producing washing machines. Our business is people and some of the rules that are easily applied in industry, like performance-related pay for example, are incredibly difficult to translate into education.

Pauline's educational values were not incompatible with the new ethos in education. She welcomed, for example, the frameworks and criteria provided by many of the innovations, since they brought the order she welcomed, but 'the art is managing the edges of those. I am paid to make the judgements at the edges'. Diana's reservations were greater:

> I must say when I was a guest of one of the local businesses and did a total quality management course with them, I was very much aware of how advanced our thinking was in schools compared with what they were saying in the business environment. The way we treat people, the way we promote people's point of view, the support we give on a personal level, the way we try to minimize the divide between management and workers. I often think business in this country has received accolades for its management it does not deserve. I am not saying I have discarded

business models. I think it is important that we recognize we have a lot to learn from business that we could adopt in our schools. I do not think, though, that the business approach is the panacea in education.

In spite of reservations, competition provided the secondary heads with a lever for bringing about what they considered to be much needed changes. They were driven by a strong desire to make 'their' school successful, even to the extent of the school becoming a model for others. They took great pride in knowing that, when their staff went elsewhere for INSET or new jobs, they soon realized how much in the vanguard of developments their own school was. Their decisions involving, for example, delegation of funds to marketing exercises were sometimes unpopular with staff who preferred to see them used for in-school purposes. This exemplifies the heads allowing their beliefs in what was good for the school as a whole to over-ride their obligations to some colleagues who held different beliefs.

POWER NOT POLITICS

A theme running through my discussions with the heads of their attitudes of power was their rejection of actions which they considered illegitimate, anti-people, self rather than school regarding and unethical. Included in the behaviours they rejected were those which Ball (1987) associates with 'adversarial political' and 'authoritarian political' management styles. His typology of headship styles to represent heads' responses to their needs for domination or integration was based on what teachers said about their heads, rather than interviews with or observation of them. While he does not indicate the prevalence of each of the four styles among heads, his observations offer a view of heads' 'political' behaviour which is in marked contrast to that demonstrated by the women heads. Within his conflict perspective of schools as arenas of struggle, micro-political behaviour dominates. He uses Hoyle's (1982, p. 88) definition of micro-politics as embracing 'those strategies by which individuals and groups in organizational contexts seek to use their resources of power and influence to further their interests'. Within this model, headship is action orientated towards maintaining political stability in the school through one of four modes: interpersonal (emphasizes community and relationships); managerial (emphasizes structures, roles and procedures); adversarial (dynamic or radical); and authoritarian (static and conservative) (Ball, 1987, p. 120).

Earlier examples of the women heads' behaviour reflected a combination of 'interpersonal' and 'managerial' approaches. Within the interpersonal mode, Ball suggests control is achieved through 'the symbolic mobilization of support' with an emphasis on commitment and persuasion. Chapters 5 and 6 showed how this was the thrust of their symbolic leadership behaviour, but without some of the covert, manipulative practices that Ball attributes to heads in their attempt to subvert opposition. His version of the 'managerial model' includes its spurious claims to neutrality and its distancing effect on head and staff. Although, as we have seen, the heads were comfortable with management techniques (e.g. teamwork, formal meetings with agendas, specified aims and objectives), they used it to enhance not control community, as Ball suggests. Thus, two of the styles he identifies contain some features of the women heads' styles but the 'political' dimension of each style was not evident. I recognize that the difficulties I faced as a researcher in collecting evidence of micro-political behaviour (defined as covert and manipulative) may have obscured its presence. As Southworth (1995, p. 144) says, researching micro-politics is not a straightforward task, precisely because it concerns hidden and disguised behaviour which might best be observed by a full-time participant observer steeped in the institution's norms. Even so, nothing I observed suggested that their response to opposition was to 'fragment and compromise' or 'channel and delay'; nor did they demonstrate the strategies of control Ball (1987) associates with the two styles. Even less evident were the features he associates with the two 'political' styles, i.e. styles in which the 'political' is to the fore, rather than an accompanying dimension to all interaction. The 'adversarial' style is mainly confrontational, something all six heads tried to circumvent. Within the adversarial style the heads' view is inevitably dominant, making a mockery of consultation, and the head operates as an active politician. For the 'authoritarian' head, statement replaces confrontation yet, as Chapter 5 showed, the women heads' use of talk was characterized more by questions and suggestions than assertions and commands.

The apparent absence of these political styles from the women's repertoires may reflect the different meanings they brought to issues relating to politics, which they distinguished from power. Interestingly, it was another woman head, writing about school leadership, who questioned whether micro-political behaviour need be all about self-interest and getting your own way by fair means or foul (Jones, 1987). Other metaphors are needed to describe women's political styles. These can then be held up as mirrors to both men and women's leadership behaviour in the same way as we currently do with typologies such as Ball's, derived mainly from examples of men's behaviour. For example, Van Nostrand (1993), looking for other metaphors for leadership that derive from women's experiences, distinguishes between the 'peacock' and 'midwife' styles. The peacock, which she associates with masculine leadership, struts and is adversarial, given to telling rather than asking. The 'midwife', which she associates with women, is responsive and advocative. Rather than telling, women listen and ask as a basis for managing others. In both models, power is being used but in substantially different ways and, most likely, with different outcomes. The relative absence of women from leadership positions means that these other styles are less familiar, less easily identified and less available to others as models. The women heads in the study were by no means 'peacocks' although they would use this style if necessary. There is nothing to say that male managers cannot be 'midwives'.

Given their negative views of power, it was not surprising that the women heads also described 'politics' pejoratively. In spite of this Vanessa was aware of becoming increasingly, albeit reluctantly, politicized by the effects of government policies on her school:

> I'm now far more politically aware than I ever was. I went through most of my upbringing not having a clue about politics. I didn't used to think politics came into education. Now I don't think you can separate them. It influences how I behave in school now. I used to think I should be politically neutral but the effects on young people of recent changes in education concern me so much I feel I have to make what I know are viewed as political statements, telling people, you have to fight for what you want to do for the students here.

For her, the powerful social context of the need to fight for the school's survival after the Education Reform Act 1988, a fight that she saw as her responsibility, had transformed her previously 'apolitical' stance. She watched the news avidly every night, lobbied members of parliament and spoke out on issues like enrolment which were affecting the success of her school: 'I feel the political views I express are not just personal but relate to the reality of the school. I'm not saying them just for the sake of saying them.' In contrast Pauline described herself as increasingly anti-politics as a result of the government's lack of support for education. Susan too was generally disillusioned, in spite of a rise in educational standards she saw as a result of some national policies:

> Apart from the testing, it's not in my head that I'm doing what the government wants. I'm not a political person in that sense. I don't think like that, I think in all the ways we've talked about, I'm interested in how those children come through and grow. It doesn't matter who's in Downing Street. OK, LMS I've made it work for me. I can see its strengths and I can also see its pitfalls, but I also know, whatever my politics, how the LEA let down the school before LMS.

Accompanying their mistrust of politics was some ambivalence about the role of the teacher unions and their relationship with them. Their self-concept as professionals included a commitment to management action that was primarily consensual and collegial, with an emphasis on individual responsibility. In so far as the teacher unions were committed to collective action, sometimes, in the heads' view, at the expense of the children, then there was the potential for conflict. They worked hard to circumvent this by maintaining open, non-conflictual relations with staff, although only Diana met regularly with the union representatives, in order to forestall problems. Pauline and Vanessa met theirs only in times of crisis and felt ambivalent about the values underpinning industrial action. Vanessa described working with the teaching unions as one area where she had real difficulty, particularly where issues had arisen as a result of outside demands (such as testing) rather than events in the school. When a conflict situation arose, as a result of a dispute between two staff members, she turned to her own professional association for advice, as well as talking with the relevant union representative. The critical incident involved a complaint from students about the behaviour of one member of staff who retaliated by complaining about the colleague who had received the complaint. At the same time, in front of students, the aggrieved teacher voiced criticisms of the management of the school. As with all the other critical incidents in which the heads were involved, Vanessa's approach was judicial, seeking out the evidence from all the parties concerned and trying to arrive at an objective judgement. She concealed her own anger at what she saw as the teacher's disloyalty and tried to listen impartially to both sides.

Only Heather described herself as a political activist, initially continuing her career-long involvement with the National Union of Teachers into headship. She had been the union representative at her previous school and, in that role, had often been in conflict with the head. When she and Barbara were separately confronted as heads by the unions, about redundancies that were needed in their schools as a result of temporary falling rolls, the experience served her well. Unlike Barbara, whose experience of working with unions was limited, Heather was more prepared for the games she saw the unions playing, as they sought to protect staff interests. In contrast, Barbara felt she was 'like a lamb to the slaughter because I wasn't prepared. I am now a hundred times more prepared for anything like that again'. Even Heather, who had years of union experience, was angered by the 'sexist and patronizing' approach taken by the (male) union officials: 'They were almost appearing to say don't worry little girl, we are very experienced in this matter, just do as we tell you.' She resented their suggestions that, as management, she did not have teachers' interests at heart: 'I'm not that naive to assume that they are going to support management totally but what I did disagree with is that in primary schools we know people are our best resources.'

In this particular situation of male union officials and women heads, the dominant norms were those relating to women as followers, not leaders. In Heather's view, they did everything they could to undermine her credibility in the situation. They arrived late, talked about union business, thereby delaying the meeting's formal purpose, and asked for budget details from the time before she took over. Barbara described them as 'playing the old games, hello Len, hello Bill, slap on the back, let's get this one over and done with, all *bonhomie*'. Both heads drew on their own support networks (their deputies and LEA advisers) but this did not reduce the threat of the situation at the time. The fact that both Heather and Barbara, with their different prior experiences of political activity, responded similarly reinforces the idea of contradictory norms influencing the interaction. Heather had always enjoyed the cut and thrust of politics, so it was not political activity itself to which she was objecting. Like the women members of parliament interviewed in Abdela (1989), she was shaken by the subversion of 'acceptable' politics by unacceptable sexist attitudes. Their usual strategies for establishing their credibility as leaders (since their own behaviour in this situation was consistent with their usual behaviour) failed in this situation where different expectations and rules operated.

OWLS, FOXES, DONKEYS OR SHEEP?

Baddeley and James (1987) use the metaphors of 'owl, fox, donkey or sheep' to capture the essence of political skills for managers. The four positions are based on an individual manager's skills in 'reading' the politics of an organization (they are identified on a continuum of awareness to naivety) and the skills they carry into a situation, predisposing them to act with integrity or play psychological games. Chapters 5 and 6 showed the heads' ability to read sensitively situations and events, as well as the value they placed on integrity, expressed through the desire to be 'authentic' and 'walk their talk'. It is not therefore surprising that, within Baddeley and James's model, they emerge not as innocent sheep, inept donkeys or clever foxes but as wise owls! Inevitably they were not always as wise as they would have liked to be, but their self-knowledge enabled them to recognize their occasional lapses in 'wisdom'.

Most of the examples given so far of women's responses to 'politics' in education suggest antipathy, suspicion and discomfort. Yet it would be misleading to suggest that the women heads were not 'political'. Faced with other people's political behaviour, incompetent colleagues, the need to push through unpopular decisions and policy challenges to their authority, they would not have survived if they had not drawn on their 'political' skills. Bacharach and Lawler (1980) describe organizational life as dominated by political interactions, so that survival in an organization becomes a political act. The women heads were determined to survive and recognized the need to be 'political' in their own terms. These, however, differed from those described by Ball (1987) or Bacharach and Lawler. The latter, for example, identify as apolitical views of organizations that see people motivated by rewards and that give importance to consensus and structural co-ordination. According to this definition, the women heads were apolitical since these were their beliefs. Political views, as represented by Ball and Bacharach and Lawler, provide a vision of organizations as politically negotiated orders in which actors are engaged in perpetual bargaining, repeatedly forming and reforming coalitions. The women heads' behaviour suggested that subscribing to an 'apolitical' view of organizational life (as defined by Bacharach and Lawler) does not rule out 'political' behaviour, though it is not the same as these writers define it. The women heads recognized and used the powers they had, by virtue of their hierarchical status, in, for example, giving teachers references and development opportunities in return for getting things done. They considered these types of acts as legitimate uses of power. They were aware of teachers' attempts to influence them, particularly

with changes in the Pay and Conditions of Teachers' Work documents
and the institution of annual performance reviews. Diana, as she toured
the school while lessons were in progress, was commonly approached
by teaching and associate staff making cases for additional resources,
recounting the demands of their work, wanting to discuss plans for other
jobs. The heads were also politically skilled in knowing how to use both
the written and unwritten rules to make things happen, as examples of
their work with governors (in Chapter 8) show. They used grapevines
and 'plants' among the staff to keep in touch with staff views, although
were circumspect in how they used the information, preferring to form
their own judgements through direct contact. Diana, for example, felt her
attempts to talk to all teaching and non-teaching staff made it unnecessary
to have 'plants'. Pauline, who visited the staffroom less frequently, had
identified her information sources early on.

Their sensitivity to people and events, described in Chapters 5 and
6, made them confident that they were aware of covert and overt
agendas, the location of the bases of power, their own power base
and the best ways of using influence. They tuned in by listening
carefully and encouraging others to talk (through eye contact, body
language, questions). This interactive style (described in more detail
in Chapter 5) could be considered a political strength in the women's
repertoire. It is neither adversarial nor authoritarian. It is about having
the necessary information on which to base decisions and actions; in
other words, reading the situation. The ability to read the situation,
particularly in the context of the political pluralism of schools where
goals are often incompatible and organizational conflict inevitable, is
paramount for successful leadership. Whether or not they used the
word political to describe what they did, they recognized and acted
on the basis of a view of organizations constituted by activities which
represent competing views, conflicting interests, competition over scarce
resources and the exercise of power. They were not politically naive.
These heads were appointed at a time of radical changes in education
and a multiplicity of versions of schooling prevailed. In order to take a
school forward, it was important that heads should have the capacity to
listen to different groups, and the sensitivity and strength to recognize
and circumvent incipient opposition where they considered it threatened
the school's progress. Even though they felt they should not enjoy being
political women, the heads were by no means innocent or blind to the
possibilities of formal power. Pauline, for example, described the middle
managers in her school as 'all strong people who run their empires but the
empires are all on the same continent'. As a result she supported separate
physical bases in the school for these 'empires' and did not feel threatened
by the subcultures that this potentially encouraged. This was in contrast
to Diana who sought to prevent the development of power bases, both
within the SMT (by extending its composition) and between other staff. In
both cases, the actions they took were different but informed by 'political'
awareness. They had, as it were, the wisdom of owls.

On the basis of such a small sample, it would be inappropriate to suggest that women are more likely to be 'wise politicians' than men, even though the six women in the study approximated closely to this behaviour. Their reinterpretation of what it means to be political in schools constitutes a challenge to those who claim that organizations can only be understood in terms of politics, and that organizational actors, to be successful, must learn to play 'political' games of a particular kind. I observed the heads engage in lobbying, get items on agendas, speak to the 'right' people, time proposals accurately. All these are what Hoyle (1986) describes as 'micro-political' behaviours. They showed that they were not averse to acting outside some values, in order to ensure other values were preserved. As Giddens (1976) suggests, individuals may or may not behave according to their values, since in most situations they have some choice over whether and how to act. The women heads associated others' (particularly men's) 'political' behaviour with the covert and illegitimate use of power to manipulate behaviour. Their negative interpretation of political was closer to those aspects of micro-politics that refer to political skills such as selective secrecy, withholding information, manipulation and suspicion. Their negative view of these came from the conflict they represented with other values they held to do with openness, trust, collaboration and teamwork. On a continuum stretching from conflict and competition at one end, to co-operation and collaboration at the other, the women could be located at the latter end, with a preference for win-win rather than win-lose outcomes.

Like the women high flyers in White *et al.* (1992), their political wisdom consisted in being aware of what was happening in the organization, and being sensitive to others' awareness of personal values and intimate knowledge of the context. Two of the primary heads were particularly concerned that their behaviour should neither be, nor be seen to be, manipulative. A political view of organizations might see this as naive or inept since management is inevitably manipulative. An alternative view of action as manipulative might see it as a conscious attempt to influence events through means or ends which are not made explicit. Susan was uncomfortable with her strategy for showing an underperforming colleague examples of others' work, because it represented a covert, though in her view legitimate, attempt to improve performance. The others were more comfortable with covert but legitimate manipulative behaviour. Their expressed distaste for dogma and politics (based on a view of their negative connotations and characteristics such as manipulation, achievement at any cost, back-stabbing and deviousness) did not prevent them from using their negotiating and bargaining skills, whenever necessary.

CONCLUSIONS

Overall, the heads appeared to perceive their power expressed mainly when their collaborative efforts did not get others to act within the parameters with which the heads felt comfortable. Their preferred approach was to use power to empower, based on their beliefs and values about collaborating. When this did not work, they reverted, reluctantly and relatively rarely, to a less preferred but more directive use of power. This meant sometimes putting values about goals (e.g. about quality teaching) above values about people (e.g. about supporting, not sanctioning). The operation of contradictory norms regarding expectations of women's behaviour as 'powerful' leaders or 'powerless' women was evident through my (rather than the heads') lens of power as transformative capacity. In other words, the heads were using power in all their interactions. They made continual adjustments to their behaviour to influence others, including adjustments as a result of being women. These included avoiding using authoritative or adversarial power in favour of sharing and consensus. Within their more restricted conception of power, they saw themselves mainly using it when things were not going smoothly. In my own view, they were using what I described earlier as 'woman power' all the time.

8.

GOVERNORS AND SENIOR COLLEAGUES: WORKING WITH OR DANCING ROUND?

INTRODUCTION

Chapter 7 looked at the heads' attitudes to power and politics and how these influenced their leadership and management styles. This chapter considers their rhetoric in action, particularly its manifestation in their relations with governing bodies and senior colleagues. It is based on observations of a small number of formal governor and SMT meetings for each head, together with observations of interactions with individual members of these two groups and discussions with the head of the issues involved. Earlier chapters argued the considerable consistency between what they said and their behaviour. Inconsistencies were the result, not of their own muddled thinking or duplicitous behaviour, but of the dynamic between how they wanted to behave and what others expected of them. Although gender was an influence on their work with governing bodies, it was not prominent. The governors talked about and behaved towards the heads in a way that suggested that respect for their authority as heads over-rode norms regarding women as leaders. It could be that, having made the (risky) decision to appoint a woman head, governors were more concerned to validate their choice, not see its loop-holes. A different study would have had no problem in identifying the many ways in which the discourse of governors' meetings and the different nature of men and women governors' participation in required tasks were evident. Men governors talked, for example, about the 'girls in the office' or needing to get permission 'from the missus at home', before embarking on an activity. At governors' meetings, women usually spoke far less than their male colleagues, including at the smaller subcommittees, where many of the decisions were made. Men and women often sat with same-sex colleagues. The heads were aware of these behaviours and attitudes as a backcloth to interaction in meetings but did not intervene other than to make attempts to arrange the setting for meetings, so that it was harder for gender-based groups to form. All worked with men in the chair of governors' role, except at Heather's second school, where the position was held by a woman.

Gender was much more prominent in the heads' relations with senior colleagues, although similarly unstated most of the time. For some it constituted a considerable constraint on their preferred ways of working, particularly in their approach to teamwork and in their attempts to support senior colleagues' professional development (discussed in Chapter 6).

WOMEN HEADS AND GOVERNING BODIES: FOLLOWING HER LEAD?

The women heads' working relations with their governing bodies provided examples of how they chose to use authority and influence, within the contradictory norms regarding women in power discussed in relation to Figure 7.1. In spite of their commitment to a team approach, working with governors was a task that they took on almost exclusively, rarely sharing with senior colleagues the difficulties they experienced in feeling accountable to both staff and governors and, through them, pupils and parents. Vanessa commented: 'I don't think staff appreciate the problems the head has in dealing with governors and the way as head you are torn in two directions. Governors expect me to know everything, be on top of everything, sometimes do their job for them.' Susan, unlike the others, chose not to be a governor so that she could avoid the difficult position of feeling strongly about an issue that governors were divided on and being forced to come down on one side.

In taking on this more exclusive role with the governors, the heads demonstrated their concern to protect staff, including senior colleagues, from additional management tasks. They were also concerned to demonstrate their centrality as leader, to reassure the governors that the ship was afloat and they were firmly at the helm. (The use of military, sporting and nautical metaphors was as much prevalent among the women heads as they are among men and, in this respect, supports the notion that managers draw on a 'man-made' language. A separate study is required of the additional metaphors that women use.)

The context for their work with governors was provided by the Education Reform Acts in the second half of the 1980s that obliged heads to share with governing bodies responsibility for the local management of schools. The anticipated demise of LEAs and competition between schools as a result of enhanced parental choice were important influences on the nature of their partnership, alongside the specific characteristics of each school and its environment. Drawing on recent research into the work of governing bodies (Thody, 1994), I have explored how the women heads talked about and worked with their governors through three perspectives. First, in what ways did their interactions with governors reflect their reported conceptions of leadership and power? Secondly, how far was the partnership between heads and governors characterized by consent and protection? Thirdly, to what extent were they intent on creating an illusion of shared management rather than a reality?

The framework for each headteacher's partnership with her governors was the expectation created by legislation that heads should be accountable to their governing body for all aspects of professional practice. Authority to manage schools is legally divided between heads and governors, the latter being able to decide how far to delegate responsibility to the former. Thody (*ibid.*, p. 12) distinguishes between the role of governing bodies within the polity, i.e. their contributions to democracy, and governing bodies within the management of schools, i.e. their contribution to the efficiency of the operation of their organizations. The focus here is mainly on this second theme, viewed through the heads' words and actions as they worked with governors. Thody (*ibid.*, p. 24) comments on the limited empirical base for conclusions about governing bodies' contributions to school effectiveness and proposes an analysis based on a distinction between their 'covert' and 'overt' responses to school efficiency. My observations of how the heads worked with their governing bodies provided support for Thody's distinction between the governors' covert contribution of 'consent' and of 'protection'. She defines governors' 'consent' as the function of legitimating the pivotal position of headteachers in the determination of policy for their schools. Governors use consent to support and legitimate the head's decisions rather than challenge and criticize, as the original legislation had intended they should. Their 'protection' role arises from the function of consent but extends beyond it. She concludes (*ibid.*): 'Legitimation by governors' consent lends support to principals and can help protect them from some of the stresses of school management. Heads can gain protection from governors providing a forum to which heads can refer decisions.'

The following analysis draws on these concepts to explore how the women headteachers acted in order to gain consent and protection. It raises the question of whether, in so doing, they were contradicting their espoused interpretation of power as empowering, shared and consensual. How far did they work with a 'participatory democracy perspective', i.e. one in which administration becomes the work of citizens or lay people acting jointly with professionals? Thody contrasts this with Sallis's (1988) insistence on the need to make professionals more accountable and less powerful. My observations showed that, while the women heads worked within a consent and protection model, it was influenced by their commitment to collaboration and teamwork. Their interactions with governors demonstrated the same attempts to motivate through empowering that informed their other interactions, but were constrained by governors' perceptions of the partnership. The dynamic was filtered through the heads' perceptions of power as 'power for' rather than 'power over'. While I observed occasions on which the governors' protection was sought, it was less likely to be as protection from staff (for the heads' collegial ties were strong) and more likely to be in relation to external demands, either local or from national government. For example, the governors' support for decisions they took as heads about whether the school should administer government-required tests was crucial, even though they arrived at the decision through consulting others and their own professional consciences.

In a study based on interviews and observations of two women (infant-school) heads and three men (junior-school) heads, Huckman (1994) concludes that heads prefer to use governors' new management responsibilities to create 'an illusion of democracy'. She attributes this mainly to governors' relative immaturity in educational management, but also to the greater political skills of the heads in dominating decision-making. Working within a 'micro-political' framework, in which heads work covertly to influence decision-making and maintain authority, she questions apparently collegial partnerships as spurious. She does not identify gender as a significant factor in the heads' management styles, but the picture of 'domination' (reportedly experienced by the governors) appears to emerge particularly from the strategies of the three male junior heads. Some of the strategies she describes were used by the women heads in this study. They used similar techniques but considered them legitmate, whether covert or overt. They let others speak when they felt the case would be strengthened by coming 'from the horse's mouth'. They interjected their professional expertise when they judged it necessary for moving the debate in desired directions. They shaped, through their rhetoric, the picture the governors had of 'our' school, at the same time offering opportunities for the governors to observe for themselves and form their own opinions. Whether they are interpreted as micro-political or not depends, I would argue, on the values and beliefs guiding the actions.

Bolam et al. (1993, p. 66) also found that the stance of governors to their management responsibilities was generally reactive rather than proactive, taking their lead from the headteacher and other education professionals. Three years on from Bolam et al.'s study, this pattern may be changing, as governors become more experienced in their new tasks and responsibilities. Like Huckman, they concluded that governors were very much junior partners in school management in the 'effectively managed schools' that were the focus of their study. They explain this, not in terms of heads' micro-political strategies, but of other pressures on governors' time and abilities to do the job properly. They suggest that even 'effective' heads should do more to forge an active partnership. Some of their suggestions for doing this were already evident in the women heads' strategies for working with their governors. I observed one join her governors in training events; another use governor subcommittees as arenas for development and teamwork; and a third included the governors in her management restructuring, so that governors were attached to particular staff groups.

WORKING WITH AND THROUGH GOVERNORS

I referred earlier to Thody's (1994) identification of the governing body's function in providing consent and protection for the head's actions. In so far as this model leaves formal power primarily with the head, it would appear to contravene the views on leadership and power described by the heads at the beginning of this chapter. There I suggested that all six heads described leadership as a process of working with people and through people. Their expressed preference in most aspects of managing a school was for collective action, for which they as heads provided leadership as a resource rather than a spearhead. They subscribed to the belief that, in management, there should be no more heroic leaders. They saw themselves neither as knights on white chargers nor Joans of Arc, although some governors would have been comfortable with them in either of these roles. Their problem in working with governors after the recent reforms was in persuading them of the desirability and feasibility of greater participation than had been usual until the late 1980s. They wanted to empower governors as partners in managing the school. Their actions supported this intention through strategies for securing their greater involvement as a result of sharing information, jointly generating ideas and consensus decision-making. Constraints on the heads' attempts to share rather than impose power arose from the obstacles to greater governor involvement in managing schools that have already been noted.

In this respect, there were differences between the primary and secondary heads as a result of different assumptions about the extent and type of desired governor involvement by their respective governing bodies. Empowering governors was hardest for Barbara whose infant-school governing body, in her view, lacked confidence in taking the reins, even with her guidance. In her school, governors had chopped and changed about as their children moved into the junior school, and she had had three chairs of governors in five years. Each time, she had to start again in supporting the governors in developing confidence in sharing the management of the school:

> My experience so far is they are quite happy as long as I keep things ticking over well. They see it as the head's job to manage the school. They are always there to back me up when I need it but they feel 'it's her school, she's the head'. Because of all the changes, and everything being new and emerging, we've gone through this metamorphosis as a group and I've had to lead in many ways, even though I was as green as the rest of them.

Her strategy for combating the frustrations caused by the turnover was to spend a lot of time keeping them informed, through letters, news-sheets and the head's report at governors' meetings. She was forced sometimes to interpret silence as approval, but used subcommittee meetings to encourage governors to take responsibility for decisions and insist they, not she, present them to the whole governing body.

The other two primary heads were also aware that they led the governors more than their commitment to collaborative decision-making made appropriate. They, too, saw themselves constrained by governors' relative lack of experience in school management, even though they, as heads, felt they were only one step ahead at times. Susan said:

> I tend to lead the governors quite a bit. The last set were good at saying, you know the workings of your team. Go ahead. I wouldn't go so far as to say we are jointly managing the school but they are being trained and I try to act as adviser.

Heather's attempts to educate her governing body about the details of school budgets, so that they would take more responsibility for financial decisions, conflicted with the welcome power over the budget she gained, as a result of their tendency to delegate those decisions entirely to her. She would deliberately include some items requiring decisions on the main agenda for the governors' meeting 'since I feel very strongly that governors don't take responsibility for anything and I want to make them realize that they're running the schools. I want to make them realize that, wherever possible, they're responsible'.

The secondary heads' relations with their governors were similarly led by a desire to involve them, followed by action to secure their participation and increase their knowledge, skills and understanding. Vanessa, in particular, had found a number of ways of strengthening governors' commitment to the school. One described his role there as 'a real privilege'. When the school went into LMS, she organized a day off-site for staff and governors to explore together the nature of the partnership they should forge. The structuring of different management groups in the school included governors, so that staff and governor task-group decisions were not taken separately. Her motivation for involving governors as much as possible in the day-to-day running of the school came, in part, from a desire to share the pressures of managing a demanding school, and meeting the high expectations she knew governors had of her. She wanted them to understand and share in the daily challenges – in her own words, to be a supporters' club but also play in the field:

> I don't think they realize that it is at great personal cost to give the school the amount of energy and devotion that I do. My problem is that the governors have very high expectations of me and I work flat out to fulfil them. On the other hand, at governors' meetings I can hand over full control because they are really informed and supportive which means I can trust them to get on with things. I don't feel I have to push things the way I want them to go with this group. I only try to be influential after they have had a chance to debate things. I would, however, say if I thought they were going to make a bad mistake and step in and make sure it didn't happen.

She favoured a collaboration strategy as long as the governors operated within the bounds of what she was comfortable with. When they moved outside she was prepared to change her use of power to fit the circumstances. Underpinning this public relationship was the work she did behind the scenes to shape the governing body as a team. This sometimes created conflict when the interests of the different teams to which she belonged, and which she had sought to shape (staff and governors), required different responses from her:

> When I go into a governors' meeting, I have to fight for my staff and professional matters that concern colleagues. I have tried to mould the governors as a team but I find it difficult, when they are trying to get to decisions, to know how much I should say.

Of the secondary heads, Pauline went furthest in overtly setting the values and principles which she felt should inform the governors' decisions. She considered herself lucky in having governors who saw her as 'paid to have the professional view' and ready to support whatever she said, within reason. For example, in common with many issues facing heads and governing bodies as a result of the Education Reform Act 1988, staffing was new territory. It required a head–governor partnership but within a framework of values and information provided by the head. I observed how at governors' meetings, she listened actively, at the same time interjecting judiciously ideas and information that would contribute to the discussion, without overtly leading it. This was in marked contrast to the male primary head in Huckman's (1994, p. 152) study, who is quoted as saying: 'I decide what I think is the best idea and I go on talking until they agree with me.' She knew their respect for her and her position would make her interjections powerful without having to dominate. She carefully managed the process by letting the governors feel they had the main control. On one occasion, she gave them sight of documents that she claimed staff had not yet had; on another, she reported that she was delaying a decision until governor views had been sought. Throughout the meetings, governors were reassured about their involvement but within a framework of unstated acquiescence to the head's right to control. She thus provided parameters for their decision-making, fed in information, clarified government policy, proposed alternative strategies and then handed over the issues for discussion, responding but not leading, giving them a sense of being equal partners in arriving at the decision. As a result, decisions often went exactly as she and her colleagues wanted. She saw her actions constituting legitimate 'political' activity, using overt and covert manipulation within the framework of what she considered a real rather than illusory democracy.

The heads' conceptions of leadership involved using resources to make things happen by empowering others within limits with which they were comfortable, being well organized, having a vision and shaping the school's culture. All this was within a framework of having authority and status, being accountable and sharing power with governors, albeit within the constraints of disparate perspectives on the desirability of hierarchy and the diverse composition of governing bodies. We have seen how their use of personal and material resources to influence and involve governors provided legitimation for their leadership actions. Gaining consent and protection implies, however, that the decisions which require these responses are the head's alone or the SMT's. The problem is in the relationship between gaining consent and consensus decision-making. This is influenced by the conception of teamwork that underpins the head's approaches to collaborative management. There were many issues for which the heads sought consent and protection, which was usually forthcoming. Barbara, who was normally able to rely on governor support for whatever she did, found it was ironically absent at a point where she needed it most. During the project, changes in school budgets meant that staff redundancies were becoming a necessity for many schools. They constituted a demand on heads (to reduce staff) to make choices (about who should go) within constraints (of professional association guidelines and their own sense of collegiality). When Barbara was faced with this situation she was forced to operate without governor support. No governor was available to come to the consultation meeting with the professional associations, 'so it was just me in what felt like the electric chair'. She set up the required panel of governors, within which she was expected to have a mediating advisory role 'although we all know what I say will have a big influence'. It appeared that it was not consent that she wanted, rather the opportunity to share the decision-making. Protection was also irrelevant, since the teaching colleagues who were identified for redundancy knew that decision-making was largely with the head, even though it would be presented as coming from the governors. Faced with the same situation in the context of a larger primary school, Heather was also concerned that her governors were not more proactive in setting the criteria for redundancy. As a result she felt she had to be absolutely sure of the advice she gave them.

In both these examples, consensus decision-making, to which the heads aspired, would have relieved some of the pressures on them. Equally, the governors sometimes used their power to delegate to the head to avoid getting involved in uncomfortable decisions. The constraints of governor inexperience and passivity meant that both heads had to go it alone, unable to share leadership in the way they would have preferred. It appeared easier for the three primary heads to work with a 'gain consent' model while they supported governors in acquiring confidence and experience in joint decision-making.

The secondary heads' relations with their governors reflected the greater experience and understanding of school management of some members of their governing body. As a result, joint decision-making was more likely. The need for protection was uppermost, for the secondary heads, when a response to the government's requirement for all schools to administer standardized tests to children at each key stage was announced. In this situation, the heads were faced with possible tensions between their own views on whether children should be tested in this way, colleagues' views and willingness to administer the tests, and governor and parental expectations about the desirability of this particular government policy. The outcome for all the heads was full support from their governors for whatever action they deemed appropriate. Rather than pushing them towards actions which might have appeared in the more immediate interests of the school and which would definitely serve the interests of government, the governors supported decisions which would prevent a probably irreparable rift between management and teachers in the school, as happened during the teacher strikes in the 1980s.

SENIOR COLLEAGUES: WHOSE DANCE IS IT?

How the heads worked with senior colleagues reflected similar choices about preferred behaviour and constraints to those characterizing their working partnership with governors. I showed in Chapter 7, and other literature supports, women's preference for working collaboratively, often through teams. Grace (1995, p. 183) found, for example, that

> While commitment to teamwork and a culture of consultation could be found in the accounts of both men and women headteachers, the discourse of the women school leaders more frequently took teamwork to be a normal, organic process whereas men referred to 'their' creation of teamwork as an important innovation in the culture of a school.

Explanations for why this might be a more natural way of working for women include their preference for shared rather than unilateral power (there are, of course, exceptions), for communion rather than competition, and for support in the potentially isolating position of being a senior manager. Even if they considered teamwork a better way to operate, they still had to convince others of its desirability. If Grace's conclusion is right, then it might be expected that male colleagues would take more convincing than women.

There are also differences in the conception of 'teamwork' at senior level, as conceived in the context of secondary and primary school settings. Most secondary heads would claim that they work with a senior management group. Calling it a team is then often a means of signalling that they work together in a specific way. In Diana's case this included sharing secretarial support with other team members rather than having 'the head's secretary'. It also included ensuring that, however time-consumimg, time and space were allowed for everyone's contributions. In both primary and secondary schools, the creation of SMTs implies superimposing new working practices for senior staff upon a hierarchy of formal status which is structurally reflected in salaries and conditions of service. The staff cultures in which this hierarchy is embedded are different for primary and secondary schools. It was not surprising, therefore, to find variations in the constraints experienced by the women heads in attempting to use teamwork as a preferred way of working. Primary heads, on the other hand, tend to work first with their deputies, then other allowance holders. For them, the dyad of head and deputy has precedence over a wider management (as opposed to teaching) group.

Given these different expectations in primary and secondary schools, how did the women heads organize their working relations with their senior colleagues: individually, as a group and as a team? How did the structures they created work out in practice and what, if any, were the influences on teamwork of tensions among hierarchy, equality and gender?

The same themes of consent and protection that characterized their own and other heads' work with governors were also features of how the heads worked with senior colleagues in the school. The need to work co-operatively with governors within an official framework of shared decision-making is externally imposed by government. It is simultaneously a demand and, depending on the particular governing body, a constraint on the head's preferred style of working. In contrast, the decision to work collaboratively as a team with senior colleagues is the head's choice in response to her perception of the demands of managing a school. The extent to which heads work within a team frame, unilaterally or in partnership with senior colleagues, depends on the head's choice of preferred strategy and the constraints deriving from the particular senior colleagues in post. These constraints relate first to the extent to which senior colleagues have a similar commitment to teamwork, or whether they feel the head is paid to be the key decision-maker. Secondly, they relate to the nature of the individual relationships heads have with senior colleagues, including features of the relationships that arise from gender. These affected whether colleagues were prepared to play along and, where they did do so, the type and strength of the partnership formed.

A key feature of teamwork is mutual empowerment as a result of shared work and shared responsibility for decision-making. By creating teams, headteachers use their power to develop a shared approach to leadership. It enables them to draw on others' expertise to strengthen them in their 'leading professional' and 'chief executive' roles (Hughes, 1985). Through the management structures they have created they can develop an overview of pedagogic issues. This includes supporting senior and middle manager colleagues as colleagues who are also leading professionals.

At the same time, working with a team can also provide some protection against the isolation of headship as well as support (through consent) for strategies that the heads favour. Paradoxically, the secondary heads, who appeared to be supported by a larger management group than the primary heads, also appeared most isolated on occasions from team support. The one-to-one relationship of the primary heads with their deputies, whatever the difficulties, provided a daily platform for sharing concerns. Similar support for the secondary heads was usually spread between two or more deputies and other senior managers, with all the possibilities for coalitions that could occur. As one secondary head said: 'I've been told I'm not always well served by my generals.' The solidarity promised by teamwork was not always evident and, when it disintegrated, all the more upsetting, since it was expected and valued. For example, Vanessa encountered slippage in good team relations when her intention to introduce a new initiative into the school foundered as a result of the team's failure to demonstrate a united front, when the proposal was put to the governing body. She felt let down, not only by the absence of support but also by the suggestion in their action that there had been miscommunication and division in the team. Her instinctive reaction (which she curbed) was to say 'we are going to do it' but this would have contravened her own values about the undesirability of unilateral decision-making. Instead, she decided to set the proposal aside, but for a while relations in the team were strained.

The primary heads chose to work more autonomously than the secondary heads from their senior colleagues. This was still within a collaborative approach but, in their view, recognized their differentiation as managers as a result of pay, availability and minimal teaching loads. They had fewer expectations of solidarity and therefore less disappointment when it did not emerge. Potentially, teamwork has the same possibility of representing a sham democracy or pseudo-sharing as was earlier associated with the involvement of governors in managing the school. In what ways did the women heads' work with their senior colleagues reflect a real commitment to collaborative management? How far was it an expression of their need for support in the difficult task of running a school? Whatever they said about their style of working with senior colleagues (the rhetoric) was fitted against what I observed to happen when they came together (the reality).

WOMEN SECONDARY HEADS AND SMTs

The three secondary heads were unequivocal about their commitment to teamwork. Opportunities provided by the LEA to develop teamwork skills merely confirmed that their instinct to work in this way had been right. Pauline's total commitment to the teamwork approach advocated by the local authority came from the possibilities it provided for quality through synergy: 'I want everyone to be operating on the bad crate of apples principle, where you might have a crate of bad apples but you can still make a damn good apple pie if you cut out all the bad bits.' Both she and Diana valued the potential of teams in arriving jointly at views and principles for behaviour, ethos and expectations of their school, staff and pupils. Teamwork provided the mechanism for moving from principle to practice. In Diana's view: 'With immediate colleagues I try to make it very clear that the importance of what we discuss and agree in the SMT is not just the outcome but the process by which we arrive at the conclusions. That's crucial and that is what they should take to others.'

SMT meetings were lengthy, reflecting her concern that they should provide opportunities for individual team members to discuss thoroughly the pros and cons of any decision within a supportive environment, where they could express reservations and insecurities.

Interviews with others in the school showed that the extent to which her team message was received as intended varied according to the receiver. For one teacher: 'One of the strengths of how Diana runs the SMT is that they are always target setting and laying down the strategies for improving the school that are shared amongst every member of staff.' Another admired the way Diana worked through the SMT and middle managers to get everyone achieving to their maximum, but felt that the vision that was pushing the school was the head's rather than the SMT's. Diana, on the other hand, found it difficult to recall a time when she had said something was going to happen. It would have contradicted her belief in consensus decisions. On one exceptional occasion, when she did take unilateral action, the team had been unable to arrive at a consensus about something that she considered a very high priority: the school's results in public examinations. Her strategy was, through the use of an added-value model which she worked on for months on her own, to demonstrate where the problem lay and persuade the SMT and heads of department concerned that changes were needed. She provided additional resources of staff and time, so that they would feel supported in undertaking the changes.

Vanessa also favoured teams, less for synergy than for strategy. She valued the support being part of a team provided, attributing this to her sports background, where teamwork represented discipline, competition to succeed and supporting each other. A strong individualist, she attributed the value of teams to the competitive edge they provided through collaboration.

Generally the secondary heads' response to their own membership of teams resembled that of the musician in a chamber-music group, who has the chance to be both team player and soloist, rather than the conductor of an orchestra, controlling and separate from the other players. They would come in and out of other teams in the school to lend their symbolic weight to what they were trying to achieve, but not intervening. They believed that if they could get the relationships right in the team, then the teams would work effectively. In fact, there were difficulties in some aspects of the relationships in all three teams. These were not about gender, although gender was an issue in Diana's team where only one other member was a woman. When this person left the team for personal reasons it was again all male.

The main source of difficulty in relationships was in the variable commitment to teamwork of other team members. From taking up post, the heads had used vacancies at senior level to appoint new senior managers, whom they judged would be sympathetic to their preferred style of working. Their greatest difficulties came from senior colleagues who had worked with the previous head and who were less happy with a teamwork approach. Diana distinguished between the 'old and new guard' and was ever vigilant not to appear to favour one over the other, even though she knew some staff saw new appointments as her special recruits.

The composition of the secondary SMTs was described in Chapter 4, including whether members had been appointed by the heads or not. Although they wanted a gender balance on the team, on the grounds that balance was a good thing, they were reluctant to use positive discrimination to ensure more women, even though it potentially provided support for themselves as women. They recognized that it also demonstrated to other women the possibilities of women as leaders, but their values about appointing on what they judged as merit were uppermost.

The ways in which they worked with core SMT colleagues was a central concern of and focus for reflection by the three secondary heads throughout. They frequently reviewed the situation and sought ways in which to overcome obstacles to teamwork and strengthen its potential for synergy. Some strategies were more successful than others.

Vanessa had chosen to extend the senior management group in order to involve existing E-allowance holders more in managing the school, as well as teaching. The strategy had not been as successful as she had hoped, since her commitment to teamwork was not shared by all members. The collaborative approach she encouraged involved not only being consulted and involved in decision-making but also taking on tasks and responsibilities, often high-profile ones. She was often frustrated by the same colleagues' failure to take advantage of the spaces she offered for involvement, so that she eventually felt forced to step in. Towards the end of the project, she was considering restructuring this level of management. She had aimed to create an SMT that included the head, but she felt it operated and was seen as the head plus the SMT. Diana's reasons for having a wider management group were to avoid the potential for a small senior management team becoming a power block in the school. Extending it to six or eight people made it too big for the kind of tight power base that she thought that the smaller group of a head and her deputies might represent.

Pauline's view was that people must be on the team in her terms: 'If they don't want to be playing my game, they don't want to be in my team.' In spite of this, she worked for years with some colleagues who did not agree with her terms. Both she and Vanessa had senior colleagues who were unconvinced by their advocacy of teamwork and yet, by virtue of position, were *de facto* members of the SMT. As a result, the heads were forced into more isolated positions than they wanted. Pauline's problem was that

> Since I came to the school my 'feminine' management technique has been tested to the limit and it's dictated in many ways how the management of the school has evolved. I've had to work out how to work round the obstacles their negativity and criticism represents. It's made impossible any kind of real team approach to managing the school.

In her own mind, if not in the minds of others, an antipathy to teamwork was associated with 'masculine' management.

Teamwork for the secondary heads manifested all the strains and gains of teamwork identified in the Wallace and Hall (1994) study. The authors conclude that the culture of teamwork is no stronger than each individual member's commitment. Having accepted team membership, the onus is on every member to take responsibility for making the team work. From the women heads' perspective that responsibility was very much on their own shoulders, since they were the source for the teamwork approach. One strain that Wallace and Hall identified was the risk to the head's credibility if teamwork failed. Given women's sense of having more to prove and further to fall, the strain of losing credibility is all the greater. Vanessa's sense of being let down by senior colleagues was exacerbated by the loss of face she felt it entailed in front of governors. Women's preferences for the kinds of collaborative approaches that teamwork represents are also high-risk strategies. Shakeshaft (1989, p. 207) has pointed out:

> The collaborative approach to decision making that shares power may cause women to be initially evaluated as weak or ineffective. Women who manage from a collaborative framework do so within a system that stresses the values of competitive individualism and personal achievement at the expense of community goals. Thus women often report that they first establish themselves and then introduce participatory styles.

The women secondary heads had to steer a tight course between demonstrating strength and being participatory. They were faced with the problem of appearing to impose collaboration. As a result of some team members' resistance, Vanessa and Pauline were pushed towards restructuring their SMTs in ways that had not been their original intention. Generally, the strains and stresses that characterized some of the dynamics of the teams working together were not evident in the meetings I observed. There, the norms relating to teamwork as joint work prevailed, with the heads structuring setting and interaction in the ways described in Chapter 5. Open displays of conflict or dissent were discouraged by the heads' business-like chairing, in the context of meetings which were characterized by much humour and exchange. Any disappointments felt by the heads with the outcome of team meetings were discussed with individuals outside the meeting. In spite of their commitment to teamwork, none made team meetings sacrosanct, so that there were often people missing or times were changed to accommodate team members' needs. The heads were reluctant to impose a way of working and preferred, through their own behaviour in meetings, to model the kind of approach they advocated. They encouraged contributions, delegated tasks, praised and generally used their position as team leader to control the process, so that the needs of both people and the task were satisfied.

WOMAN PRIMARY HEADS AND SENIOR COLLEAGUES

Partnership rather than teamwork is more appropriate for describing how the primary heads worked with their senior colleagues, although they expressed a preference for team approaches. In each case, they saw their relationship with their deputies as pivotal. Potentially, it constituted the biggest support or biggest constraint on their preferred way of working.

Some problems which arose in the relationship of primary heads with their deputies derived from their deputies' different perceptions of the scope and nature of the management tasks. All six heads had been socialized professionally within their own sector and had been exposed to common expectations about, and arrangements for, sharing management responsibilities. Both primary and secondary schools have been faced with a multiplicity of tasks, implicit in the reforms of the past decade. These have put heavy pressures on the heads in both sectors to delegate, but delegation is easier for secondary heads than primary, because the appropriate roles, structures and expectations are already in place. Middle and senior managers in secondary schools expect to share management tasks through delegation. The more favourable funding of secondary schools means there are more posts of responsibility and more non-contact time. In primary schools, allowance holders (including deputies and, in small schools, heads) have full teaching timetables and no time to manage. As a result, primary heads, including the three on the study, feel they must protect colleagues from additional management tasks. At the same time, as the three primary heads demonstrated, they wanted to work as a team with senior colleagues, in spite of the constraints on doing so. In working out how to share some of the responsibilities for managing the school, they sought first to establish the parameters of their working partnership with their deputies. It was important to them that the respective roles and responsibilities should be clearly defined. This is in contrast to the lack of role definition which earlier literature has described as characterizing the deputy's role (Clerkin, 1985; Nias, 1989). On the basis of that partnership, and the kind and extent of sharing it entailed, they made decisions about how far to involve others in the school's management team.

In each of the three primary schools studied, the dyad (of head and deputy) or 'core' senior management group was distinct from the wider group. Depending on the success of that partnership, membership of the senior group was extended to include others. The most striking feature of Heather's use of teams to share management was the difference between the situation at her first and second schools. In both cases, she had a male deputy, but was only involved in his appointment at the second school. Differences in attitudes to management, management style and the extent to which management tasks should be shared led her, at Edgehill, to establish a wider management team to give her more support in managing a very challenging school. At her second school, where she judged her deputy would share her preferred management style, she did not consider it necessary to create the wider group. The consent and protection, as well as the capacity for creative management, were already present in her relationship with the new deputy to the extent that, at critical moments, she would share her uncertainties with him in a way she would not, and could not, have done with her previous deputy. She saw her new deputy's skills and qualities as complementing her own, including his facility (which she saw as a masculine trait) of being able to compartmentalize and become highly focused when necessary.

Susan was also faced with the challenge of working with and working round her senior colleagues. In common with the other heads, her preference was to use the head–deputy relationship for mutual empowerment. This is only feasible, however, if the other's consent to seeing the relationship in this way has been gained, and there is agreement on the desired outcomes of the collaboration. In her discussion of women teachers as 'pin-money professionals', Al-Khalifa (1988) has argued, from her work with women teachers, that the support given by male heads to their female deputies is likely to be influenced by gender stereotypes of women's role. They may assume that women's work takes lower priority than their families and, as a result, accord their development a lower priority than that of men teachers. In their concern to support the development of their senior colleagues, the women primary heads showed an equal concern with both men and women teachers. Development, as we saw in Chapter 6, was a high priority for them, whatever the person's gender or status in the school. Their attempts to encourage their deputies towards promotion were sometimes thwarted by the deputies' own preferences for remaining in the classroom, and reluctance to share management tasks. The heads' power in defining the kind of headteacher–deputy partnership they preferred was limited by their dependency on the deputies agreeing to share management tasks in the way the heads wanted.

Barbara worked with a woman deputy head who had been acting head, when Barbara was appointed to the headship. Their working partnership was characterized by close collaboration on all tasks but, as a non-teaching head, Barbara felt she should shoulder most of the management responsibilities herself. This desire to be fair conflicted with her desire to share power and created a tension for her. The lifestyle priorities of her deputy meant she had chosen not to seek her own headship. She was always willing to provide a sounding board for Barbara's intentions and warning device for any occasions when Barbara's actions provoked a negative reaction. Most disagreements between them were openly discussed and within the framework of a united front 'because you are the head'. In the dialectic of control between these two women, Barbara was accorded more power because of her position.

While the primary heads experienced some frustration in their attempts to groom their deputies towards headship, Vanessa was concerned that the very fact that she was a woman got in the way of her male deputies' promotion prospects. When I talked with the heads' senior colleagues, most had reservations about their abilities to do the job with the same single-mindedness and total commitment that the heads demonstrated. In this respect their strategy of being positive role models in order to empower backfired, when colleagues were left with an impression of headship requiring superhuman strengths.

ONE WOMAN'S POWER IS ANOTHER MAN'S IMPOTENCE?

As I suggested in Chapter 2, research that openly declares itself to be about gender tends to bring down shutters on the willingness of men and women to acknowledge it as a factor in their interaction, at least where those working in education are concerned. For this reason alone, it was not easy to explore how far the working relations of heads and their senior colleagues were influenced by gender, whomever's perceptions were sought. The heads tended to say 'I wasn't aware of being a woman in that situation but you may have perceived it differently'. The men tended to deny that their behaviour was any different as a result of the head being a woman, whereas the women who were interviewed commented quite freely on the head as a woman. As noted earlier, this reluctance might be seen to reflect the culture of education, where teachers feel inhibited in expressing views on gender, in case they appear sexist. Judging by research into women managers in other occuptions (e.g. Cockburn, 1991), inhibitions about discussing gender relations are fewer. Also, where SMTs are concerned, Wallace and Hall (1994, p. 38) note that the team members' shared values about collaboration, equity and collective responsibility dominated their separate, private beliefs about men and women's behaviour at work. They conclude:

> We would be naive to accept the almost total denial by most respondents [women and men] of the influence of gender on team behaviour as evidence that gender differentiation does not exist. On the other hand, the value that teamwork places on equal contribution appears to make it more likely that individuals will try to suppress or refrain from acting on values that subscribe to gender inequalities or differences in the workplace.

Difficulties in working together were attributed by the heads mainly to personality or different perceptions of the boundaries of the head's role. Sometimes, they acknowledged that the fact that they were women did play a part, whether the senior colleague was male or female. Vanessa, for example, expressed 'a sense of unease and consciousness of being a woman telling a man what to do. You automatically feel more confident with a woman'. It is claimed that one man's power is another man's impotence, if the latter must forego his will on behalf of the former. How much more resonant the claim becomes when it is transposed to 'one woman's power is another man's impotence', with all the implications that has for men–women power relations from cradle to grave. As Park (1995, p. 212) shows, in his study of mother–son relationships, the mother defines her son's reality for so long 'that even the style of his rebellions is shaped by her', including the style of his future relationships with women.

The implication is that women with formal power may have to work twice as hard at leaving people, particularly men, feeling potent. As Kanter's (1977) research showed, both men and women are more prepared to 'forego their will' for men than women bosses. Even if it cannot be proven, it is an assumption that women who lead make. It influences the strategies they adopt. In the same way as many men tread carefully in order not to make women colleagues cry (Shakeshaft, 1993), some women are cautious about not threatening male egos.

The need to be attentive to this dimension of relations with senior colleagues was apparent in much that the heads said and did. Criticism might be softened by smiles; unpleasant requests accompanied by flattery. Being sensitive to men's egos suggested that openness (which the heads valued) was harder to sustain with men than women, because of anticipated different agendas and the clash between hierarchy and gender norms. The heads themselves were ambivalent. Pauline said that she preferred working with women but sought the approval of men colleagues. Heather described herself as always having got on better with men, but was aware of becoming increasingly feminist in her perceptions as a result of a growing distrust of many of their actions. All the heads, in some respects, found men easier to deal with because they felt they knew how to deal with them, for example by using flattery. In her discussion of Margaret Thatcher's sources of power, Webster (1990) suggests that some of her control of ministers came from their unfamiliarity with women in power and consequent lack of strategies for dealing with them. She could capitalize on their disorientation by drawing on her greater familiarity with men and power. On the other hand, where the men with whom the heads worked were antagonistic towards the kind of behaviour they valued, the heads found it necessary to work round rather than through them. Although the heads expressed these sentiments and concerns to me as researcher, their preferences were not manifest in their interactive style, which was the same whether with men or women senior colleagues. With colleagues, being professional (which included not disclosing personal preferences) took precedence over being open.

In her study of gender-responsible leadership, Van Nostrand (1993) discusses the ways in which women are taught from childhood to accommodate men. At the same time, men are taught they will be accommodated to. Men expect to be understood and women work to understand. Detachment and defensiveness become masculine tools for control, when confronted with women's assertiveness and resistance to being purely accommodating (ibid., p. 33). An incident between one head and her deputy illustrates how some of these tensions were manifest in the heads' interactions with men colleagues. Coming out of a governors' meeting, which had lasted for three hours, she was met by her male deputy who described his frenetic afternoon, in which two fights had broken out and two sets of angry parents had consequently come to the school. She listened carefully to what he had to say, making sympathetic noises and confirming the rightness of the actions he had taken. When he had gone, she offered an alternative interpretation of what the exchange had been about. In her view, it had been full of undercurrents to do with her relationship with him as deputy. What he was saying, in telling her about the naughty boys, was 'while you were sitting in that governing body doing all sorts of things that aren't important, I'm out here dealing with the really important issues of the school which are those to do with children'. Her sense that he did not see her way of doing her job as appropriate to running a school meant that she felt she must continuously justify her actions to him. The game she then played, when he was telling her the things she ought to know if she weren't busy doing things that were unimportant, was to tell him that he should know that she did know what was going on. After three years she still did not feel that she had got to grips with the undercurrents of their relationship. At different times, each of the other heads expressed an awareness of similar nuances influencing some aspects of their relationship with male colleagues, though not necessarily their deputies. In Diana's view, the undercurrents were to do with the chemistry between personalities more than gender, and her strategies for dealing with men and women varied according to the individual. Her working principle was that the personal was an integral part of working with someone as a professional. She acknowledged that, unconsciously, her behaviour might be influenced by whether they were a man or woman.

If women are taught from childhood to accommodate to men (and the heads' biographies testified to the importance of the father's approval), it follows that, when women become leaders, they have either to unlearn those accommodating characteristics (where they are conscious of them) or they may use them as powerful weapons in bringing about desired behaviour. On a number of occasions, the women heads referred to their use of 'feminine wiles'. The reference was usually accompanied by an apology, declaring these behaviours as inappropriate for the principled leadership they tried to represent, but acknowledging them as necessary part of their management repertoire. In Heather's view, it was unwise to be confrontational with men 'because if you are going to have a fight they are going to win. So I use other methods for getting what I want, such as flattery'. Flattery emerged from their descriptions of its use as a covert but legitimate form of manipulation, to be distinguished from giving praise which was overt. There is a close relationship between flattering and flirting, which makes it more likely to be used by the women heads with men than with other women.

The undercurrents were there with women too, but took a different form. They arose, for example, in what the heads perceived as some resentment of their personal success or disapproval of their management style. Problems in one head's partnership with a woman senior colleague arose from mutual disappointment, as a result of frustrated expectations on both sides that were not addressed openly, in spite of the head's usual commitment to being open and honest. The situation was complicated by another's intervention that made it difficult for the head to pursue her preferred strategy. Her woman colleague's disappointment was all the greater because she felt she had been let down by another woman. Judgements about when it was appropriate to be open or not were not peculiar to women working together. They were necessary at one time or another with both men and women, particularly with those who were closest to them in the management hierarchy. The constraint on openness was less to do with gender, more to do with hierarchy.

As we saw in Chapter 5, the heads were continuously concerned to present an image of strength and control and reluctant to share their weaknesses with others. Most sharing occurred between the heads and the deputies they had appointed, whether men or women. It suggests that the influence of gender in the head–senior colleague partnership related to a head's expectations of that partnership in the context of her view of herself as a woman head. On the one hand, as heads who were women, they wanted to be open and sharing. On the other hand, as women who were heads, they wanted to conceal their vulnerability and retain their credibility. Their desire not to be hierarchical was sometimes thwarted by the failure of senior colleagues 'to be on the same wavelength'. It was not simply a case of colleagues disagreeing about what needed to be done, but often not seeing what was appropriate. Barbara, for example, had strong views about the need for a handwriting policy in the school, but had equally strong views about not imposing or using what she considered undue influence: 'I had to restrain myself from flexing my headteacher muscles.' In these situations the heads were torn between needing things done and not wanting to ask or tell. The ability to say something openly depended on the strength of the relationship and, in three cases involving male deputies, their feeling was that they had not yet 'got the relationship quite right'.

CONCLUSIONS

The heads' working relationships with their senior colleagues mainly reflected the priority they gave to collaborative leadership styles, characterized by openness and shared decision-making. Although at times they sought consent and protection within the relationship, it was a subordinate motive compared to their relationship with governors where it was dominant. Attempts to dominate were rarely evident, and then only when all other strategies had failed. Marshall (1984) has suggested that, in other employment sectors, a preference for collaborative or communion-based styles might be an obstacle to reaching the top. In the different workplace cultures of schools, where people rather than products are the goals, this is less likely to be the case. Once at the top in schools, women are in a position to enact and model their chosen style, within the constraints of a small minority of colleagues who were either not equipped or unwilling to act in the expected ways. Observations of their interactions with senior colleagues and governors supported the claims they made about their preferred uses of power to promote teamwork rather than to dominate.

SUMMARY AND CONCLUSIONS: WOMEN LEADING THE DANCE

INTRODUCTION

A theme throughout the book has been the ways in which the women heads enacted practical educational leadership. I have argued that their approach to school leadership shared many common features, even though they were also six individuals in six different school contexts. This final chapter begins with an overview of the findings, which are then discussed in the context of other studies of women in management, as well as those of men and women in education management. It proposes some explanations for the form their leadership takes, including the influence of their gender identity and experience of being a woman leading an organization. It also considers the extent to which working in primary or secondary schools created different constraints on their practice. The chapter goes on to examine how far the concepts of 'praxis', 'emancipatory praxis' and 'critical leadership' apply to their interpretation of the role. Finally, the implications of the study and its findings for women and men in education management are reviewed, in the light of conclusions about managing schools that have emerged from the research.

Differences between women and men are the focus of neither the book nor the study on which it is based. The emphasis has been on the women heads' similarities and differences from each other in their interpretation and enactment of school leadership. In this way I have aimed to correct the androcentrism of most descriptions of educational managers and present what Shakeshaft (1989) calls 'the female world of school administration'. Ignoring the 'differences' question does not, however, make it go away. In this final chapter, I intend to raise my guard against its pervasiveness and look at some aspects of the findings in the light of what other studies have shown about men as school leaders. This contributes to a reconceptualization of education management that recognizes a broader repertoire of skills and qualities as fundamental to effective school leadership. The components of the repertoire are not new to the literature, but they are usually presented in a way which is divorced from the personal and professional development experiences of school leaders as performers. The book has shown how the art of headship as performed by six women heads has its roots in childhood and educational and career experiences that cannot be divorced from their gender identity as women. I have argued that, in order to understand them as heads, it is necessary to understand them as women. In this final chapter I argue that, in order to understand men as heads, it is necessary to understand them as men. In order to understand leaders and managers in education, we must also understand them as people. This is the point we will finally reach, and it should be the jumping-off ground for future research.

OVERVIEW OF THE FINDINGS

What, then, is the picture of practical educational leadership that emerges from studying six women heads? What does it add to our understanding of women and men as educational managers? In Chapter 1, I suggested that the women heads' behaviour and values about school leadership showed them to prefer a 'practical action' model in which power for is preferred to power over and development goals are favoured over accountability. The claim was also asserted that managers' behaviour cannot and should not be understood separately from the experiences that influence the foundation of values and beliefs on which it is based.

In reviewing the women heads' career paths, Chapter 3 concluded that they were characterized as individuals by the development of an inner locus of control. This evolved from their responses to experiences in their family of origin, through school, college and their teaching careers. The inter-relationships of these different factors in the formation of personal identity is not, of course, new, but it is still relatively rare to see discussed the implications of these factors for the formation of 'manager' or 'leader' identities. Similarly, any discussions of the gendered character of organizations have to be based on a more detailed understanding of how men and women as individual employees have arrived at their conceptions of appropriate work-based behaviour. While experiences of family life are unique, a review of their childhood experiences showed that, as a result of the different influences of each parent, women are exposed to a diverse set of role options and behaviours. Although tasks and roles within families were mainly differentiated along gender lines, the father's strong influence in each case encouraged them towards achievement and self-sufficiency. Within the family, they learned from both their mother and father about using power and influence, i.e. drawing on different resources to achieve desired ends. All enjoyed their school careers and, by the time they were eighteen, had differentiated themselves in the family by being the first (or first woman) in their generation to go on to higher education and a profession.

The primary heads differed from their secondary colleagues in choosing teaching because of the opportunities it provided to work with children.

Interest in their subject was initially the main motivator for the secondary heads. A driving force in the heads' choice of career, as opposed to whether to have a career or not, was their commitment to the central purpose of their work: young people's education as a valuable enterprise. In common with the career progression of other women teachers, they made lifestyle choices that enabled them to combine work and family commitments, whether or not they had children. At different times, one or other was a priority and influenced how they did the job. Support from others for childcare responsibilities was variable and influenced their attitudes later as heads to supporting colleagues with similar demands. All worked exceptionally hard to compensate for any time they needed to take away from work, as a result of having children. The high standards of work which they developed in childhood and at school carried through into their performance at work and the cultivation of 'a perfect front'. They felt that their success as women depended on their own efforts and not displaying weaknesses. They took both men and women as positive and negative role models but were never aware of feeling the need to be 'like a man' to achieve career success. They were mainly self-directed in choosing and negotiating their career paths, determined to succeed on their own merits rather than as a result of others' help.

Although they were aware of their impact as women on others, as they sought promotion (and used this to their advantage if necessary), they considered barriers to be surmountable by their own efforts. They were reliant on 'a strong inner locus of control' that supported them in taking responsibility for their own progress. Proud in having achieved headships, they judged their professional success in terms of success as a teacher, then manager, then leader. They attributed their success at job interviews for headship to their decisions not to apply until they felt ready, willing and able to do the job. Career moves were based as much on this 'inner path to headship' as on external factors constraining or promoting career choices.

Using a range of models developed to explain women's careers highlighted the androcentrism of other models and their limitations in understanding men and women's careers. The questions that were asked of women (about family influences, educational experiences, lifestyle choices, values underpinning career moves, etc.) need to be asked also of men, as well as other women, for a full understanding of educational leadership.

Once in post, a distinction was made between the early years when they were testing the water and deciding appropriate strategies in the context of their school and later, when they had got to grips with the school's demands, and were confident about their choices of preferred strategies for taking the school forward. Chapter 4 traced one primary head's transition from one school to another and the issues involved when a woman takes over a school from a man. It confirmed that all heads, irrespective of gender, have to deal initially with the legacy of their predecessor and the extent to which it lives on in the expectations of some staff and others associated with the school. The heads saw the changes they were appointed to implement, as a result of the Education Reform Act 1988, as supporting rather than constraining their own evolving vision for the school. The individual case study showed that the repertoire of skills and qualities that Heather brought to managing one school successfully was sufficiently flexible and comprehensive to meet the very different demands of the next. Her effectiveness depended on her sense of self-efficacy combined with support from others which allowed her 'to be herself'. This possibility, important to all the heads, varied according to the situation of the school when they took over and the extent to which their senior colleagues approved of their style. The difference between taking over a headship and other stages of their careers was in the acquisition of formal power and authority to influence events, in addition to their preferred way of working with people to achieve results. Like adding new clothes to a wardrobe, they experimented initially with these new 'powers' to see how they fitted with those they already had, in the form of 'personal power' and other resources of expertise, skills and experience. They had a clear idea of what they wanted the school to be like, but trod carefully in working with what was already there in the school's culture. All the schools were judged to have developed successfully in their time as heads. Their styles and management skills were seen as necessary contributions to that success and far outweighing any initial reservations about their gender.

They aimed to create and support organizational cultures characterized by trust, openness, involvement and a sense of self-worth. Chapter 5 looked at how they tried to model, through their own behaviours, how they wanted others to work and relate with each other in the school. At the heart of managing others was their continued vigilance in managing themselves as leaders and as women. I hypothesized that any interaction is influenced by contradictory norms about being a head and being a woman. Observing the heads at work revealed numerous, usually subtle, adjustments of their behaviour. These were directed either towards strengthening their influence as leaders (by playing down being a woman) or towards removing any discomfort people might feel, because they were women.

Their self-management strategies (of self-presentation, self-organization and self-development) were honed to enable them to demonstrate self-control as a legitimation of their claim to be in charge of the school. They valued being 'authentic' and being 'consistent' at work, to give credibility to the role models they provided for others. Through self-reflection and engagement in self-development, they held up mirrors to their own performance, though regretted others' diffidence in giving them honest feedback. Their symbolic leadership behaviour depended for its effectiveness on their sensitive readings of others and of the situation.

I associated this sensitivity with their earlier socialization as girls and women. They paid close attention to how they dressed, moved and used body languge to ensure that the messages they communicated as leaders were not undermined by responses to them as women. They used strategies for keeping in touch that involved balancing distance and closeness, formality and intimacy. Differences in the school cultures made this easier for the primary than secondary heads. It appeared that they were more likely to use talk in a consistent fashion, across different environments, though primary heads talked differently with children.

Given that schools generally have a preponderance of women staff, the notion of contradictory norms, including gender, raises questions about what is happening when men are managing women, or men are managing men. Men's behaviour as leaders is as much symbolic of their masculinity as I have shown the women's to be of their femininity, yet its impact is rarely explored in those terms. If men as managers are as concerned to know and manage 'self' as the women were shown to be, more research is needed into the relationship between their self-concept and their educational leadership practice.

As human resource managers, the women heads' approaches to selecting, motivating, developing and reviewing performance were aimed at bringing out the best in people, without discriminating in favour of women or men. 'Bringing out the best' meant working with a developmental model of adults as 'resourceful humans', whose commitment, proactivity and trust were best harnessed through the provision of continual opportunities for development. Primary heads led more from the front, where selection was concerned, though they shared with the secondary heads a common purpose of using selection to strengthen teamwork in the school, as well as bring in expertise. In this way, they all used their power and influence to shape the school's culture by choosing like-minded, yet creative people.

Their strategies for motivating others were based on an understanding of their own motivation towards better performance, including using praise, giving autonomy, high expectations and providing material and other kinds of support. They were aware of the danger that their high standards for their own performance might deter rather than encourage some others. It was easier for the primary than for the secondary heads to reassure colleagues that they were human too, particularly where family responsibilities were concerned.

Having become what Levine (1989) calls 'autonomous adults' in their own development, the heads were able to understand and respond in the main appropriately to others' development needs, although they did not recognize women as having different needs from men. Their vision for staff development included using performance review systems for developmental rather than accountability purposes. While their HRM practices resembled those of corporate management represented in the Peters and Waterman tradition (1982), I have argued that their personal values regarding authenticity, consistency and the centrality of educational goals rescue them from being tarred by a 'managerialist' brush.

Throughout the study, power was defined as the use of resources to secure desired outcomes. Chapters 7 and 8 focused specifically on how women heads interpreted power and politics and used both formal and informal power in their work with governors and senior colleagues. Unlike most women in organizations, the heads had formal power which they used in the same context of contradictory norms about women and power that characterized the interactions described in Chapters 5 and 6. They demonstrated a need to establish the legitimacy of their authority as leaders without damaging their acceptability as women. This is a gender dimension of leadership which is not addressed regarding men's use of power or discussions of power based mainly on men, yet it has considerable implications for the relationship between leaders and followers.

The same congruence between values and behaviour that characterized their HRM activities was also evident in the relationship between the rhetoric and the reality of their use of power. They were ever vigilant against what they felt were the potential abuses of power (particularly the primary heads), which they associated more with negative than positive outcomes. Their suspicion of the power that came with the position of headteacher, and the conflict it created with other deeply held values about preferred ways of working, led them to reformulate it in ways they found more acceptable. These included preferring 'power for' rather than 'power over', using power to empower, sharing power. Their reluctance to take power for granted made them sensitive to its components and its consequences. Their leadership styles reflected choices about how they wanted to be and felt they should be, within the constraints of what they recognized as sometimes conflicting instinctual behaviours.

Their approach to managing and leading a school led me to question the 'management is masculine' argument, since they demonstrated a comfort with the role which they saw as sufficiently flexible not to require compromising their beliefs as education professionals and women. Their style reflected the characteristics of androgynous management, which I have reinterpreted as being about possessing a broad integrated repertoire of management skills rather than 'masculine' and 'feminine' characteristics. As Bem (1975, p. 6) says:

> The concept of androgyny contains an inner contradiction and, hence, the seeds of its own destruction . . . Androgyny necessarily presupposes that the concepts of masculinity and femininity themselves have distinct and substantive content. But to the extent that the androgynous message is absorbed by the culture, the concepts of masculinity and femininity will cease to have such content and the distinctions to which they refer will blur into invisibility. Thus, when androgyny becomes a reality, the concept of androgyny will have been transcended.

The primary heads were less concerned about competition with other schools but anticipated being uncomfortable with it, should it arise. The secondary heads accepted the need to be competitive externally, while encouraging collaboration within the school. All the heads were familiar through reading and training with management practices outside schools and willing to listen to their messages, as long as they were interpreted in the context of educational values.

The 'political' component to management styles identified by writers like Ball and Hoyle was less evident than these two writers suggest. This was not least because of the women heads' antipathy to what they described as 'political' (as opposed to powerful) behaviour. Generally, they let what they saw as negative political behaviour remain dormant in their repertoires, drawing on it if necessary but preferring to be what I have called 'wise' politicians, concerned to act with integrity and eschewing negative micro-political activity in favour of consistency, fairness and caring. Learning to be 'wise' was crucial in dealing with the contradictory norms imposed by some teacher union officials on their interactions with them as heads (less important to the officials) who were women (more important to them since they assumed that manipulation would be easier). The women heads' preferred interactive style gave them political strength by enabling them to 'read' the organization mainly accurately, without being adversarial or authoritarian or playing 'political' games. They sought win-win rather than win-lose outcomes, through co-operation and collaboration rather than conflict and competition.

Their work with governing bodies and senior colleagues (described in Chapter 8) showed how they enacted their interpretation of power and the constraints on its preferred uses. In common with other heads, they sought the governors' consent and protection within a partnership which required them at times to lead more than they wanted. The primary heads, in particular, found it difficult to share decision-making as much as they felt they ought to. While acknowledging the greater power this gave them, they would have been more comfortable with more power sharing. The secondary heads found it easier to work within the boundaries of their own interpretation of legitmate governor manipulation. Their governors had more confidence about challenging and taking responsibility, albeit within a framework constructed by the head.

In common with other studies of women managers, the women heads' preference for working collaboratively was manifest in their support for teamwork, particularly when working with senior colleagues. It was expressed differently in each sector: in primary schools through the partnership with the deputy head, and in secondary schools through the SMT. The contradictory norms that operated in the context of teamwork related to equity and hierarchy (as in the Wallace and Hall, 1994, study) and less frequently to gender, particularly for the primary heads. The main source of difficulty in relationships with senior colleagues was in their variable commitment to teamwork. Where commitment was not shared, a major constraint lay in the degree of openness that existed between the head and colleague(s) concerned. Being open was harder, where the colleague was a man, as a result of the different strains that can characterize men–women working relationships, arising from different experiences and expectations. These were more likely to be attributed by those concerned to a different 'chemistry' rather than gender.

FINDING NEW METAPHORS FOR LEADERSHIP

A picture emerges of women heads enacting strong leadership within a collaborative framework. In spite of this, the women heads (in common with men and women heads in the studies by Southworth and Grace) were firmly committed to the belief that sharing leadership still required them to take the lead when appropriate, including having a personal vision for the school. They saw themselves (and were seen) as key players, co-ordinating, developing and using others' efforts to the benefit of the school's purpose. I suggested in Chapter 1 that they were, with others, the choreographers of the school's performance. Their actions for achieving these purposes were collaborative rather than directive, but within a conception of the headship role that included clarifying the direction and ensuring people were reminded of where they were going.

In the introduction I pointed out that Jenkins's (1991) prescriptions for 'getting school leadership right' associated only one prescription with 'female' characteristics: caring for and valuing staff. When the women heads' behaviour is viewed in the light of his summary of the competencies of school leadership (shown in Table 9.1), then it is clear that their performance closely matches all the prescriptions.

Different chapters have shown examples of the typical behaviours (proposed in the right-hand column) which Jenkins describes as manifestations of 'the transforming post-heroic leader'. Since Jenkins's prescriptions and the models on which they are based were drawn from predominantly androcentric versions of management (in so far as they did not address gender as a significant factor in their accounts), then the women heads' apparent conformity to all the prescriptions would suggest that they are at least as likely as men to be successful as school leaders. The point of the women heads' study was also to examine whether, as leaders of the dance, they changed or modified the dance steps. Their accounts and my observations strongly refuted the notion that making the dance floor their own meant dancing like a man.

Their version of school leadership shows their intention to represent the kind of post-heroic leaders who, rather than riding like knights on white chargers to the rescue, seek 'the far greater power and potential for excellence available in the commitment and abilities of their whole group' (Bradford and Cohen, 1984, p. 61). Asked to sum up in a word their own leadership style, they talked of being 'exemplars', 'motivators', 'interpreters', 'opportunists', 'reflectors', 'facilitators'.

Table 9.1 Competencies for school leadership

Prescription/competence area	Typical behaviour
See the future	• Develop and articulate a vision • Live the vision • Plan within the vision
Empower the staff	• Design new structures • Relinquish power • Create self-managing teams
Create fair and caring systems	• Care for and value staff • Create a climate of integrity • Select and promote staff on a fair basis
Offer strong instructional leadership	• Enact a coherent educational philosophy • Be a leading professional • Take an interventionist role
Demand high quality	• Put total quality management into operation • Introduce quality measurement • Treat staff as the key to quality
Delight the customer	• Put customer care into operation • Create constructive partnership with customers • Try collaboration rather than competition
Take risks	• Create an entrepreneurial climate • Break down barriers to change • Support champions of change

Source: Jenkins, 1991, p. 164.

Further research into women as leaders might build on this study and explore the images, metaphors and stereotypes of leadership that shape our notions of who leaders (including educational leaders) are, and what they do. As Weber and Mitchell (1995) show, in exploring the impact of images of teachers in popular culture, metaphors are powerful in conceptualizing teaching. They are ideological in carrying meaning derived from the historical and cultural contexts in which they are rooted. This is precisely the problem with the post-heroic leader title in that it is still resonant of its feudal origins. The role has changed from rescuing to helping but the knight remains a knight. We need a new mythology and set of metaphors to represent the new model. I suggested how the heads themselves worked with their own images of 'looking like a head' and 'being like a head'. How they saw themselves as heads was an important part of constructing their headship identity. I showed (in Chapter 4) how they attempted to dismantle and re-create images of headship, while making sense of their new roles and forging their personal and professional identities in a new context.

The six women heads in this study were successful as heads. Their success lay in harnessing the capacity of their colleagues to work towards educational goals within the framework of the new entrepreneurialism that characterizes schools today. This success, however, begs the question posed by Grace (1995, p. 192) about the extent to which they represent conceptions of educational leadership that 'are not simply technical formulations for making schools effective as organizations, they are also fundamental expressions of cultural and political values' (ibid., p. 26). Grace talks about the changing discourse of English schooling 'as leadership is first constituted in the nineteenth century in moral terms and is reconstructed over time in market relation terms'. We saw in Chapter 1 how the centenary account of headmistresses emphasized their responsiveness to different demands throughout the century. As the discussion of the women heads as entrepreneurs in subsequent chapters shows, there was little evidence of the reversion to strong leadership characterized by rapid executive action, low tolerance of opposition and little commitment to consultative procedures that Grace (ibid., p. 45) pessimistically envisages.

ALTERNATIVE ENTREPRENEURS?

Emerging from this account of women heads is a version of the new educational entrepreneur which is not managerialist. From some perspectives such a position is untenable, since the values on which entrepreneurialism is based have their roots in the same soil as managerialism. Yet, from the heads' own perspective, it is possible to be entrepreneurial in striving for their schools' success (or even survival), and simultaneously resist the effects of government reforms on the transformation of staff and students from resourceful humans to human resources. They demonstrated a model of educational entrepreneurialism that eschews manageralism, in order to preserve the integrity of the educational enterprise and its ultimate goal: young people's learning and development. How does this relate to critical leadership which we saw in Chapter 1 to be associated with emancipatory praxis?

   Although this account did not set out to be a feminist construction of the concept of an educational leader, the picture that emerges reflects some of the characteristics which Blackmore (1989), for example, associates with feminist discourse and practice. From the perspective of critical leadership theory, feminist praxis challenges the assumptions of a market-led education system and the patriarchal, 'masculine' attitudes to power that underpin it. As Chapter 7 showed, the women heads sought to act with others rather than exert power over them. They encouraged a culture based on caring and reciprocal relations and resisted the push towards corporate managerialism that government reforms have instigated. While they may not have gone as far beyond patriarchy as some feminists would advocate, the integrity of their leadership styles would appear to have given them the strength to transform (through working with rather than against) New Right educational reforms. Grace (1995, p. 23) distinguishes between those who are attracted by the new playing field (the equivalent of my dance floor) with the opportunities and excitement of new roles to be practised, and those for whom the professional aspects of headship are specially important, and who must either adjust or flee. Whereas few of the women in his sample were 'headteacher-managers', all of mine were. They demonstrated the possibility of playing the game but according to their rules which are not always the same as the other players'. To return to the metaphor at the beginning of the book, we are observing a dance floor on which women are suggesting new steps to men and women partners, whom they are leading, not following. That is why the gender features of headteacher behaviour were always most apparent at mixed headteacher groups, particularly at secondary-school level. In those situations all the players were involved in the same game, but playing to different rules. There were a few cross-gender alliances but lines were usually (invisibly) drawn according to gender.

CHANGING THE STEPS?

The different chapters have shown the ways in which the women heads built up a repertoire of behaviours which would allow them, suitably dressed and partnered, to lead the school dance. The components of the repertoire were selected from what was available to them as girls and women, and what would equip them to become managers and leaders in place of men. In Chapter 1, I questioned whether the experiences of being what Marshall (1984) calls 'travellers in a male world' would necessarily lead to a repertoire which included 'emancipatory praxis'. I implied, and subsequent chapters have shown, that their commitment to 'practical educational leadership' was not situated in a socially critical framework that challenges the meanings and practices that shape our consciousness.

Matthews (1984, p. 13) talks of a 'gender order' in which the differences between men and women form the ideological and material grids from which social meaning is created. She suggests that the existence of such an order is not necessarily acknowledged by the players themselves but their actions contribute to its maintenance. The heads' denial of awareness of being a woman in many of the situations I observed meant that they were also less likely to challenge the gender order of the school. In their view, they had contributed to challenging stereotypes by allowing women to be seen in a position of authority (e.g. themselves) and men in positions of support (e.g. their male deputies).

They demonstrated the same fear of feminism that Grace (1995) identified in his sample: as an explicit social label that would identify the heads with unwelcome stereotypes. 'I am a personist not a feminist', said one. But denying a personal association with feminist beliefs does not necessarily mean denying a commitment to equal opportunities generally or towards supporting women at work in particular. The denial is understandably an anathema to radical and socialist feminists, though more acceptable to those working within the liberal feminist tradition, even though it is, by their already more tolerant standards, still shaky as a commitment. The descriptions of women heads' behaviour showed how, whatever their private thoughts about gender differences and constraints on their performance as a result of being women, they were committed to a professionalism which took care not to discriminate against or in favour of either men or women. Their support for all staff, not just women, was based on recognizing and tapping into the potential within the school and encouraging anyone who was capable but possibly lacking in confidence.

By so doing they appear to fail the feminist critique's test of emancipatory praxis by not acting as advocates for women's rights or taking necessary steps to advance women's particular interests. But, as Cockburn (1991) points out in her study of sex equality in organizations, a person can be pro-women without declaring himself or herself as feminist. Similarly, the women heads (particularly the primary heads) supported women colleagues in a variety of ways, which were sometimes different but not more than the support they gave to men. Van Nostrand (1993) talks of gender-responsible leadership as leadership that promotes equality and avoids collusion. The heads' ambivalence about public commitment to the need for greater gender equality did not come as a surprise, given what Cockburn, for example, has shown to be men's resistance to sex equality in organizations. Cunnison's (1994) survey of men's reactions to one LEA's attempts to apply positive discrimination when appointing to headships showed their resentment and assumption that those appointed were not necessarily the best candidates. This reflects exactly what the women heads feared, leading to their concern to demonstrate a conception of justice that did not include giving advantage to one group rather than another. Having surmounted barriers to their own career progression without positive discrimination, they felt others should be able to do the same. The heads were therefore supportive of each individual's development regardless of gender. In order to lead both men and women they had to establish their credibility with both. They tended to assume they had it more easily with most women, as a result of gender, although even this they did not take for granted. There was irony, however, in the women heads' demonstrations of a leadership style that sought to empower but did not specially seek to empower those (i.e. other women) who are more likely to be organizationally powerless.

One explanation for their reluctance to be identified too closely with women's interests lies in their own career experiences. Like the women managers in Marshall's (1984) study, they were against identifying themselves as disadvantaged because they were women. Their self-efficacy came from believing they had succeeded as a result of their own efforts and achievements, not by being given help or special consideration. If they discriminated in favour of other women, people would think they had gained their positions through the same means and not as a result of their own talents. Cockburn (1991) came to the same conclusion in her study of four large organizations, where she found continuing resistance to sex equality, in spite of equal opportunities initiatives. She concludes (*ibid.*, p. 216): 'Positive discrimination in favour of individual women is unpopular with women, who feel obscurely that it adds one more unfairness to an unfair organization. Yet they welcome the idea of transformative change that could improve things, they believe, for women and men.' From the heads' perspectives, to favour other women would also deny the right of those women to develop self-efficacy and possibly be damaging to the school by putting people in post who were not ready or able. Further, to appear to favour women would create antagonism and a sense of injustice among men colleagues. The alternative argument for women in power becoming advocates for other disadvantaged individuals and groups took second place to the need to preserve their own self-image, keep men on their side (even at the risk of alienating some women) and to keep the school running smoothly. As a result the school's systems and structures reflected a commitment to positive action but not positive discrimination. Their challenge to the perpetuation of male privilege came, in their view, from the very fact of their presence and performance as leaders. Their personal and professional experiences as women led them to hold values about management and leadership that they hoped would influence others and thereby demonstrate the value of women's contributions. We have seen, in their actions to change the schools which they led, an emphasis on cultures in which hierarchy, competition and conflict are minimized and equal contribution, collaboration and harmony are encouraged. On the basis of her research, Cockburn (*ibid.*) describes a new 'voice' in organizations, among women and of women, speaking for a different way of doing things. She concludes: 'It may not be well articulated and it may sometimes be utopian but it embodies a vision of something new' (*ibid.*, p. 71). Critics might argue that any real impact the women heads made on their schools, from the point of view of emancipatory praxis, would be evident in a culture informed by what Coleman (1991) calls 'wider forms of knowing and doing'. She argues (*ibid.*, p. 68) for organizations to become processes of inclusion, not exclusion, characterized by organizational risk-taking:

> Such risk-taking will show itself in initially small ways: a preparedness to make appointments and promotions on the basis of non-conventional skills and experiences, and willingness to engage in discussion on the use of power and definitions of normalcy within the organization, a preparedness to confront both organizational practices which prevent movement and to confront people who rest in their comfort.

The women heads demonstrated some of the behaviours Coleman associates with other forms of organizational thinking, knowing and doing: they listened, they involved, they provided time, they encouraged process as well as task skills, they provided personal support. These were the choices they made. In spite of their professional confidence they had not, however, attained (or even sought) a level of consciousness that would enable them to trust and express what they 'knew' as women. They sought to create the caring, nurturing, responsive culture advocated in the management thinking of the 1980s (e.g. Peters and Waterman, 1982) but within a framework of high individual commitment to organizational goals and purposes.

A study like this, which focuses so closely on the work of six women heads, becomes like an oasis in the desert. The palm tree becomes the prototype of trees that will flourish in that environment. Similarly, these women appear as prototypes of success in the current educational climate. As such, they emerge as and are expected to be role models for other women aspiring to leadership in schools and potentially for other men. The point was made in Chapter 3 that some women's repertoires of leadership skills are enhanced by their access to qualities demonstrated by both parents and influential in their development. Even though, as they move further through their teaching careers, their opportunities to observe women in senior positions diminish, the broader repertoire has already been set. In contrast, men as boys are more likely to pattern their behaviours on fathers and other male figures who, as they progress in their careers, increasingly dominate the higher echelons of the profession. As a result, an already narrower repertoire becomes increasingly specialized and difficult to open up. Discussions of men, masculinity and management (e.g. Gray, 1989) point to the challenge to management development to enable men to open up and develop a wider range and a new language of feelings.

The question about how far men should be more like women is particularly pertinent to education. Mac An Ghaill (1994) has cogently demonstrated that the process of 'the making of men' starts early, as schools actively produce, through the official and hidden curriculum, a range of masculinities which young men come to inhabit. The same is true for girls and the making of women, as illustrated in studies like Weber and Mitchell's (1995) *That's Funny, You Don't Look Like A Teacher?* As they point out, although teachers figure in the play and popular culture of both boys and girls, they occupy a particularized, gendered space in the play and popular culture of girls. They comment on the effect on boys of men's absence from the classroom (particularly at primary-school level) and dominance of the principal's office; but do not comment on the effects on boys and girls of women's absence from the principal's office and dominance of the classroom, as inter-related factors.

Virginia Woolf speaks of the need to be neither pure man nor pure woman, but 'a woman manly', or 'a man womanly.' Being 'woman manly', as the heads showed themselves to be, was the outcome of both innate and learned characteristics. My own position, confirmed by the study, is that the innate characteristics which may be relevant to being an effective manager and leader are not linked to gender. Blumberg and Greenfield (1980), for example, describe the 'ontological security' that characterized the eight 'effective principals' in their study. It is a characteristic which is as likely to be present in men as women. Rejecting the notion that women are innately predisposed to superior performance in some areas also means rejecting what Byrne-Whyte (1987) calls the 'moral superiority' argument. She associates it with the neo-feminists who claim a fundamental, innate personality dichotomy between men and women, demonstrated in women being more skilled socially, more peaceable and civilized and in their rejection of hierarchies. Within this paradigm, similarities between men and women are underestimated and the possibilities of collaboration between the sexes to transform social institutions ruled out.

I have, however, argued from the evidence that there are factors in girls' upbringing that may encourage some girls to develop a broader repertoire of responses, if and when they become managers, than is available to most boys. This has repercussions for future work styles, particularly when they are in positions of power and influence in relation to other adults. Are these qualities more appropriate to education than other management spheres? They were, after all, first honed through the medium of being a teacher. The generation represented by the heads in the study also appears to have had the luxury of time to evolve towards headship, enjoying on the way the full developmental potential of self-actualizing work. As I showed in Chapter 3, men are pushed by expectations of job first, family second, rapid promotion and continuous working (assuming employment is available). In highlighting the choices the women heads made I have not intended to underplay the continued existence of barriers to women's career advancement, in spite of legislation. In common with other women, the heads faced problems of sexist attitudes and behaviour, lack of support for conflicting demands, lack of career advice. Though some of these can also be problems for men, it would be misleading to suggest they have anything like the same impact as they do on women's lives and women's consciousness.

Reviewing his earlier work on team roles at work, Belbin (1993, p. 82) questions the value of role models and the notion that managers can learn from outstanding managers and leaders 'by osmosis'. Rather than seeking to become pale shadows of others, he exhorts managers to find their 'real' selves, based on two strands of information: self-assessment and assessment from others. I prefer not to follow his lead in rejecting the value of role models and thereby running the risk of throwing the baby out with the bath water. We saw, for example, in Chapter 5 how the women heads prioritized self-knowledge as a basis for action and, in this respect, they offered very cogent role models for women and men developing as managers and leaders. A limitation in the model they presented arose from the difficulty of receiving information about self from the assessment of others. As we have seen, this limitation was in part the result of hierarchy and their formal position as heads; in part a result of the defences they erected as women leading the organization. The real value of staff appraisal in schools is in the possibility it provides for generating information derived from perception of self and of others that can be integrated, as Belbin (*ibid.*) suggests, into 'a working profile that can act as a reference base for decision-making.' I wonder whether the greater 'external' orientation of men, referred to earlier, makes it easier for them to obtain (though not necessarily 'hear') others' feedback but less easy to review self? Similarly, women's greater 'internal' orientation may predispose them to listen to their inner voice about themselves, but be less proactive in seeking others' assessments. For both men and women, as Southworth (1995, p. 216) concludes:

> The scale and depth needed for critical leadership to blossom is considerable. The scale is extensive because critical leadership rests not only on developing headteachers, but also on altering assumptions of teachers and deputies. The depth of change in headship is great because deep-seated role conventions must be challenged. The occupational identities of teachers and heads need to be questioned.

In the same way as women have argued for decades for positive female role models for girls, so men are now arguing for a different kind of role model for boys. Harris (1995, p. 193) suggests that men need role models of other men who have courageously challenged the assumptions of patriarchy. The characteristics he associates with this new role model including self-nurturing, conscious choices about how to live their lives, able to parent self and others, admitting mistakes, listening well, expressing feelings. All these resemble closely the characteristics I discerned in the women heads' approach to leadership. Gray (1993, p. 114) concludes from his work with headteachers that 'women's awareness is greater than men's' (regarding gender and sexuality) and men 'fail to understand themselves'. In his view (*ibid.*), 'as heads become more aware of the importance of gender issues in schools, there will be a change in the way men and women think about one another and how teachers think about children'. Although I have described the women heads' rejection of gender as a strong issue in their careers, I have also tried to show their consciousness and understanding of themselves as women, which provides the basis for their performance as heads.

RECONCEPTUALIZING EDUCATIONAL LEADERSHIP

I have referred a number of times to Southworth's research-based interpretation of one male primary head. Its value in arriving at my own conclusions lies in its integration of an empirical base with a theoretical framework for understanding educational leadership. With two different starting-points, but similar research concerns and research design and operating within the same educational culture, both my own and Southworth's study appear to arrive at very similar conclusions about school headship now. This is in spite of his exclusive focus on men and headship and mine on women and headship. This apparent convergence may appear to undermine my claims to gender as a factor in explaining the women heads' behaviour. Yet, Southworth (1995, p. 147) describes the primary head's role as 'largely a male conception', explored mainly by male researchers and writers. He shows Ron to have a 'masculine' view of headship reflected in his vertical and staged career path and exclusively men role models. He attributes Ron's paternalistic view of headship to the fact that he is a product of the social conditioning which sustains male seniority in some schools. He shows him to combine successfully political guile with caring and consultation. He concludes that Ron dominated the school and that his conception of headship was as an identity and not a role; that is, he saw his work as part of his professional self. So far, he appears to have little in common with the women heads I have described.

However, Ron's 'domination' of his school, arising from his centrality, resembles the women primary heads though not the secondary heads. This similarity between men and women primary heads suggests that this form of 'domination' may be a feature of primary headship (not gender), which arises from heads' responses to primary teachers' expectations about how heads should operate. On the other hand, there was strong evidence in the primary schools in my study that, as teachers became empowered through the head's leadership style, expectations rose about involvement in and responsibility for shared decision-making. This response does not appear in Southworth's study. This might be attributed to schools and teachers' expectations having changed since Southworth collected his data (in the 1980s), or it might reflect different responses to different leadership styles. Southworth describes Ron's work as underpinned by a male view of power, to which staff (mainly women) were mainly submissive and about which there was little dissent. The women heads, however, asserted their belief in 'power for' as opposed to 'power over'. This contrasted with Southworth's headteacher whose acceptance of his right to dominate was part of his professional identity (ibid., p. 164).

It is on the issue of identity that the two studies both converge and diverge. Southworth rests his case for Ron's 'male view of power' on his professional identity, which he defines in terms of the characteristics of his 'situational selves' (how he is in interaction with others). These characteristics can be attributed to his occupation and are manifest in his workplace behaviour. Similarly (albeit coincidentally) I chose to focus on professional identity as the key to understanding women and headship. Earlier chapters show how the women's professional identities were socially constructed from interaction with significant others (e.g. family, friends, teachers) both within and outside education. From these experiences they developed their sense of how they wanted to be as heads.

The fact that they shared so much in common with each other, in spite of context differences, suggests patterns in the nature of those interactions which related to gender. In particular, they appeared to be differentiated from male heads in their conception and use of power.

Southworth attributes a considerable part of Ron's professional identity to his continuing commitment to his self-concept as a teacher. Southworth describes the four elements of a teacher's identity (being natural, feeling responsible and concerned for the children, needing to feel in control and wanting to reach children) as characterizing Ron's headship behaviour, so that he was able to be a head and remain a teacher. The same features characterized the women as heads but had their roots in different soil. Unlike the women, Ron was promoted straight from the classroom into headship. There was thus no disjunction between being a teacher and becoming a head. He was, in fact, a head by the time he was twenty-nine, much younger than the women heads. Although such a transition from classroom teacher to head would never happen in secondary schools, both the primary and secondary women heads had had considerable management experience before becoming heads. Therefore, although they resembled Ron in carrying their self-concept as teachers into their new role, they also took with it an evolving understanding of themselves as managers. This meant that, on taking over a school, they were partly prepared for the challenges involved. Chapters 3 and 5 showed how, as women, they had also developed further the self-reliance and self-referencing (described there as an 'inner locus of control') that is crucial for combating some of the consequences of the potential isolation of headship. Their success in attaining headship confirmed their self-belief, which in turn supported their assertiveness, in implementing strategies they considered appropriate for taking the school forward (Chapter 4). Their visions and missions were not messianic, as Southworth attributes to his case-study head. They were concerned to communicate and share them in a way that they became the staff's visions and missions, albeit emanating initially from the head (Chapter 7). Unlike Ron who, Southworth (1995, p. 176) says, had developed the capacity as headteacher to supervise and control his colleagues, they were uncomfortable with the top-down implications of 'supervision' and 'control' and strove to stress the processes as collegial rather than judgemental.

To rest conclusions on the evidence of one case study (Southworth's) may appear shaky, yet a review of the literature describing headship in Britain mainly confirms his conclusions about the nature of domination and power in school leadership. At the same time, Bolam et al.'s (1993) study of effective school management reiterates the importance of characteristics that both Ron and the women in this study possess. Bolam et al. identify these as strong leadership, having clear vision shared with staff, being consultative and accessible, able to motivate and support staff, modelling desired behaviour, planning ahead, supporting staff development and being in touch with students (ibid., p. 123). What Bolam et al.'s study does not address fully, however, is the interpretation and context of power and culture within which these characteristics are demonstrated. Further, the project on which it was based considered it inappropriate to distinguish gender as a factor in the effective management of schools.

LOOKING BACK, LOOKING FORWARD

Much has changed in education since I completed with colleagues a study of secondary headship in the early 1980s (Hall *et al.*, 1986). Much, too, was different in how the women heads in my later study tackled the tasks of running a school. The problems with making comparisons are in knowing whether the differences are attributable to gender (six women rather than four men), the context (pre and post the Education Reform Act 1988) or personalities, since both studies involved only a few heads. Looking at similarities and differences emerging from the two studies tells us about both the conceptual frameworks we used for the research and headship behaviours. In the light of the women heads' study, there were two substantial limitations to the earlier research on 'headteachers at work'.

First, although the male heads were perceived to resemble and differ from each other, no account was taken of the gender bases of their behaviours, i.e. what they had in common as men and how that influenced the way they worked. If, as other research shows, men construct their masculinity and identity as a worker from messages that are different from those heard by women, then it might be anticipated that their construction of headship would also be different. At the same time, conceptions of headship are influenced by messages from the educational culture within which both men and women teachers work. That scenario changes from decade to decade, so that the women heads in this study were working within a very different context from the men heads in the earlier study. We concluded that the four men heads represented four recurring interpretations, i.e. the differences between them were greater than the similarities. The women heads, in contrast, represented one recurring interpretation, in spite of differences in personality and context. In other words, the similarities between them were greater than the differences. I have suggested that what they held in common were the value systems underpinning their management and leadership behaviours, combined with the skills and competences they have developed throughout their careers.

Another limitation of the earlier study was its failure to locate the description of headship it provided within the context of the values of the individual heads concerned. They were left implicit and shadowy. Here I have argued that, in order to understand the heads' behaviour, we must identify the values they hold about people, leadership, education. Further research is needed to establish both the content of men and women heads' values and the extent to which they are reflected in behaviour.

In his discussion of 'the moral art' of educational leadership, Hodgkinson (1991) also uses 'praxis' to describe leadership which combines management science with ethics and value theory: in his view, philosophy-in-action. Like the feminists who are concerned with emancipatory praxis (see Chapter 1), Hodgkinson challenges those education leaders who retreat into managerialism and separate ends from means, apportioning the latter to management. Instead, he argues, leaders have a continous duty to monitor their organizations 'to seek best means for given ends and best conduct for given means' (ibid., p. 115). This, in turn, means monitoring their own interests, motivation and concept of human nature, as well as identifying the collective interest. Within this model, Hodgkinson claims, 'the quality of leadership is functionally related to the moral climate of the organization and this, in turn, to the moral complexity and skills of the leader' (ibid., p. 129).

On the basis of evidence from the study, I would argue that the women heads emerged as 'ethical entrepreneurs' functioning in the same way as some firms are described as 'ethical businesses'. Means were important, as well as ends, and conduct was continuously subject to scrutiny. Even though the scale of the study did not allow for the in-depth exploration of values that a proper test of Hodgkinson's hypothesis would require, it revealed the behaviour of women heads to have some of the characteristics of leadership 'as a moral art'. Hodgkinson highlights 'authenticity' as a central feature of moral leadership, something I have shown the women heads to value. He says (ibid., p. 133):

> In my view, the authenticity of the leader stems first from the quality of private commitment to a personal set of values . . . and second, from the relating of these values to the followership. How is this second thing done? Primarily, I suspect, from the insights generated through sensitive participation, observation, interaction and reflection; by human and humane intercourse . . . the leader's relationship to the led must at all times be authentic.

Within the continuum of interest that stretches from self to society, the heads demonstrated the self-knowledge of their personal values by private reflection (see Chapter 5) that Hodgkinson suggests is the prerequisite for reviewing the metavalues of the organization. Their concern for values was not, however, the result of greater exposure to the skills of 'value auditing' that Hodgkinson proposes. There is little in current management training opportunities in Britain to cause school leaders to reflect on the ethical dimensions of their work and consider other ways of leading (Southworth, 1995, p. 215). Nor do I intend to suggest that authenticity is a woman's prerogative, but it does appear to be part of a female view of leadership, as demonstrated by these six woman heads. So too is reflection on the value issues underlying management actions. This concern emerged, for example, in how they dealt with redundancy issues, conflict between staff members, pupil discipline, relations with colleagues.

Hodgkinson (1991, p. 139) talks of the leader's need to 'know thyself'. Part of each head's rationale for engaging in the research was to deepen this knowledge of herself as a leader. Self-knowledge is never absolute and there were blindspots in every case, for example in terms of knowing their impact on others. As we saw in Chapter 5, the heads were driven by their position as women at the top to keep control of what they saw as the negative features of their affective responses. Varied as these were, they can be summed up in terms of impatience, manifested (rarely) through anger, withdrawal, irritability, taking over control. The source of the impatience was in the gap between their high expectations of people and others' failure or reluctance, in spite of support, to realize them. If there is a gender component, then it is in women's high expectations of their own and others' performance that also create the possibilities for their disappointment when things do not work out.

Hodgkinson concludes with four 'megamaxims': know the task, know the situation, know the followership, know oneself. It cannot be claimed that any of the six women heads knew as much as they wanted to know about any of these. They recognized, however, the 'need to know' as a basis for leadership which aims to be both moral and effective. Chapter 3 showed how they sought leadership at the point in their careers when they judged they 'knew the task' reasonably well. Chapter 4 looked at how 'knowing the situation' formed the basis for their actions in taking over the headship of a school. Chapters 5 and 6 described the emphasis they put on 'knowing self' as a basis for 'knowing the followership'. Critical perspectives on educational leadership will question the morality of knowledge that is not used to challenge organizational and social structures, but within the heads' own perspectives, the kind of entrepreneurship they demonstrated was a moral act.

IMPLICATIONS FOR FUTURE RESEARCH

I have tried to show in this chapter how using a triple metaphor of power, culture and gender to examine women's performance as school leaders provides insights into the phenomenon that any one perspective might fail to yield. It showed how men and women's interactions were influenced not only by different uses of power and allegiance to particular cultural norms but also by often contradictory expectations relating to gender. Any interaction was simultaneously an expression of the use of power, cultural norms and gender expectations.

I have argued that making gender 'figure' rather than 'ground' in a study of school leadership contributes to a more comprehensive picture of current practice than those studies which omit it. This is important for women in education, who need to know whether how they want to lead is legitimate and appropriate. It provides a mirror for their reflections. It is important, too, for men who want to explore further the possibilities of their own leadership practice. It has highlighted the possible transformations of formal power, when it is held by women, and the obstacles they face in maintaining collaborative relationships when they are in a position of power. Reading the final draft of what I had written about them, the heads were pleased and relieved to see the broad patterns of what they took to be idiosyncratic experiences. As a result of such realizations, Schmuck and Shubert (1995) claim, women are enabled to comprehend how gender serves as a segregating factor in the culture of educational institutions.

Focusing on gender and school leadership, and giving a voice to women's perspectives, provides a model for future studies of both men and women as educational leaders. Questions were raised about the relationships between home and work, family and career, early socialization and later performance that need to be asked of a larger sample of women and of men. The power-culture-gender focus challenges the taken-for-grantedness of how men use power and the kinds of culture women with power will seek to shape. As in the study in which the cultural and political perspective was first developed (Wallace and Hall, 1994), the conceptualization here (with gender added) is exploratory. Combined with life-history approaches and data collection through observation as well as interview, it provides a powerful lens for examining educational leadership not only in schools but in further and higher education as well.

Finally, the women heads described here were part of the tradition in English schooling that individualizes the leader's position and, as Grace (1995, p. 201) says, looks for its manifestation in exceptional individuals or in limited constituencies of 'responsible' citizens. The individualism of the leaders' position was accentuated, in their case, by their sense of being different from other women (in having made it 'to the top') and from men (in being their leaders rather than followers). Not surprisingly, they embodied a number of contradictions. They valued individualism but were also committed to collaboration and flatter hierarchies. They sought to recognize women's experience in the 'private' sphere and, as Blackmore (1989, p. 124) suggests, give it equal status to male experience in the 'public' sphere. On the other hand, their commitment to collective action did not embrace a view of women's collectivity, but referred to the staff and school as a whole.

Whether headteachers are, in Grace's terms, managers, professionals or resistors, the continuation of this individualistic tradition has considerable implications for developing school managers and leaders of the future. The origins of my research on women headteachers were in the need to identify and develop teachers as managers, and it is to this point that I finally return. The statistics show women still proportionally under-represented at all levels of management in schools, colleges and universities. I have tried throughout the book to address at least three of the concerns that are claimed to lead to this particular form of inequity: selectors' ambivalence about women 'in charge'; women's ambivalence about the congruence between being a manager and being a woman; and the absence of women as role models in educational leadership. What I hope this study has shown is that selectors, managers and women themselves can take the risk and let women lead the dance. Some of the steps may be different and the rhythm at first may feel uncomfortable, but with time, trust and an even tempo, a skilled and successful partnership can evolve.

REFERENCES

Abdela, L. (1989) *Women with X Appeal: Women Politicians in Britain Today,* Macdonald Optima, London.

Acker, S. (1992) Gender, collegiality and teachers' workplace culture in Britain: in search of the women's culture. Paper presented at the American Educational Research Association annual meeting, San Francisco, Calif.

Acker, S. (1993) Feminized or feminist? Teachers' workplace culture in an English primary school. Paper presented at the annual meeting of the Canadian Sociology and Anthropology Association, Ottawa, 7 June.

Acker, S. (1994) *Gendered Education: Sociological Reflections on Women, Teaching and Feminism,* Open University Press, Buckingham.

Adler, S., Laney, J. and Packer, M. (1993) *Managing Women: Feminism and Power in Educational Management,* Open University Press, Buckingham.

Al-Khalifa, E. (1988) Pin-money professionals? Women teaching for a change, in A. Coyle and J. Skinner (eds) *Women in Work: Positive Action for Change,* Macmillan, London.

Al-Khalifa, E. (1989) Management by halves: women teachers and school management, in H. De Lyon and F. Migniuolo (eds) *Women Teachers,* Open University, Milton Keynes.

Al-Khalifa, E. and Migniuolo, F. (1990) United Kingdom: messages for management, the experience of women's training. Paper presented at the Equal Advances in Education Management Conference, Council of Europe, Vienna.

Apslund, G. (1988) *Women Managers: Changing Organizational Culture,* Wiley, Chichester.

Astin, H.S. and Leland, C. (1991) *Women of Influence Women of Vision,* Jossey-Bass, San Francisco, Calif.

Astuto, T.A. and Clark, D.L. (1986) Achieving effective schools, in E. Hoyle and A. McMahon (eds) *World Yearbook of Education: The Management of Schools,* Kogan Page, London.

Bacharach, S.B. and Lawler, E.J. (1980) *Power and Politics in Organizations,* Jossey-Bass, San Francisco, Calif.

Baddeley, S. and James, K. (1987) Owl, fox, donkey or sheep: political skills for managers, *Management Education and Development*, Vol. 18, pp. 3–19.

Ball, S. (1987) *The Micropolitics of the School*, Methuen, London.

Beauvoir, S. de (1953) *The Second Sex*, Jonathan Cape, London.

Beck, J. and Steele, M. (1989) *Beyond the Great Divide: Introducing Equality into the Company*, Pitman, London.

Belbin, M. (1993) *Team Roles at Work*, Butterworth-Heinemann, Oxford.

Bem, S. (1975) Androgyny and mental health. Paper presented at the American Psychological Association, Chicago, Ill.

Berman, J. (1982) The managerial behavior of female high school principals. Paper presented at the American Educational Research Association annual meeting, New York.

Blackmore, J. (1989) Educational leadership: a feminist critique and reconstruction, in J. Smyth (ed.), *op. cit.*

Blackmore, J. and Kenway, J. (eds) (1993) *Gender Matters in Educational Administration and Policy: A Feminist Introduction*, Falmer Press, London.

Blase, J. and Kirby, P.C. (1992) *Bringing out the Best in Teachers: What Effective Principals Do*, Corwin Press, Newbury Park, Calif.

Blumberg, A. and Greenfield, W. (1980) *The Effective Principal: Perspectives in School Leadership*, Allyn & Bacon, Needham Heights, MA.

Bolam, R., McMahon, A., Pocklington, K. and Weindling, D. (1993) *Effective Management of Schools: A Report for the Department for Education via the School Management Task Force Professional Working Party*, HMSO, London.

Bolin, F. (1989) Empowering leadership, *Teachers College Record*, Vol. 91, pp. 81–96.

Bottery, M. (1992) *The Ethics of Educational Management*, Cassell, London.

Bowers, C.A. (1980) Curriculum as cultural reproduction: an examination of metaphor as a carrier of ideology, *Teachers College Record*, Vol. 82, pp. 267–89.

Bradford, D.L. and Cohen, A.R. (1984) *Managing for Excellence*, Wiley, New York.

Bush, T. and West-Burnham, J. (eds) (1994) *The Principles of Educational Management*, Longman, Harlow.

Byrne-Whyte, J. (1987) Under-representation of women in management posts in education: a critique of two theoretical explanatory accounts, in L. Unterkircher and I. Wagner (eds) *Die Andre halfte der Gesellschaft*, Verlag des Osterreichischen Gewerkschaftsbunden.

Cantor, D. and Bernay, T. (1992) *Women in Power: The Secrets of Leadership*, Houghton Mifflin, Boston, Mass.

Clerkin, C. (1985) What do primary heads actually do all day? *School Organization*, Vol. 5, pp. 287–300.

Cockburn, C. (1991) *In the Way of Women: Men's Resistance to Sex Equality in Organizations*, Macmillan, Basingstoke.

Coleman, G. (1991) *Investigating Organizations: A Feminist Approach. Occasional Paper 37*, School for Advanced Urban Studies, University of Bristol, Bristol.

Corson, D.J. (1992) Language, gender and education: a critical review linking social justice and power, *Gender and Education*, Vol. 4, pp. 229–54.

Cunnison, S. (1985) *Making it in a Man's World: Women Teachers in a Senior High School, Occasional Paper 1*, University of Hull, Hull.

Cunnison, S. (1994) Women teachers: career identity and perceptions of family constraints – changes over a recent decade, *Research Papers in Education*, Vol. 9, pp. 81–105.

Davies, L. (1992) School power cultures under economic constraint, *Educational Review*, Vol. 43, pp. 127–36.

Delamont, S. (1989) *Knowledgeable Women: Structuration and the Reproduction of Elites*, Routledge, London.

Department of Education and Science (1991) *Statistics of Education: Schools 1991*, DES, London.

Dunlap, D. and Schmuck, P. (eds) (1995) *Women Leading in Education*, Suny Press, Albany, NY.

Evetts, J. (1990) *Women in Primary Teaching: Career Contexts and Strategies*, Unwin Hyman, London.

Fagenson, E. (ed.) (1993) *Women in Management: Trends, Issues and Challenges in Managerial Diversity*, Sage, Newbury Park, Calif.

Fiedler, F.E. (1967) *A Theory of Leadership Effectiveness*, McGraw-Hill, New York.

Foster, W. (1989) Towards a critical path of leadership? In J. Smyth (ed.) *op. cit.*

Fullan, M. (1991) *The New Meaning of Educational Change*, Cassell, London.

Genovese, M.A. (ed.) (1993) *Women as National Leaders*, Sage, Newbury Park, Calif.

Giddens, A. (1976) *New Rules of Sociological Method*, Hutchinson, London.

Giddens, A. (1984) *The Constitution of Society*, Polity Press, Cambridge.

Giddens, A. (1991) *Modernity and Self-identity: Self and Society in the Late Modern Age*, Stanford University Press, Stanford, Calif.

Glenday, N. and Price, M. (1974) *Reluctant Revolutionaries: A Century of Headmistresses 1874–1974*, Pitman, London.

Grace, G. (1995) *School Leadership: Beyond Education Management: An Essay in Policy Scholarship*, Falmer Press, London.

Grant, R. (1989) Women teachers' career pathways: towards an alternative model of career, in Acker, S. (ed) (1989) *Teachers, Gender and Career*, Falmer Press, Lewes.

Gray, H. (1989) Gender considerations in school management: masculine and feminine leadership styles, in C. Riches and C. Morgan (eds), *op. cit.*

Gray, H. (1993) Gender issues in management training, in J. Ozga (ed.) *Women in Educational Management*, Open University Press, Buckingham.

Gronn, P. (1984) On studying administrators at work, *Educational Administration Quarterly*, Vol. 20, pp. 115–29.

Grundy, S. (1993) Educational leadership as emancipatory praxis, in J. Blackmore and J. Kenway (eds) *op. cit.*

Habermas, J. (1972) *Knowledge and Human Interests*, Heinemann, London.

Hall, V. (1978) Women in journalism. Unpublished PhD thesis, University of Essex.

Hall, V. (1990) Gender issues in primary school headship and deputy headship in the light of the Educational Reform Act (1988) England and Wales. Paper presented at the American Educational Research Association annual meeting, Boston, Mass.

Hall, V. (1993) Women in educational management: a review of research in Britain, in J. Ouston (ed.) *Women in Education Management*, Longman, Harlow.

Hall, V., Cromey-Hawke, N. and Oldroyd, D. (1995) *Management Self-Development: A Distance Learning Programme*, NDCEMP, University of Bristol.

Hall, V., Mackay, H., and Morgan, C. (1986) *Headteachers at Work*, Open University Press, Milton Keynes.

Harding, S. (1986) *The Science Question in Feminism*, Open University Press, Milton Keynes.

Hargreaves, A. (1994) Development and desire: a postmodern perspective. Paper presented at the American Educational Research Association annual meeting, New Orleans, La.

Harris, I.M. (1995) *Messages Men Hear: Constructing Masculinities*, Taylor & Francis, London.

Hearn, J., Sheppard, D.L., Tancred-Sheriff, P. and Burrell, G. (1989) *The Sexuality of Organization*, Sage, London.

Hennig, M. and Jardim, A. (1977) *The Managerial Woman*, Anchor Press/Doubleday, Garden City, NY.

Hersey, P. and Blanchard, K.H. (1988) *Management of Organizational Behavior: Utilizing Human Resources* (5th edn), Prentice-Hall, Englewood Cliffs, NJ.

Hodgkinson, C. (1991) *Educational Leadership: The Moral Art*, State University of New York Press, Albany, NY.

Hoyle, E. (1974) Professionality, professionalism and control in teaching, *London Educational Review*, Vol. 3, pp. 13–19.

Hoyle, E. (1982) Micropolitics of educational organizations, *Educational Management and Administration*, Vol. 10, pp. 87–98.

Hoyle, E. (1986) *The Politics of School Management*, Hodder & Stoughton, London.

Hoyle, E. (1989) Teacher appraisal and collaborative professionalisation, in A. Evans and J. Tomlinson (eds) *Teacher Appraisal: A Nationwide Approach*, Jessica Kingsley, London.

Huckman, L. (1994) Developing roles and relationships in primary school governance, in A. Thody (ed.), *op. cit.*

Hughes, M. (1985) Leadership in professionally staffed organizations, in M. Hughes *et al.* (eds) *Managing Education: The System and the Institution*, Holt, Rinehart & Winston, London.

Jenkins, H.O. (1991) *Getting it Right: A Handbook for Successful School Leadership*, Blackwell, Oxford.

Johnston, J. (1986) Gender differences in teachers' preferences for primary school leadership, *Educational Management and Administration*, Vol. 14, pp. 219–26.

Jones, A. (1987) *Leadership for Tomorrow's Schools*, Blackwell, Oxford.

Kanter, R. (1977) *Men and Women of the Corporation*, Basic Books, New York.

Kanter, R. (1990) *When Giants Learn to Dance*, Unwin Hyman, London.

Krüger, M. (1994) Leadership and gender in different school cultures, in K. Hämäläinen and F. Van Wieringen (eds) *Reforming Educational Management in Europe*, Academic Book Center, De Lier, The Netherlands.

Legge, K. (1995) HRM: rhetoric, reality and hidden agendas, in J. Storey (ed.) *Human Resource Management: A Critical Text*, Routledge, London.

Leithwood, K., Begley, P. and Cousins, J. (1992) *Developing Expert Leadership for Future Schools*, Falmer Press, London.

Levine, S.L. (1989) *Promoting Adult Growth in Schools: The Promise of Professional Development*, Allyn & Bacon, Boston, Mass.

Lipham, J.M. and Francke, D.C. (1966) Non-verbal behaviour of administrators, *Educational Administration Quarterly*, Vol. 2, pp. 101–9.

Lipson, J. (1994) Ethical issues in ethnography, in J.M. Morse (ed.) *Critical Issues in Qualitative Research Methods*, Sage, Thousand Oaks, CA.

Litawski, R (1993) The 'nappy and noses' brigade, *The Times Educational Supplement*, 2 April, p. 6.

Lortie, D. (1975) *Schoolteacher: A Sociological Study*, University of Chicago Press, Chicago, Ill.

Lyons, G. (1981) *Teachers' Careers and Career Perceptions*, National Foundation for Educational Research, Slough.

Mac An Ghaill, M. (1994) *The Making of Men: Masculinity, Sexualities and Schooling*, Open University Press, Buckingham.

Marshall, C. (1985) From culturally defined to self-defined. Career stages for women administrators, *The Journal of Educational Thought*, Vol. 19, pp. 134–47.

Marshall, J. (1984) *Women Managers: Travellers in a Male World*, Wiley, Chichester.

Matthews, J. (1984) *Good and Mad Women: The Historical Construction of Femininity in Twentieth Century Australia*, Allen & Unwin, Sidney.

Maynard, M. and Purvis, J. (1994) *Researching Women's Lives from a Feminist Perspective*, Taylor & Francis, London.

Mintzberg, H. (1973) *The Nature of Managerial Work*, Harper & Row, New York.

Morgan, C., Hall, V. and Mackay, H. (1983) *The Selection of Secondary Heads*, Open University Press, Milton Keynes.

Mortimore, P. and Mortimore, J. (1988) *The Secondary Head: Roles, Responsibilities and Reflections*, Paul Chapman, London.

National Union of Teachers/Equal Opportunities Commission (1980) *Promotion and the Woman Teacher*, NUT, London.

Nias, J. (1989) *Primary Teachers Talking: a Study of Teaching as Work*, Routledge, London.

Oldroyd, D. and Hall, V. (1991) *Managing Staff Development: A Handbook for Secondary Schools*, Paul Chapman, London.

Park, J. (1995) *Sons, Mothers and Other Lovers*, Little, Brown, London.

Pedler, M. and Boydell, T. (1985) *Managing Yourself*, Fontana, London.

Peters, T. and Waterman, R. (1982) *In Search of Excellence*, Harper Collins, London.

Poplin, P.P. (1995) and Rusch, E. (1995) Re-examining educational leadership: challenging assumptions, in D. Dunlap and P. Schmuck (eds.), *op. cit.*

Powney, J. and Weiner, G. (1991) *Outside of the Norm: Equity and Management in Educational Institutions*, South Bank Polytechnic, Department of Education, London.

Reason, P. and Rowan, J. (eds) (1981) *Human Inquiry: A Sourcebook of New Paradigm Research*, Wiley, Chichester.

Reizung, U.C. and Reeves, J.E. (1992) 'Miss Lincoln doesn't teach here': a descriptive narrative and conceptual analysis of a principal's symbolic leadership behaviour, *Education Administration Quarterly*, Vol. 28, pp. 185–219.

Riches, C. and Morgan, C. (1989) *Human Resource Management in Education*, Open University Press, Milton Keynes.

Rosener, S. (1990) Ways women lead, *Harvard Business Review*, November/December, pp. 119–25.

Rothwell, S. (1985) Is management a masculine role? *Management Education and Development*, Vol. 16, pp. 79–98.

Sallis, J. (1988) *Schools, Parents and Governors: A New Approach to Accountability*, Routledge, London.

Sarason, S.B. (1982) *The Culture of the School and the Problem of Change* (2nd edn), Allyn & Bacon, Boston, Mass.

Sargent, A. (1983) *The Androgynous Manager: Blending Male and Female Management Styles for Today's Organization*, American Management Association, New York.

Schein, V.E. (1989) Would women lead differently? in W.E. Rosenbach and R.L. Taylor (eds) *Contemporary Issues in Leadership* (2nd edn), Westview Press, Boulder, Colo.

Schmuck, P. (1986) School management and administration: an analysis by gender, in E. Hoyle and A. McMahon (eds) *World Yearbook: The Management of Schools*, Kogan Page, London.

Schmuck, P. and Shubert, J. (1995) Women principals' views on sex equity: exploring issues of integration and information, in D. Dunlap and P. Schmuck (eds) *op. cit.*

Sergiovanni, T. (1991) *The Principalship: A Reflective Practice Perspective* (2nd edn), Allyn & Bacon, Newton, Mass.

Shakeshaft, C. (1989) *Women in Educational Administration* (2nd edn), Sage, Newbury Park, Calif.

Shakeshaft, C. (1993) Women in educational management in the United States, in J. Ouston (ed.) *Women in Education Management*, Longman, Harlow.

Sheppard, D. (1989) Organizations, power and sexuality: the image and self-image of women managers, in J. Hearn *et al.* (eds) *op. cit.*

Silverman, D. (1993) *Interpreting Qualitative Data: Methods for Analysing Text, Talk and Interaction*, Sage, London.

Smyth, J. (ed.) (1989) *Critical Perspectives on Educational Leadership*, Falmer Press, London.

Southworth, G. (1987) Staff selection or by appointment? A case study of the appointment of a teacher to a primary school, in G. Southworth (ed.) *Readings in Primary School Management*, Falmer Press, Lewes.

Southworth, G. (1995) *Looking into Primary Headship: A Research Based Interpretation*, Falmer Press, London.

Spender, D. (1980) *Man-made Language*, Unwin Hyman, London.

Stanley, L. and Wise, S. (1993) *Breaking Out Again*, Routledge, London.

Stechert, K.B. (1986) *The Credibility Gap*, Thorsons, Wellingborough.

Storey, J. (1987) *Developments in the Management of Human Resources: An Interim Report, Warwick Papers in Industrial Relations* 17, IRRU, School of Industrial and Business Studies, University of Warwick, Coventry.

Strachan, J. (1994) Contesting and struggling? The New Right, locally managed schools and feminist leadership. Paper presented at the Women in Leadership Conference, Edith Cowan University, Perth, November–December.

Tannen, D. (1990) *You Just Don't Understand: Women and Men in Conversation*, Virago Press, London.

Tannen, D. (1995) *Talking from Nine to Five*, Virago Press, London.

Thody, A. (ed.) (1994) *School Governors: Leaders or Followers?* Harlow, Longman.

Turner, G. and Clift, P. (1988) *Studies in Teacher Appraisal*, Falmer Press, London.

Van Nostrand, C. (1993) *Gender Responsible Leadership: Detecting Bias, Implementing Interventions*, Sage, Newbury Park, Calif.

Vinnecombe, S. (1989) What exactly are the differences in male and female working styles? *Women in Management Review*, Vol. 3, pp. 13–21.

Wallace, M. and Hall, V. (1989) Management development and training for schools in England and Wales: an overview, *Educational Management and Administration*, Vol. 17, pp. 163–75.

Wallace, M. and Hall, V. (1994) *Inside the SMT: Teamwork in Secondary School Management*, Paul Chapman, London.

Weaver-Hart, A. (1995) Women ascending to leadership: the organizational socialization of principals, in D.M. Dunlap and P.A. Schmuck (eds) *op. cit.*

Weber, S. and Mitchell, C. (1995) *'That's Funny, You Don't Look Like a Teacher?' Interrogating Images and Identity in Popular Culture*, Falmer Press, London.

Webster, W. (1990) *Not a Man to Match Her*, The Woman's Press, London.

Weiler, K. (1988) *Women Teaching for Change: Gender, Class and Power*, Bergin & Garvey, New York.

Weindling, D. and Earley, P. (1987) *Secondary Headship: The First Years*, NFER-Nelson, Slough.

White, B., Cox, C. and Cooper, C. (1992) *Women's Career Development: A Study of High Flyers*, Blackwell, Oxford.

Wolcott, H. (1973) *The Man in the Principal's office: An Ethnography*, Waveland Press, Prospect Heights, Ill.

Wolcott, H. (1982) Mirrors, models and monitors: educator adaptation of the ethnographic innovation, in G. Spindler (ed.) *Doing the Ethnography of Schooling, Holt*, Rinehart & Winston, New York.

Wolcott, H. (1990) On seeking – and rejecting – validity in qualitative research, in E.W. Eisner and A. Peshkin (eds.) *Qualitative Inquiry into Education: The Continuing Debate*, Teachers College Press, New York.

Woods, P. (1987) Life histories and teacher knowledge, in J. Smyth (ed.) *Educating Teachers: Changing the Nature of Pedagogical Knowledge*, Falmer Press, London.

Yates, L. (1993) The theory-practice relationship in schooling, academia and feminist theory, in J. Blackmore and J. Kenway (eds), *op. cit.*

Young, H. (1990) *One of Us: A Study of Margaret Thatcher*, Pan, London.

INDEX